Everything
Is OK

Everything

Is OK

Debbie Tung

Andrews McMeel
PUBLISHING®

For anyone who is going through a tough time.
You are not alone. You matter.
You are enough just as you are right now.

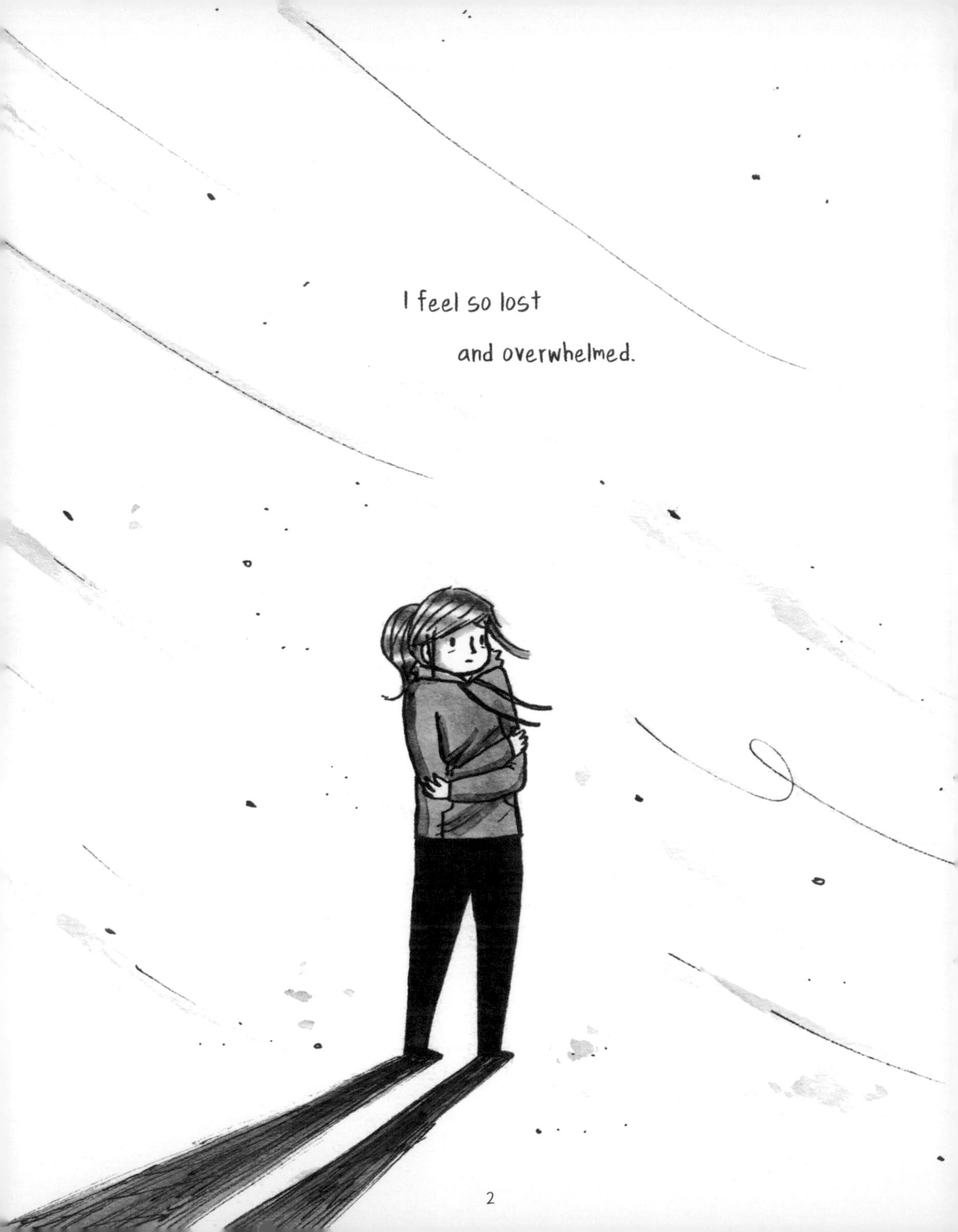
I feel so lost
and overwhelmed.

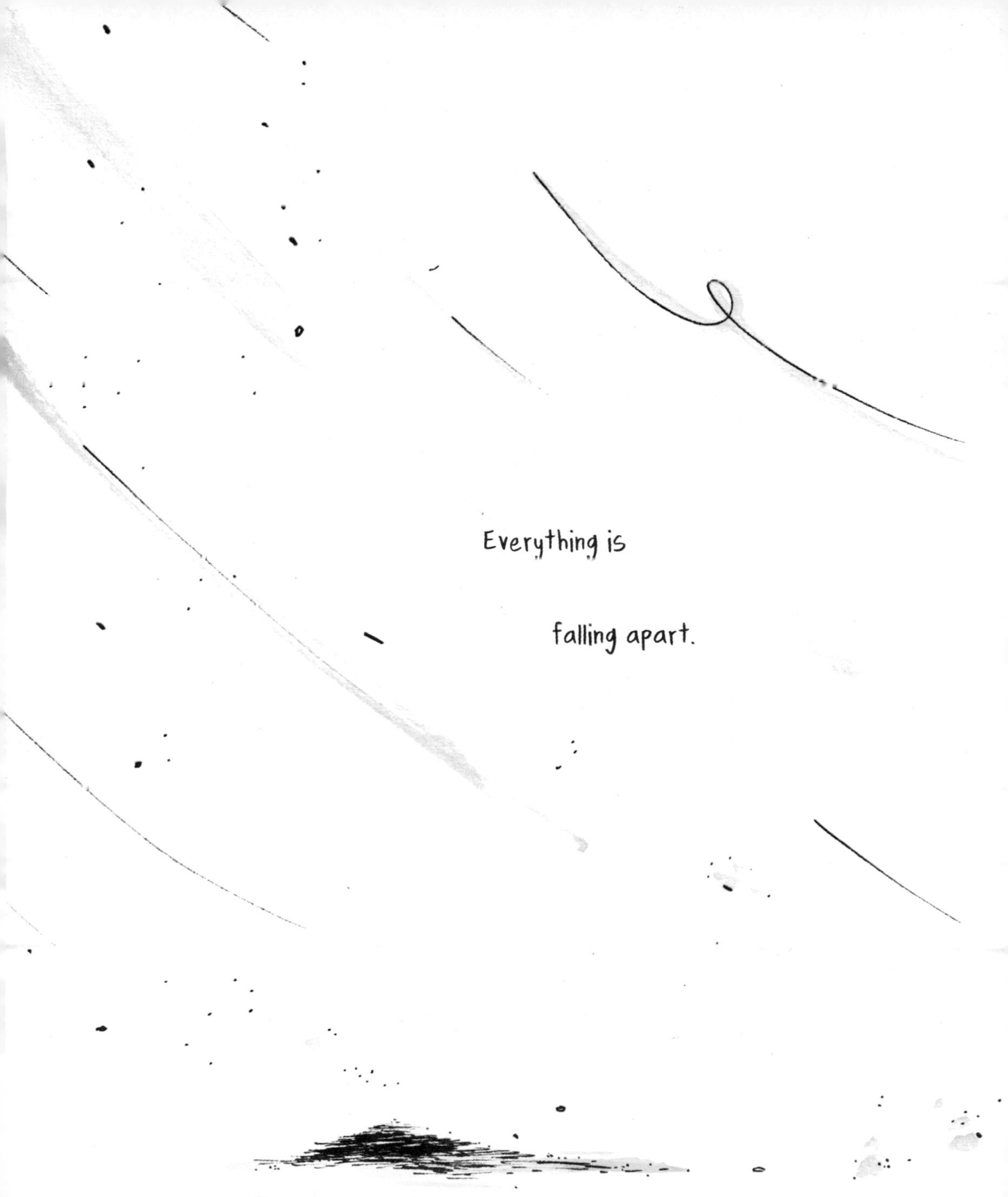
Everything is
falling apart.

How will I ever get through this?

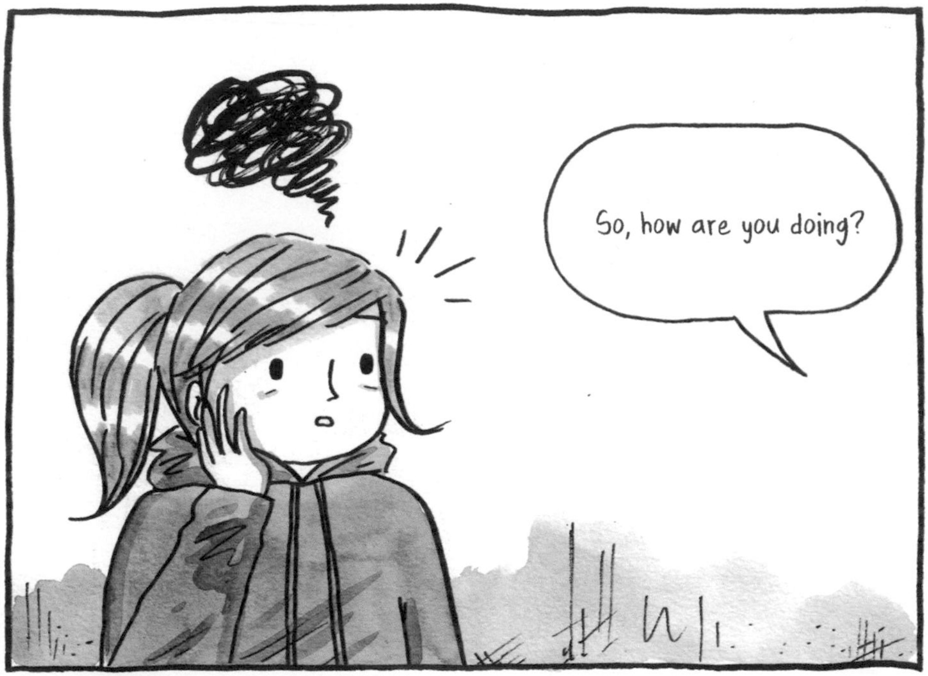
So, how are you doing?

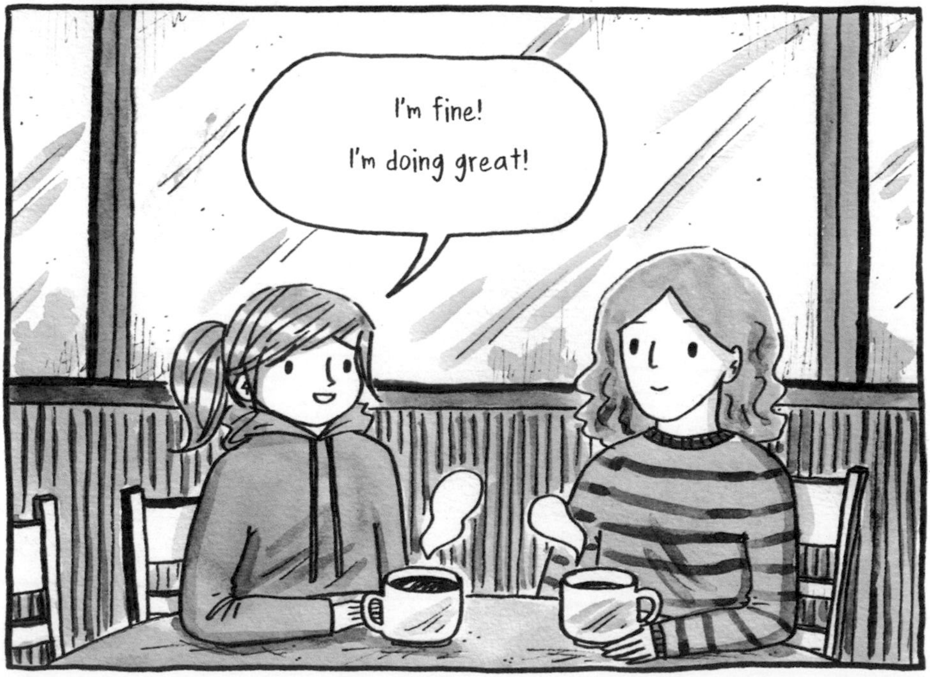
I'm fine!
I'm doing great!

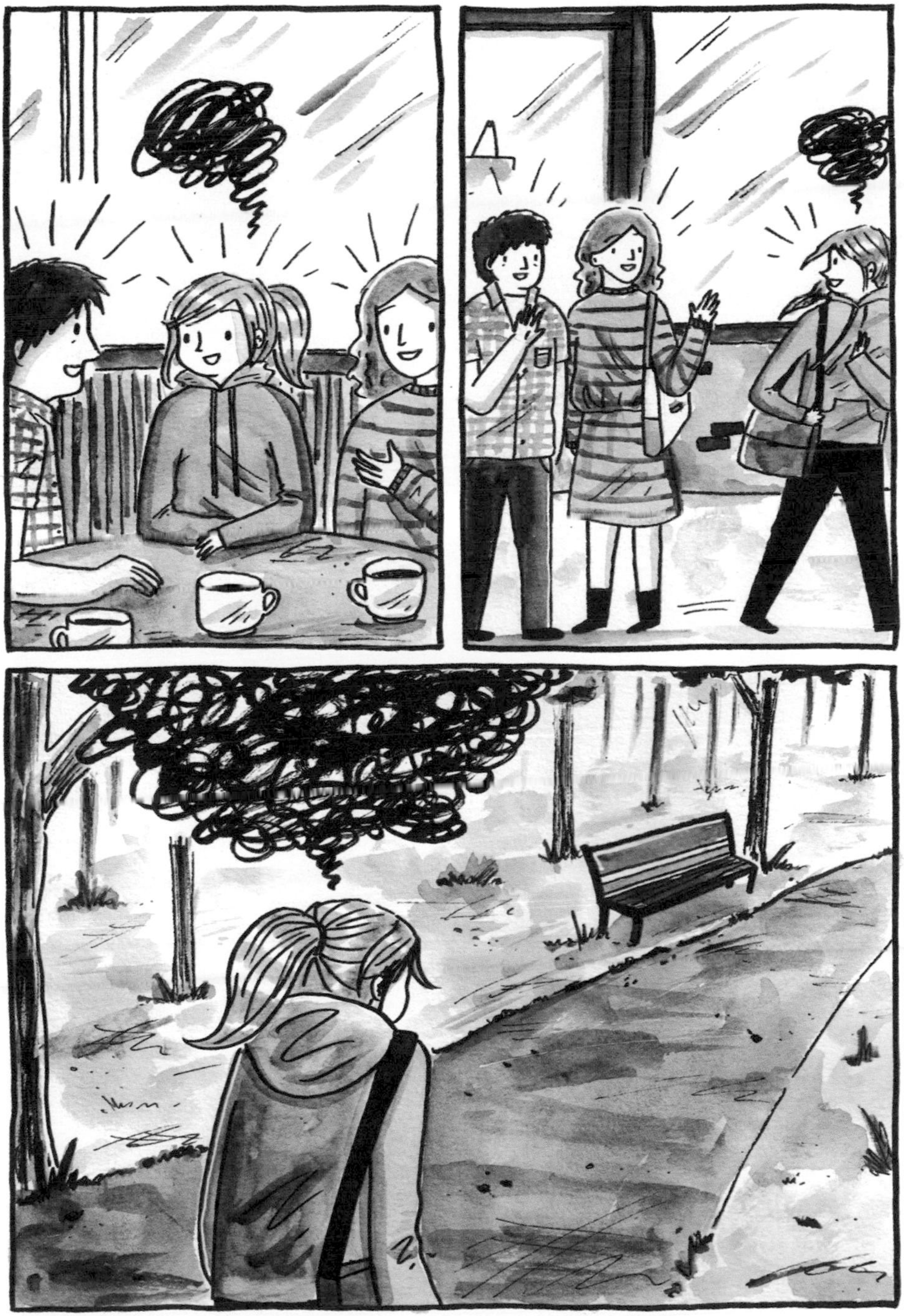

Ugh... I think I said something really weird
at that meeting today...

I shouldn't have canceled dinner with my friends.

I've probably hurt their feelings with
that lame excuse I gave.

They're all going to leave me eventually.

I should call my parents.

I forgot to call them back last week... and the week before that.

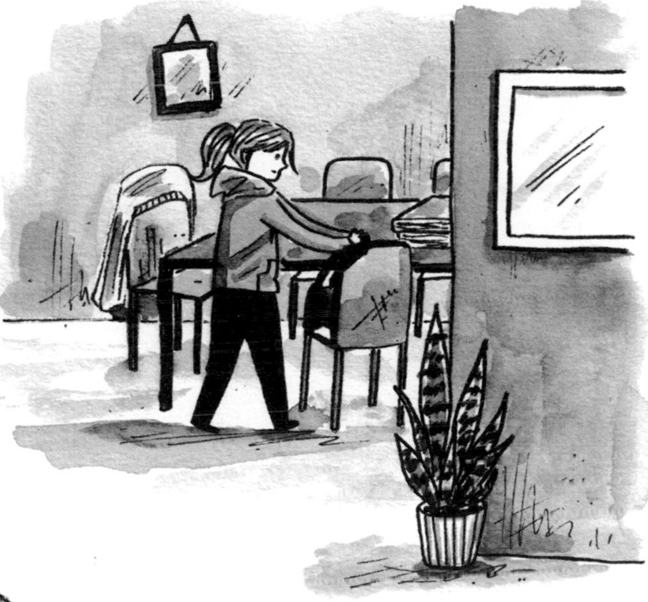

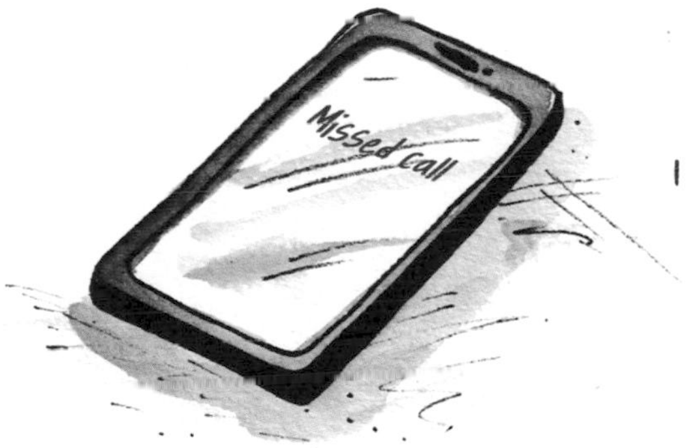
Missed call

I meant to help my dad buy something he needed online.

I wonder if they're proud of me.

I'm the worst daughter ever.

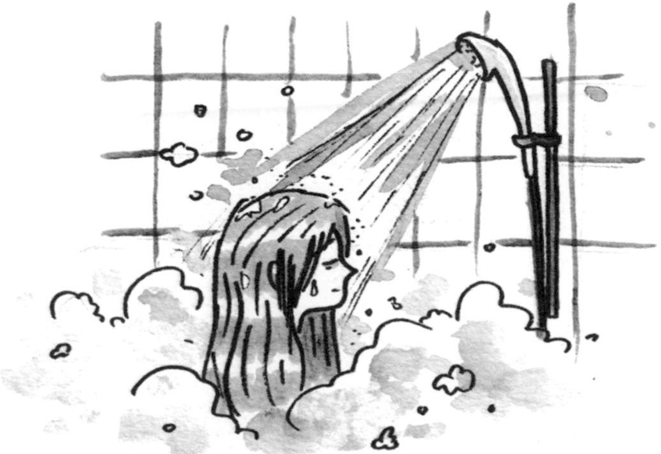

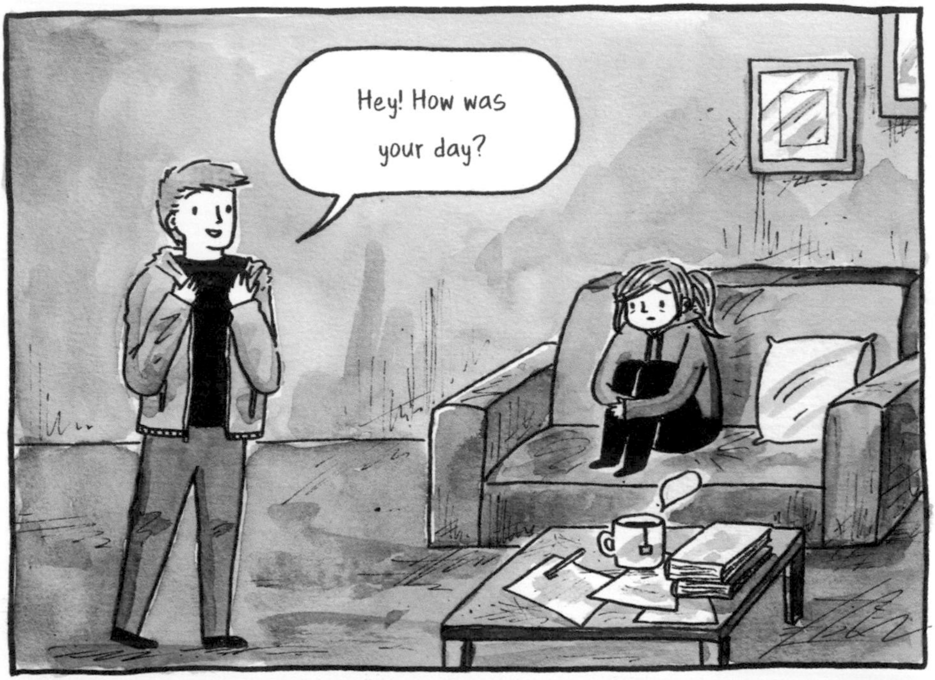
Hey! How was your day?

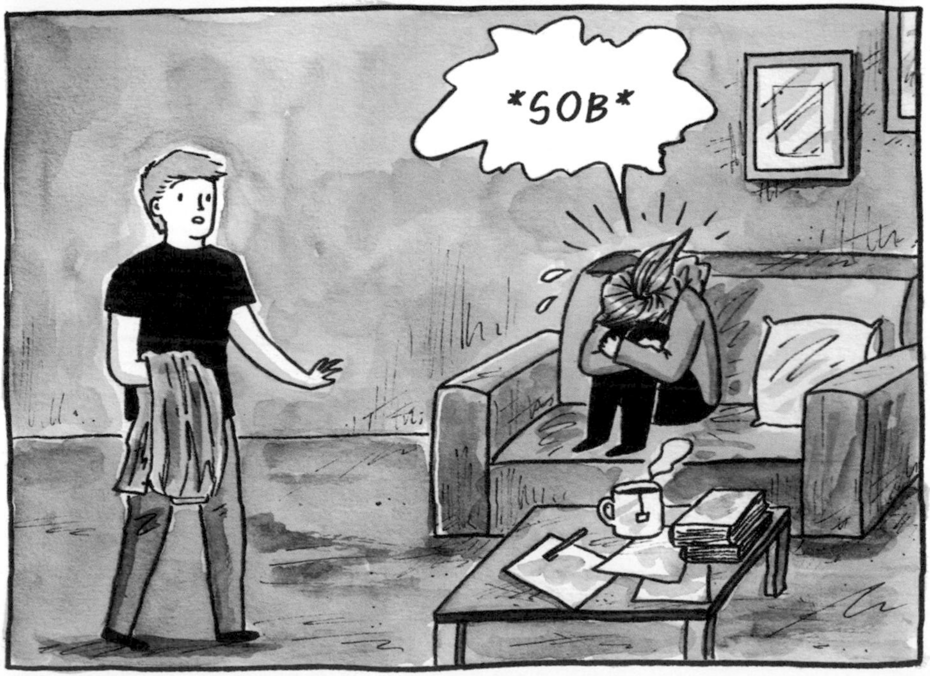
SOB

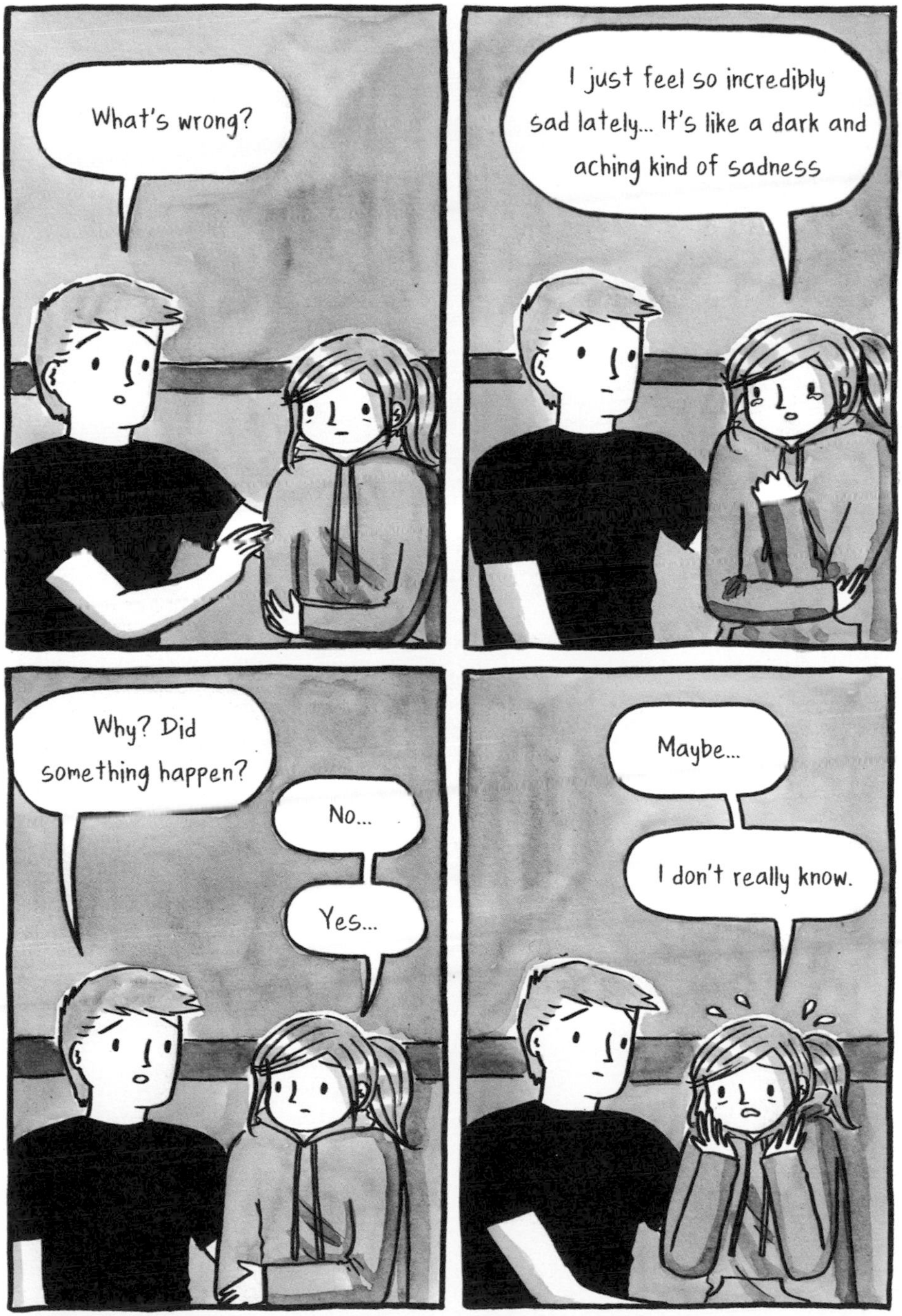
What's wrong?
I just feel so incredibly sad lately... It's like a dark and aching kind of sadness
Why? Did something happen?
No...
Yes...
Maybe...
I don't really know.

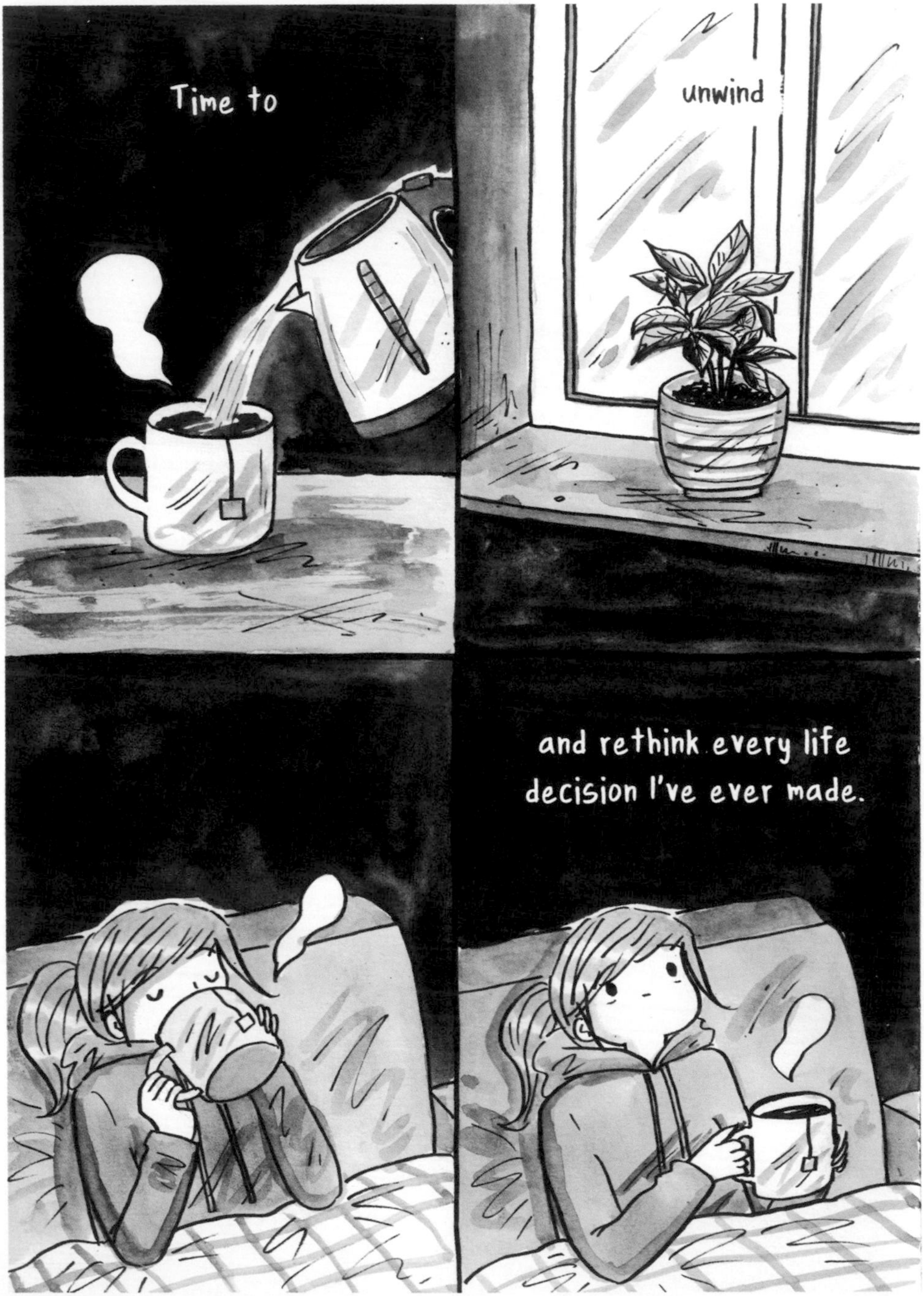
Time to
unwind
and rethink every life decision I've ever made.

Sometimes the thoughts in my head

can get too overwhelming.

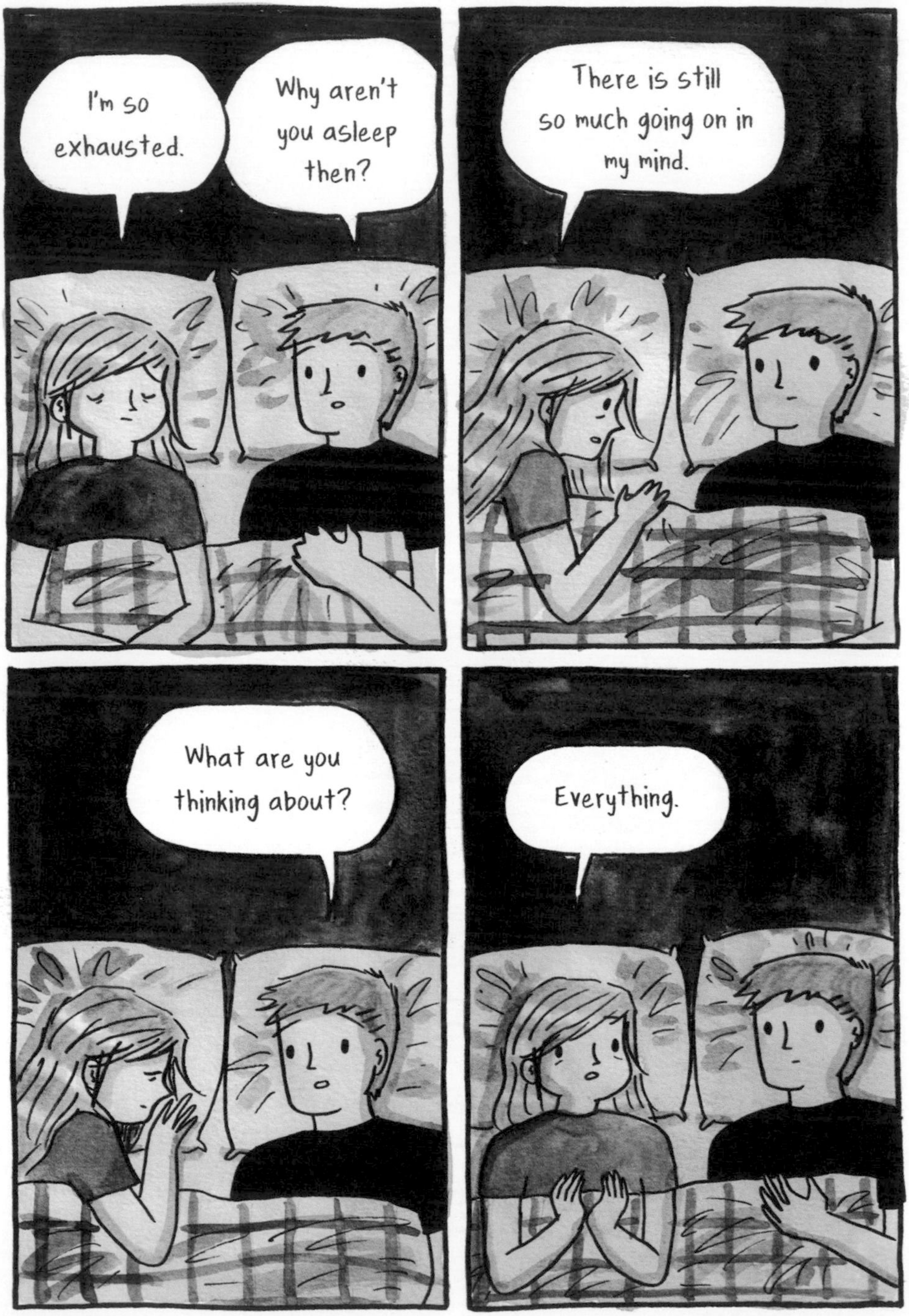
I'm so exhausted.
Why aren't you asleep then?
There is still so much going on in my mind.
What are you thinking about?
Everything.

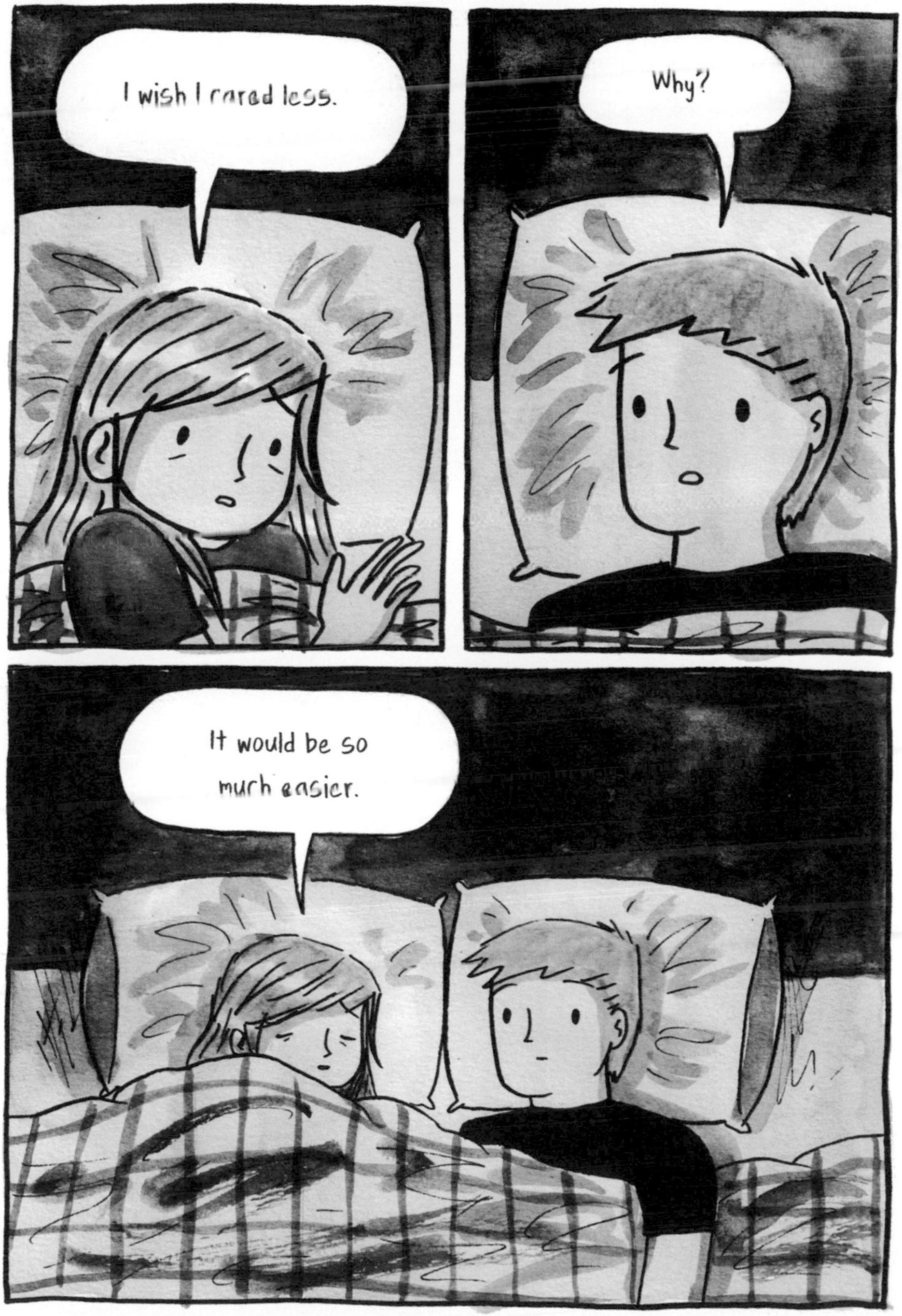
I wish I cared less.
Why?
It would be so much easier.

I've had bad days. As we all do.

Days where you're fuming because you missed a bus...

or exhausted because of endless deadlines at work.

But this time, it feels different.

It's been too long and it hurts too much.

What is wrong with me?!

Why can't I just be happy and carefree like everyone else?

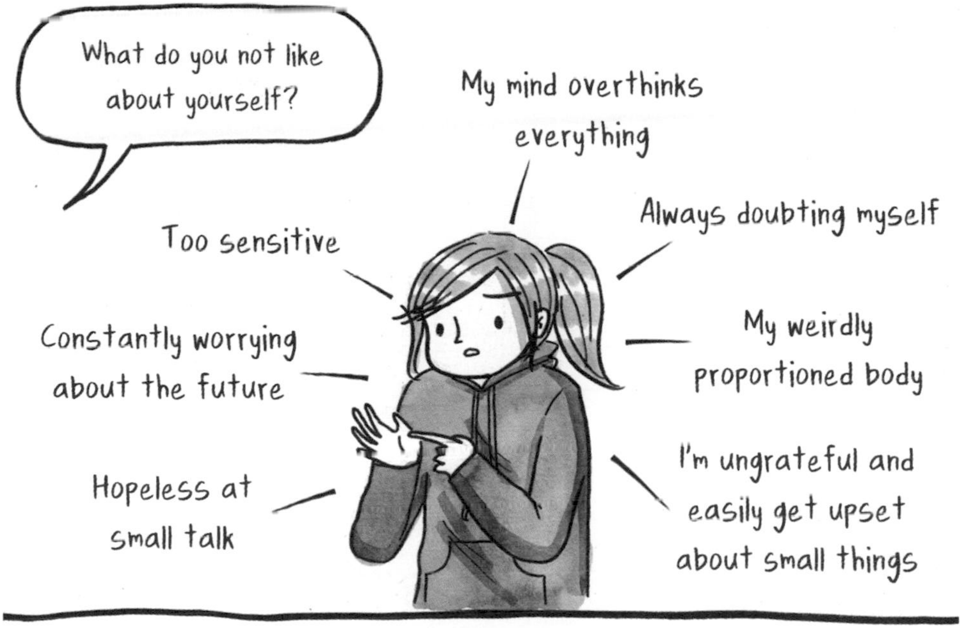
What do you not like about yourself?
My mind overthinks everything
Too sensitive
Always doubting myself
Constantly worrying about the future
My weirdly proportioned body
Hopeless at small talk
I'm ungrateful and easily get upset about small things

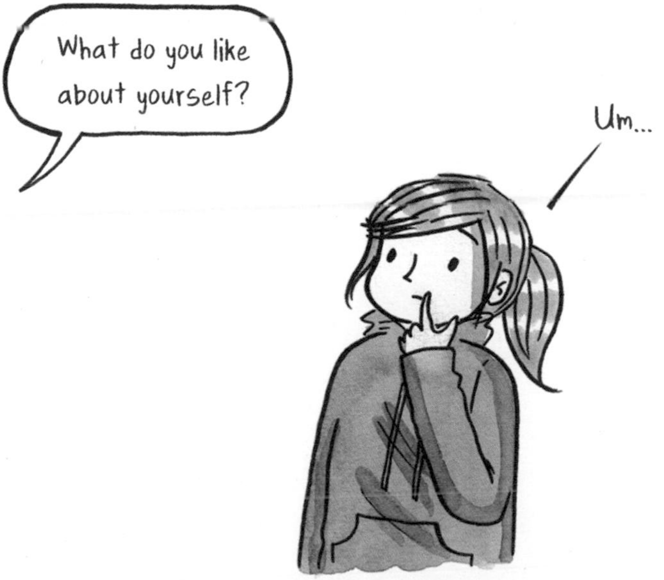
What do you like about yourself?
Um...

Some days I feel like I'm ready to take on the world.

Let's get this show on the road!

Other days I struggle to get out of bed.

Ugh... Is it morning already?

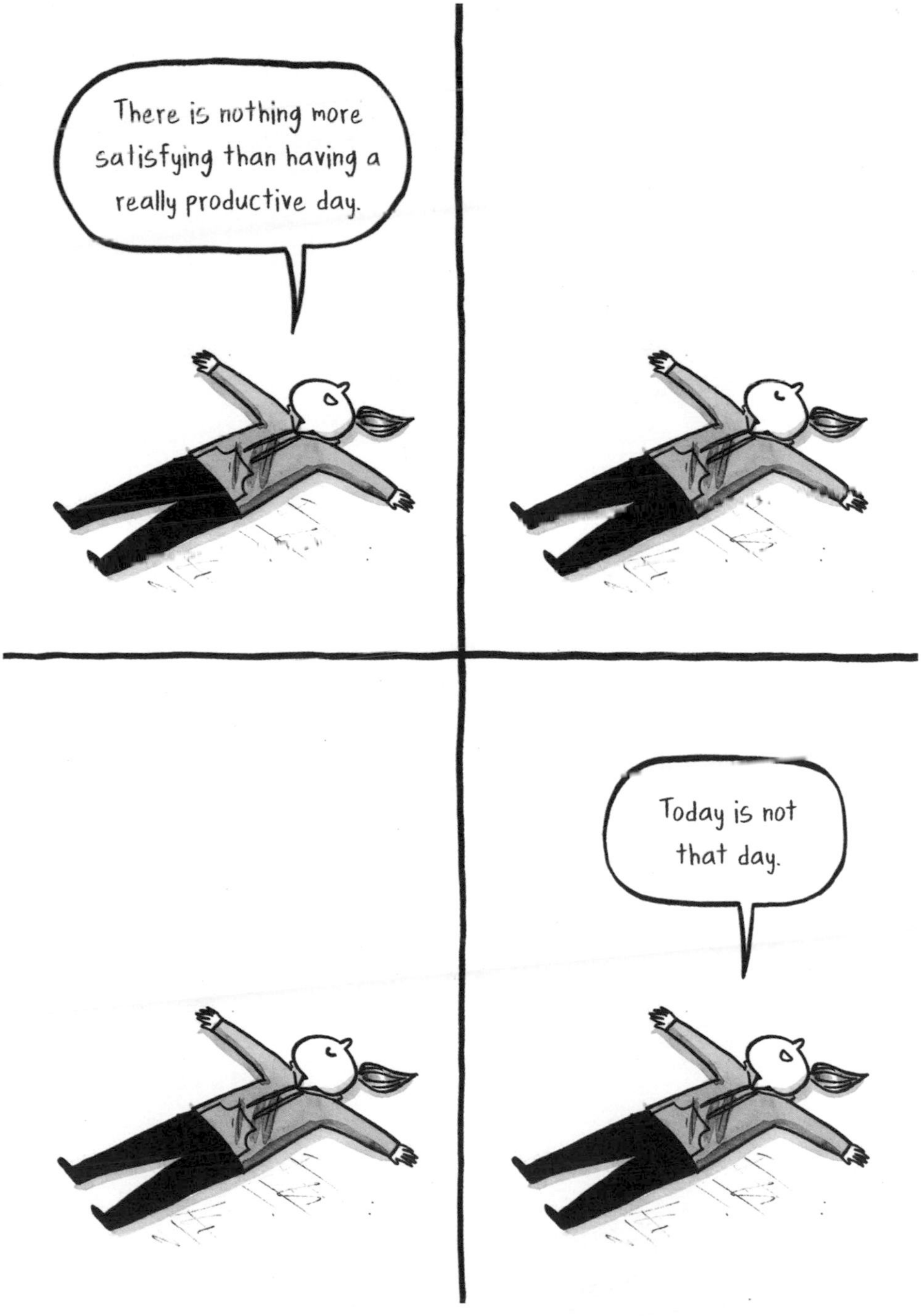
There is nothing more satisfying than having a really productive day.
Today is not that day.

It was almost a physical struggle to get up this morning.

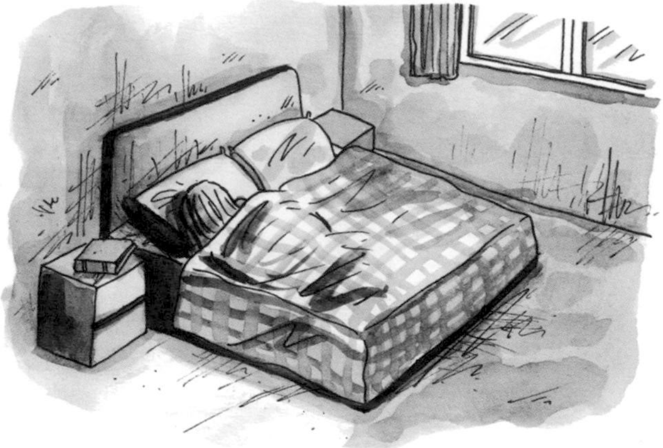

I had to force myself to open my eyes and drag myself to the bathroom.

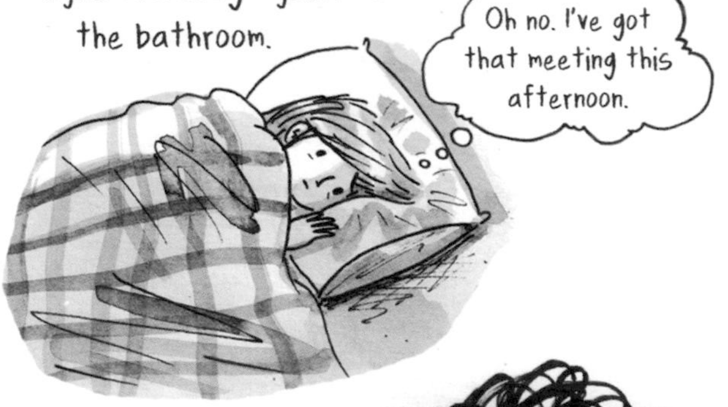
Oh no. I've got that meeting this afternoon.

I feel so weak and empty.

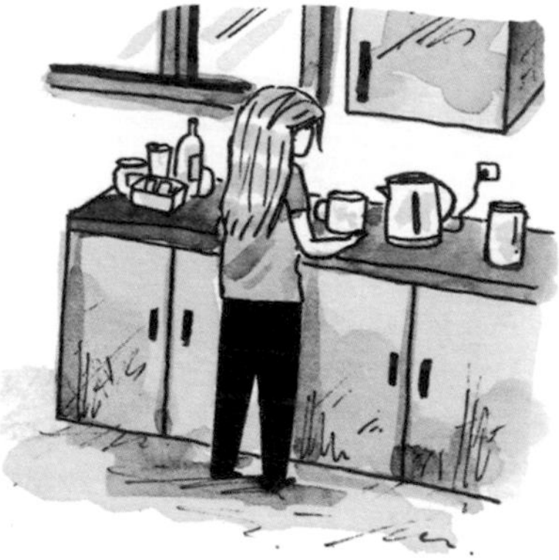

Or maybe...

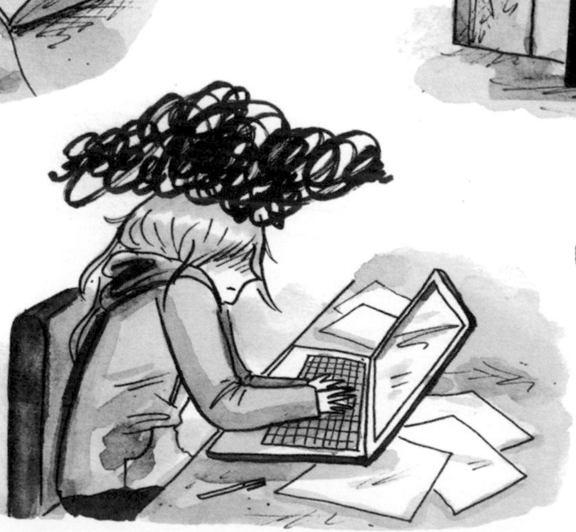

I'm just incredibly lazy.

Just another day
of pretending.

Fake that

smile!!!

Remember to keep
your head up.

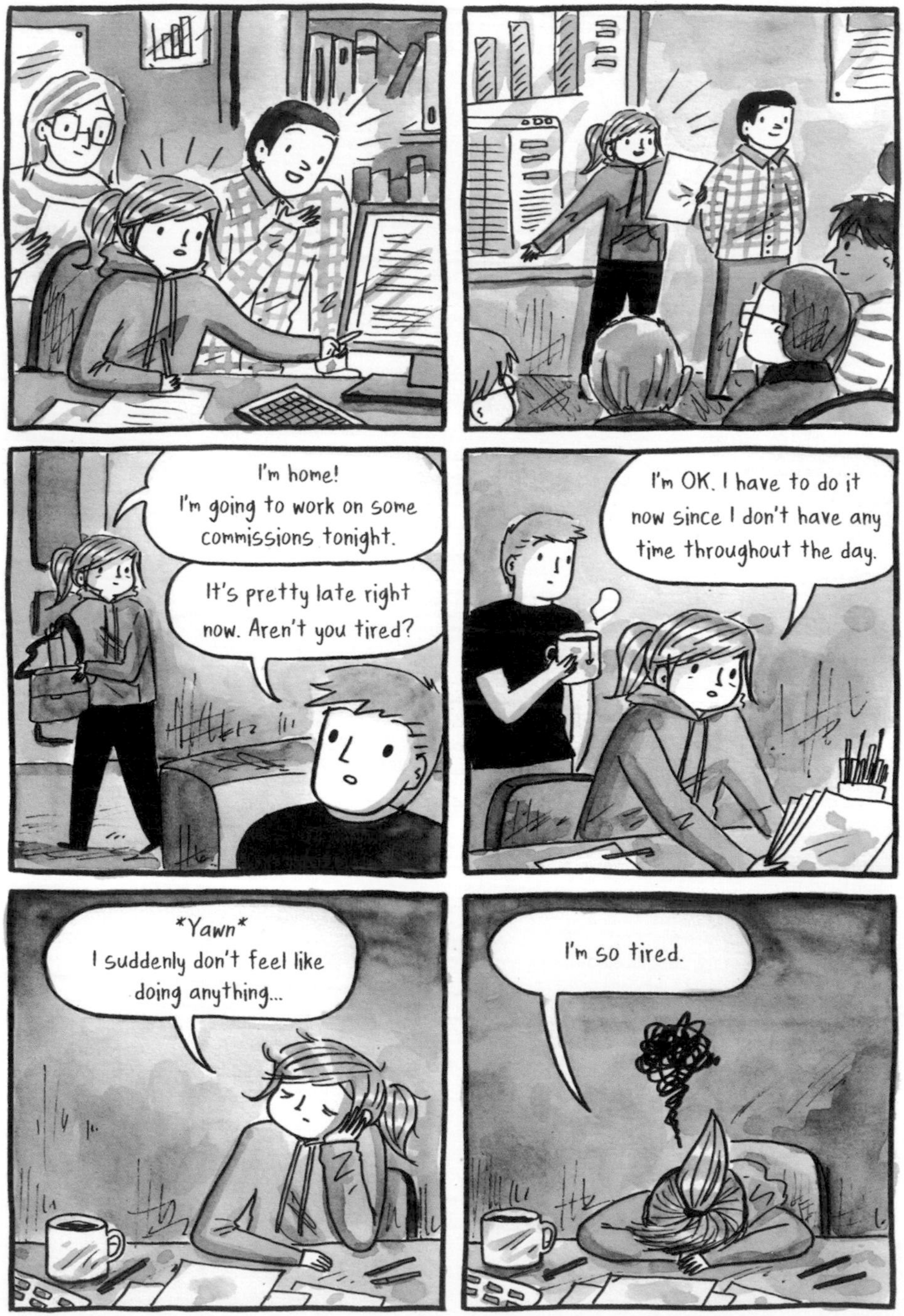
I'm home!
I'm going to work on some commissions tonight.
It's pretty late right now. Aren't you tired?
I'm OK. I have to do it now since I don't have any time throughout the day.
Yawn
I suddenly don't feel like doing anything...
I'm so tired.

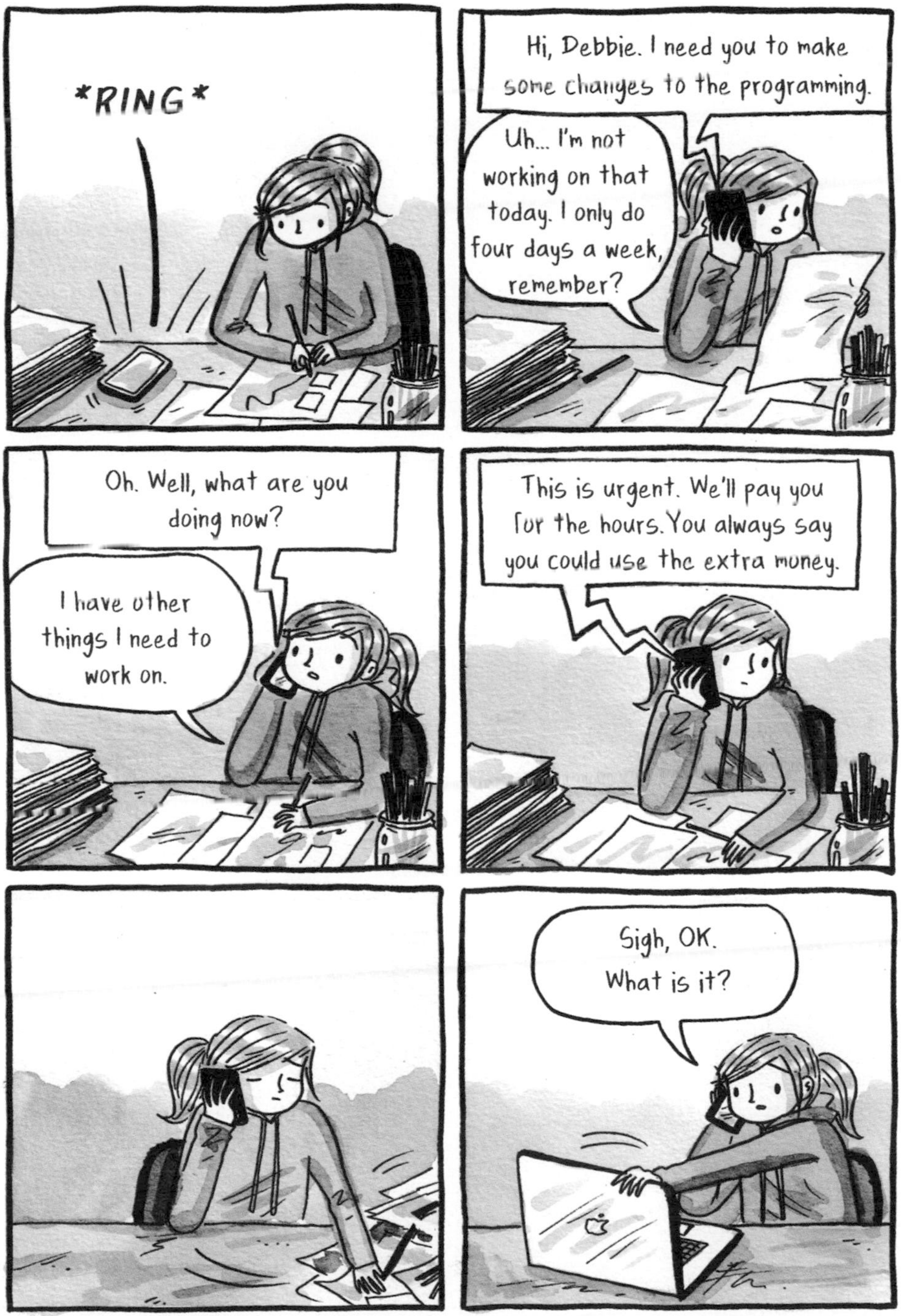
RING
Hi, Debbie. I need you to make some changes to the programming.
Uh... I'm not working on that today. I only do four days a week, remember?
Oh. Well, what are you doing now?
I have other things I need to work on.
This is urgent. We'll pay you for the hours. You always say you could use the extra money.
Sigh, OK. What is it?

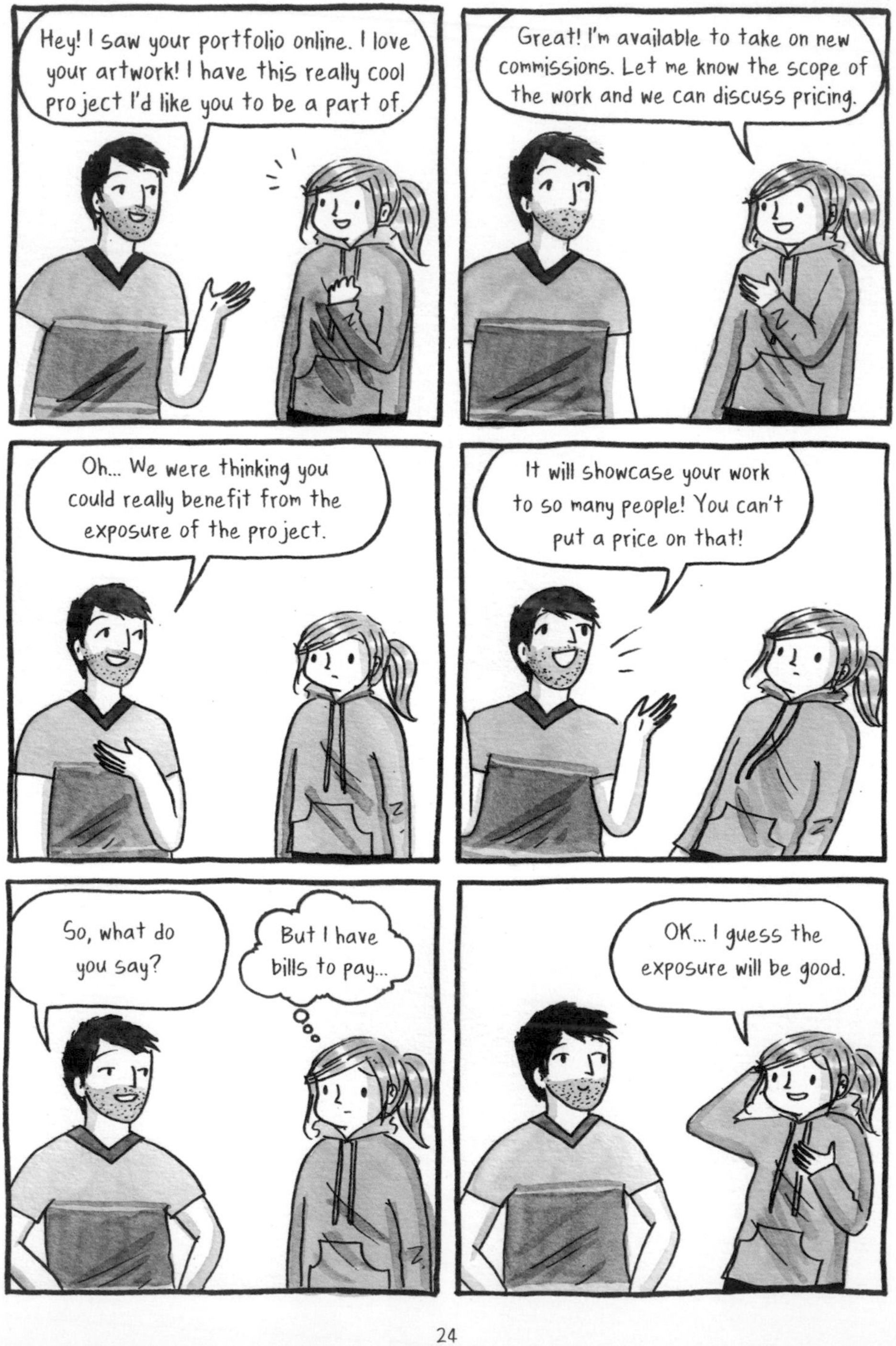
Hey! I saw your portfolio online. I love your artwork! I have this really cool project I'd like you to be a part of.
Great! I'm available to take on new commissions. Let me know the scope of the work and we can discuss pricing.
Oh... We were thinking you could really benefit from the exposure of the project.
It will showcase your work to so many people! You can't put a price on that!
So, what do you say?
But I have bills to pay...
OK... I guess the exposure will be good.

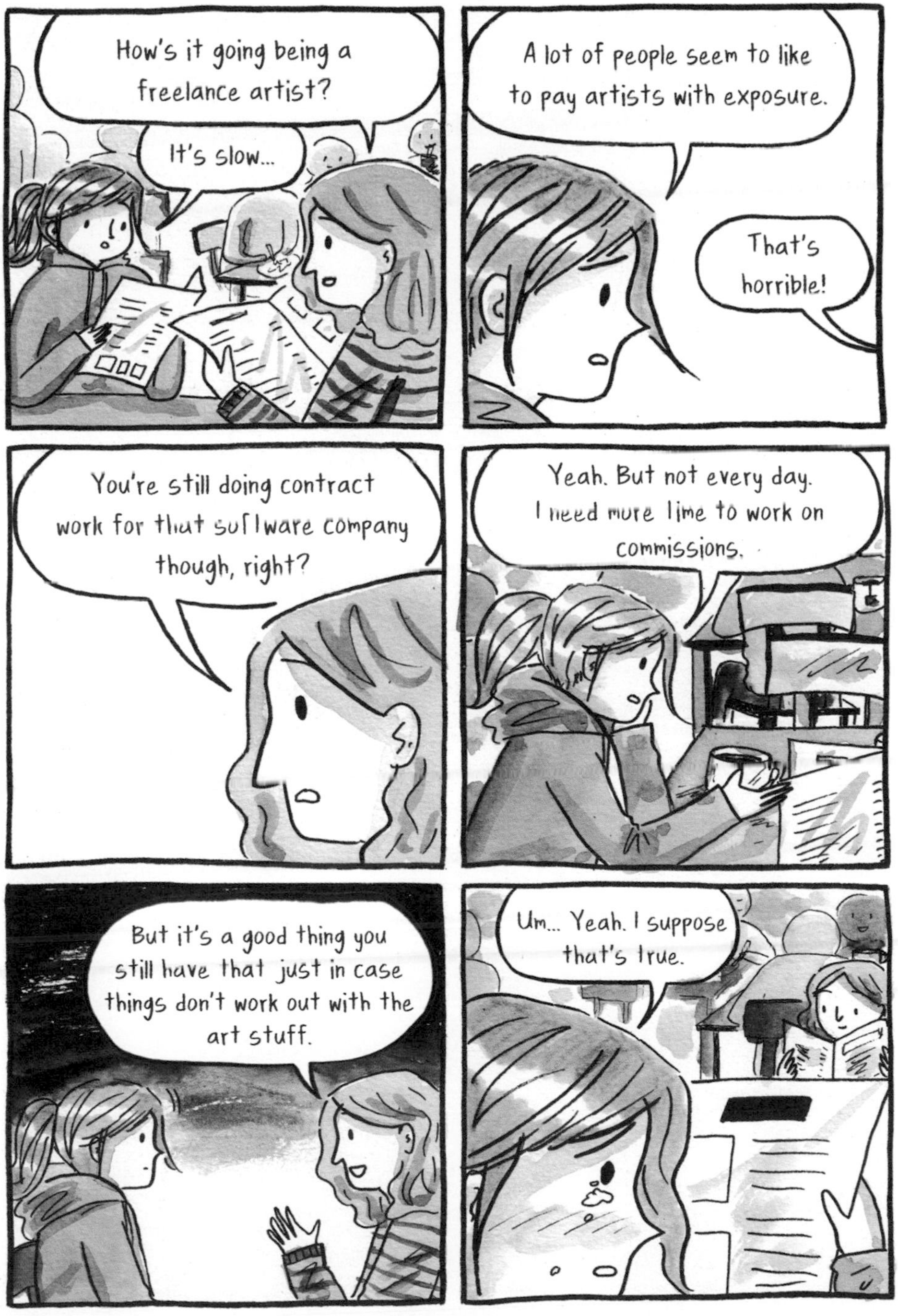
How's it going being a freelance artist?
It's slow...
A lot of people seem to like to pay artists with exposure.
That's horrible!
You're still doing contract work for that software company though, right?
Yeah. But not every day. I need more time to work on commissions.
But it's a good thing you still have that just in case things don't work out with the art stuff.
Um... Yeah. I suppose that's true.

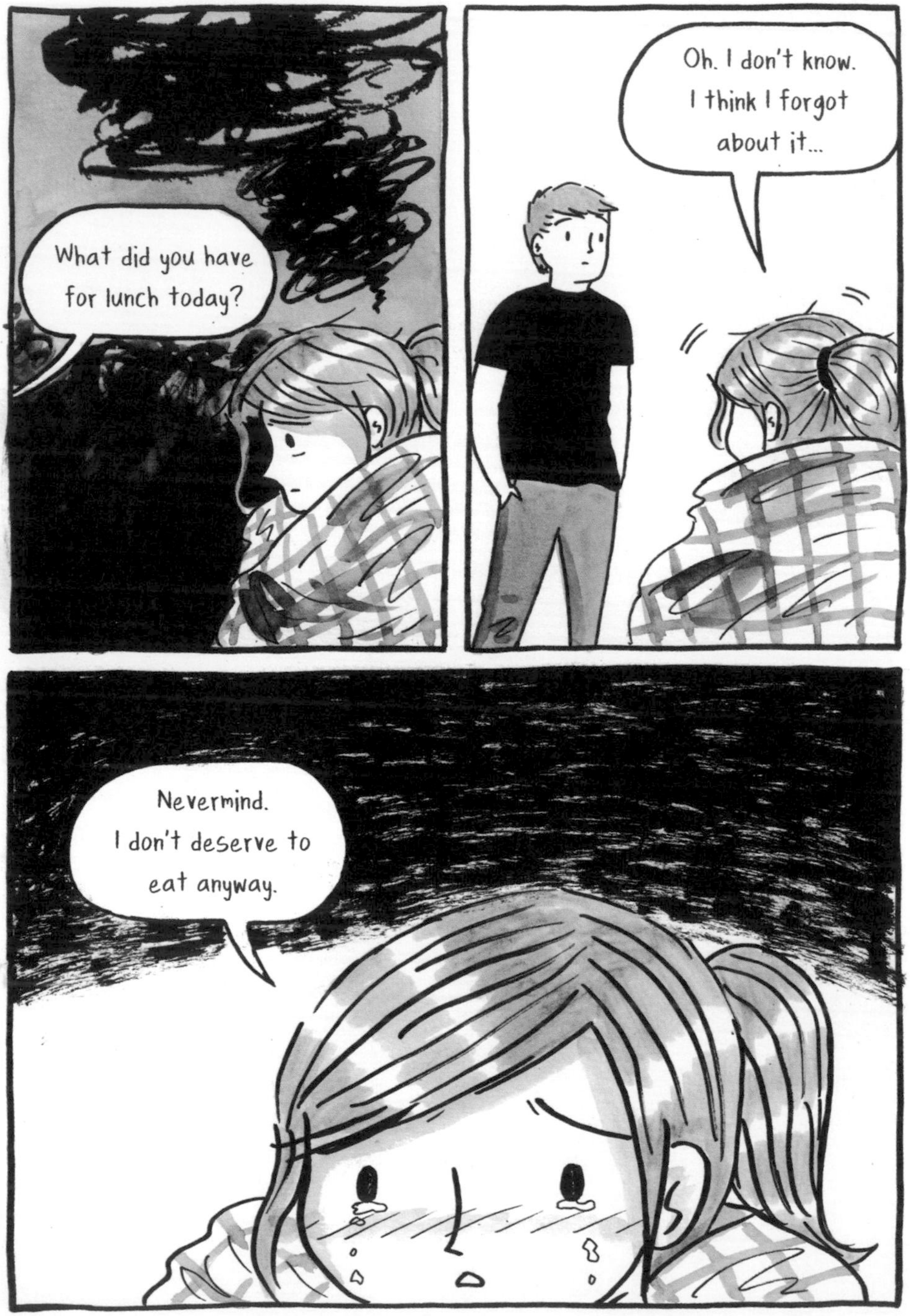
What did you have for lunch today?
Oh. I don't know. I think I forgot about it...
Nevermind. I don't deserve to eat anyway.

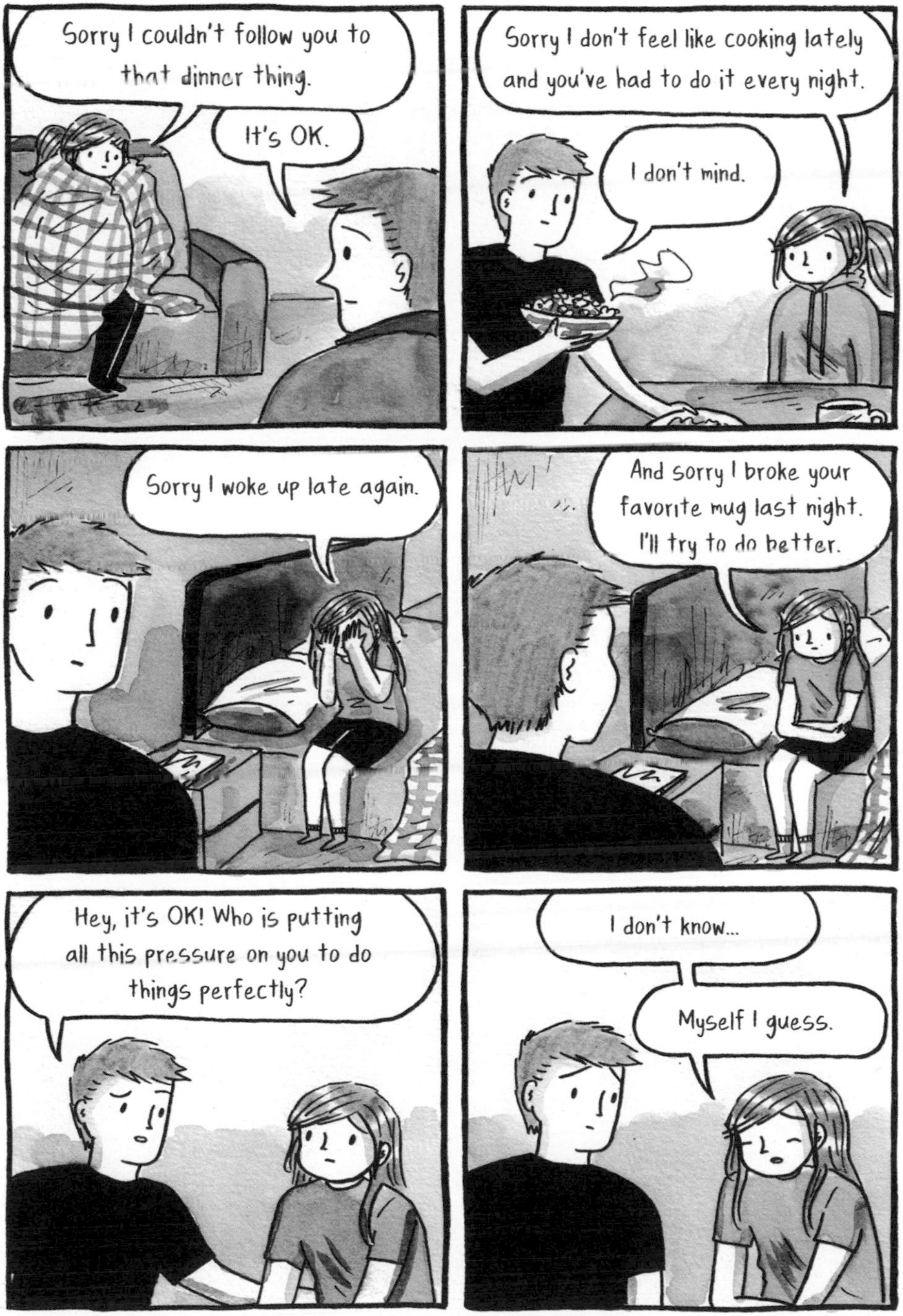
Sorry I couldn't follow you to that dinner thing.
It's OK.
Sorry I don't feel like cooking lately and you've had to do it every night.
I don't mind.
Sorry I woke up late again.
And sorry I broke your favorite mug last night. I'll try to do better.
Hey, it's OK! Who is putting all this pressure on you to do things perfectly?
I don't know...
Myself I guess.

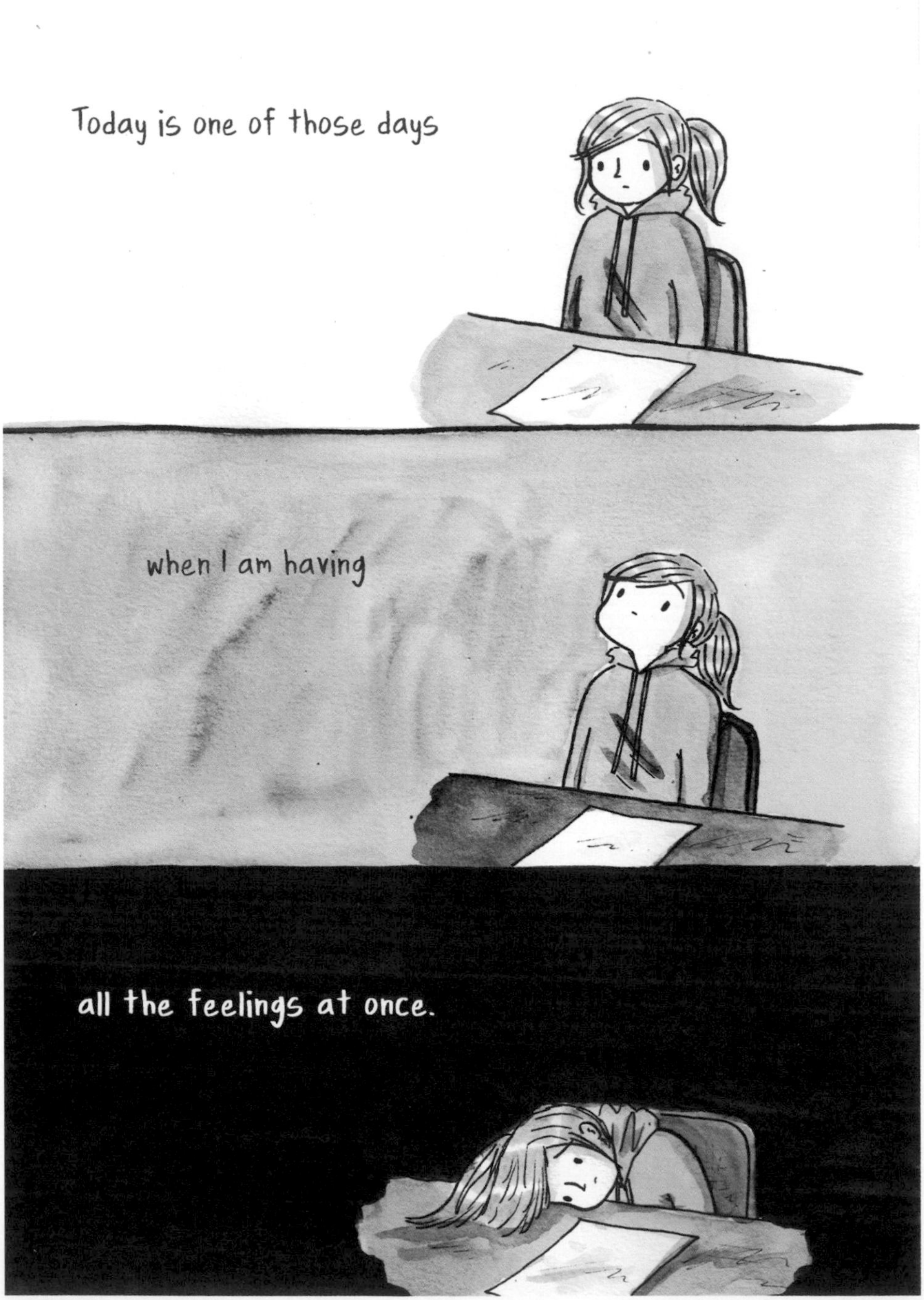
Today is one of those days
when I am having
all the feelings at once.

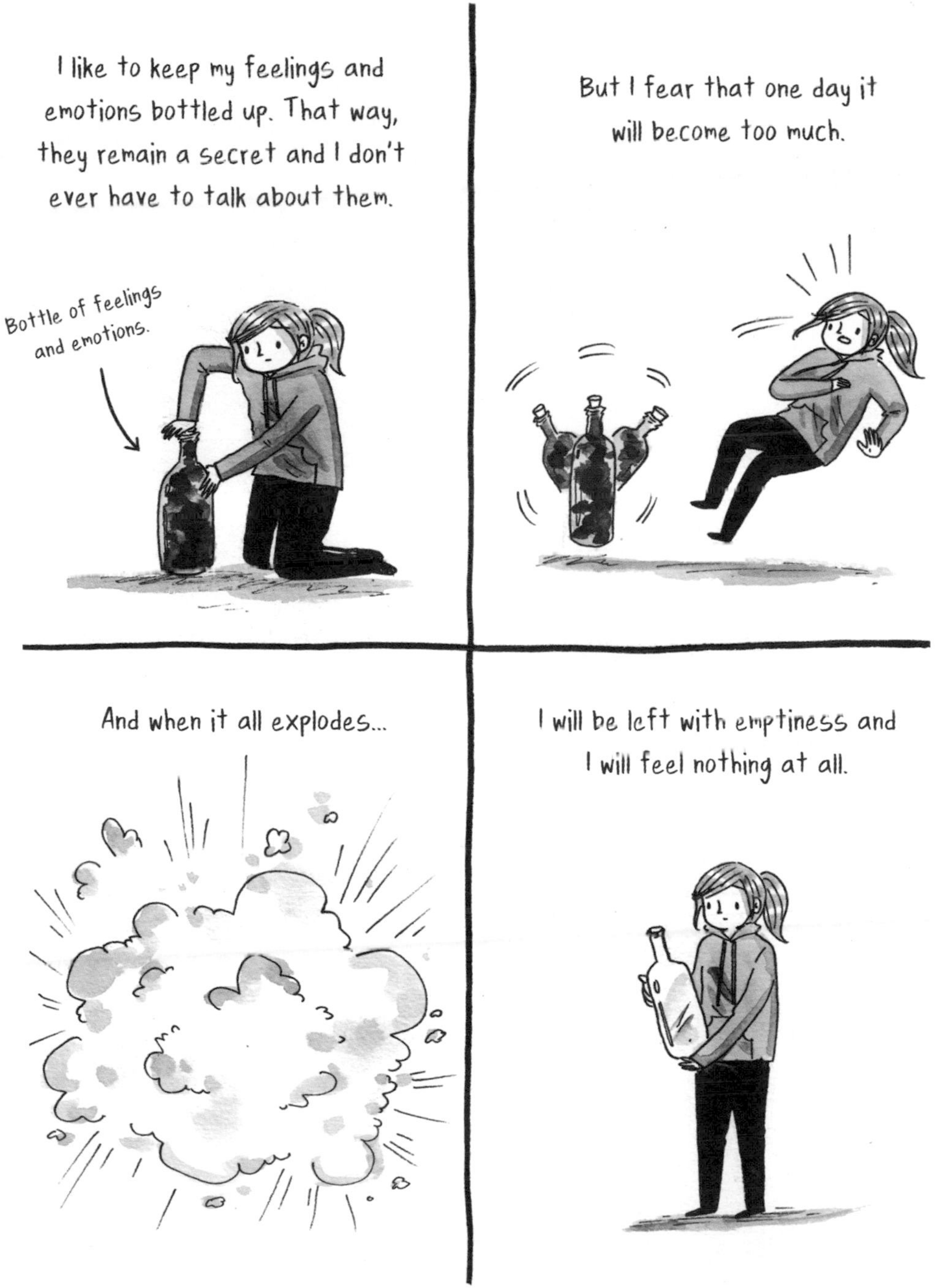
I like to keep my feelings and emotions bottled up. That way, they remain a secret and I don't ever have to talk about them.
Bottle of feelings and emotions.
But I fear that one day it will become too much.
And when it all explodes...
I will be left with emptiness and I will feel nothing at all.

Over the next few weeks, when I woke up every morning,

it was there.

This gut-wrenching sorrow...
Intense grief and pain.

Fear and anxiety radiating through me.

I felt like an alien in this world.

Disconnected from reality.

Observing life from behind a thick, blurry glass wall.

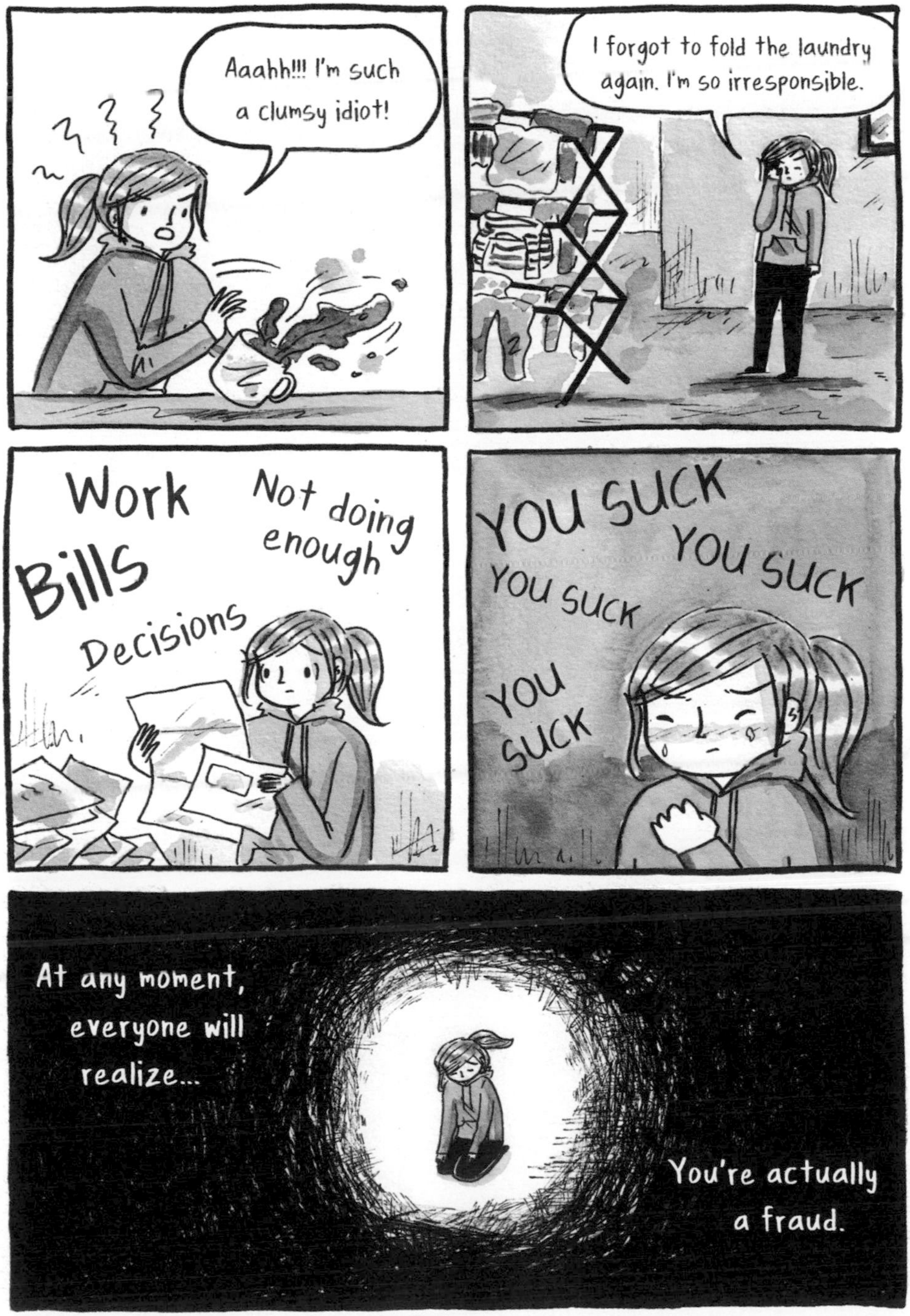

Aaahh!!! I'm such a clumsy idiot!
I forgot to fold the laundry again. I'm so irresponsible.
Work
Not doing enough
Bills
Decisions
YOU SUCK
YOU SUCK
YOU SUCK
YOU SUCK
At any moment, everyone will realize...
You're actually a fraud.

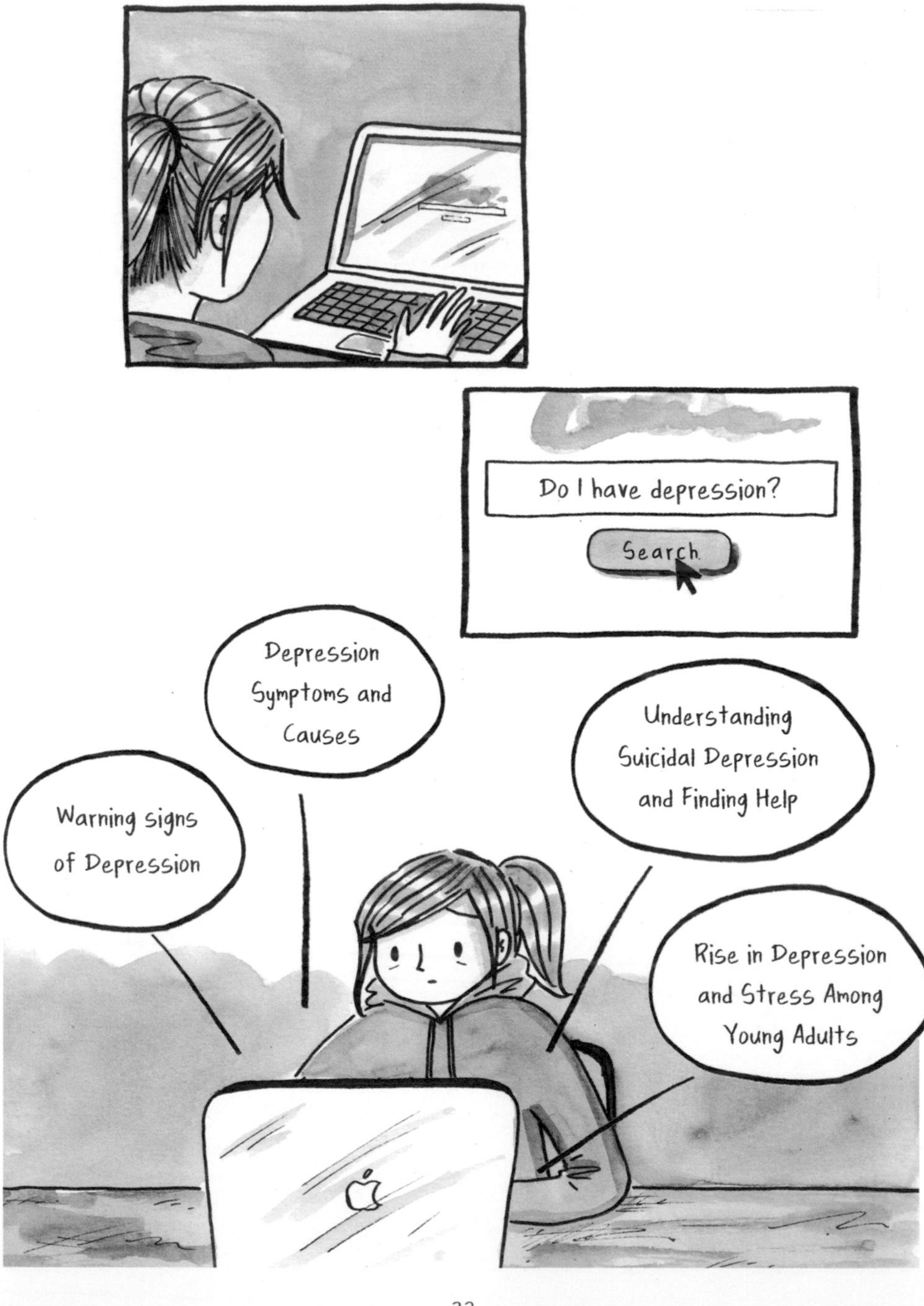
Do I have depression?
Search
Depression Symptoms and Causes
Understanding Suicidal Depression and Finding Help
Warning signs of Depression
Rise in Depression and Stress Among Young Adults

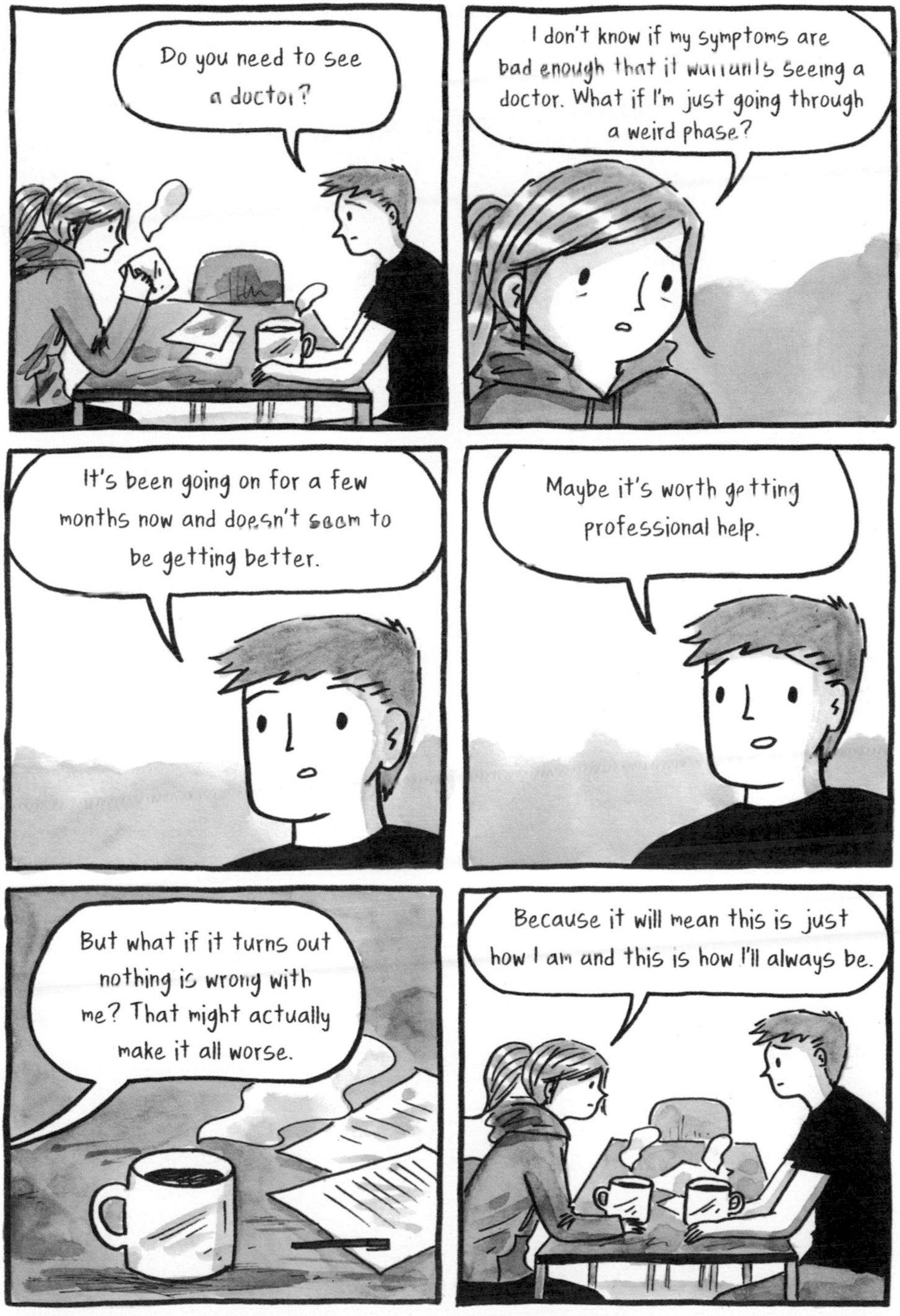
Do you need to see a doctor?
I don't know if my symptoms are bad enough that it warrants seeing a doctor. What if I'm just going through a weird phase?
It's been going on for a few months now and doesn't seem to be getting better.
Maybe it's worth getting professional help.
But what if it turns out nothing is wrong with me? That might actually make it all worse.
Because it will mean this is just how I am and this is how I'll always be.

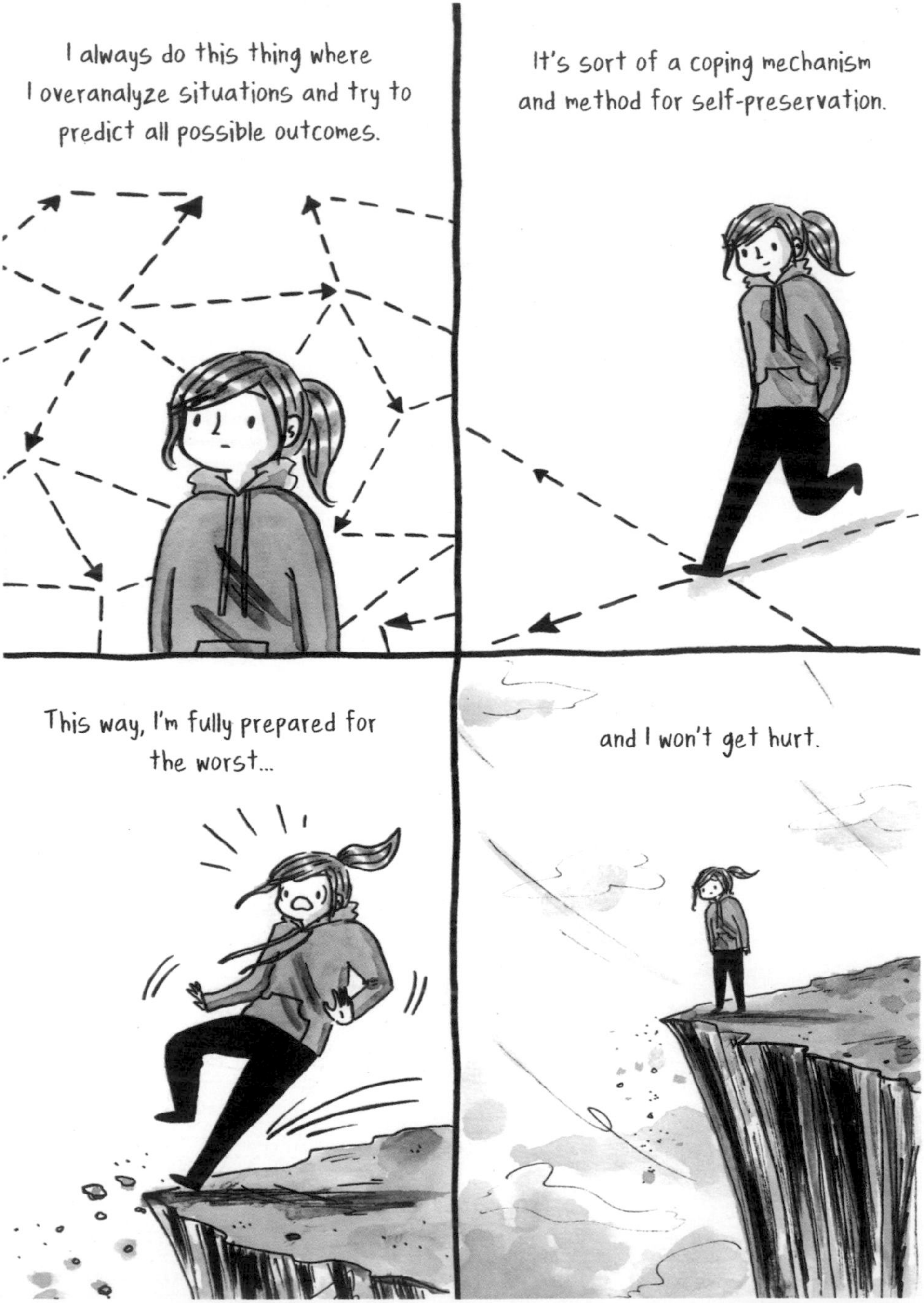
I always do this thing where I overanalyze situations and try to predict all possible outcomes.
It's sort of a coping mechanism and method for self-preservation.
This way, I'm fully prepared for the worst...
and I won't get hurt.

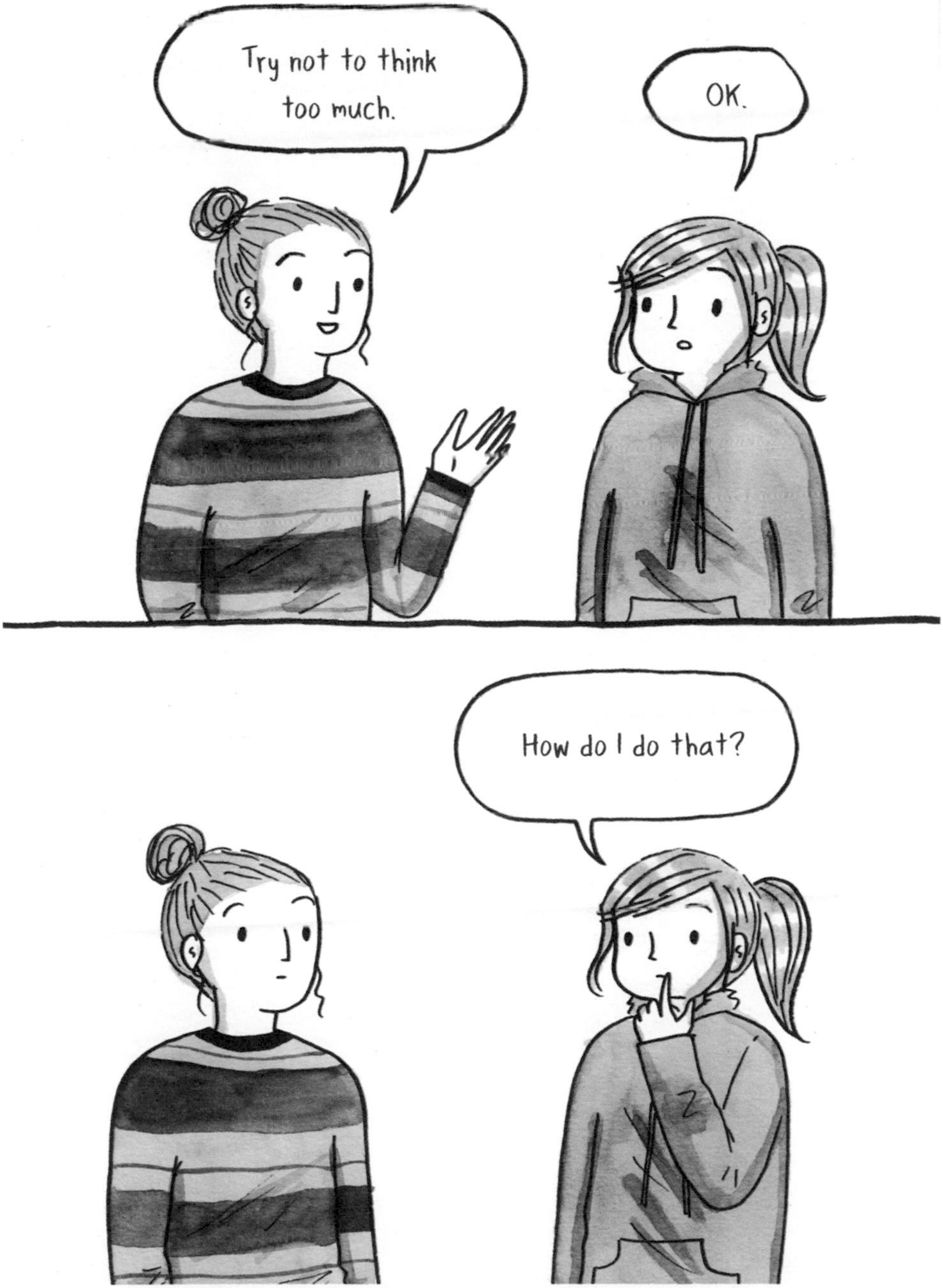
Try not to think too much.
OK.
How do I do that?

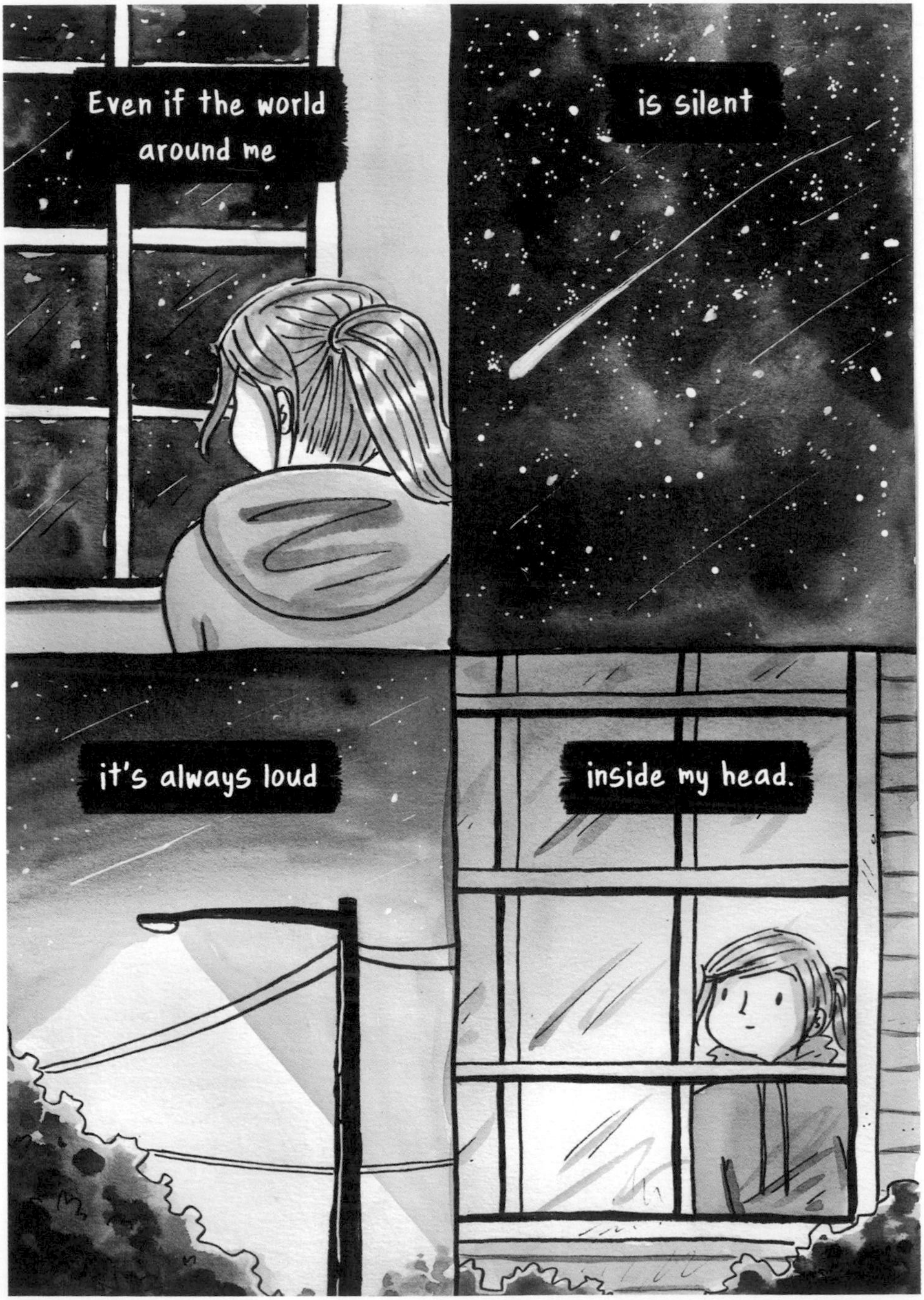

Even if the world around me
is silent
it's always loud
inside my head.

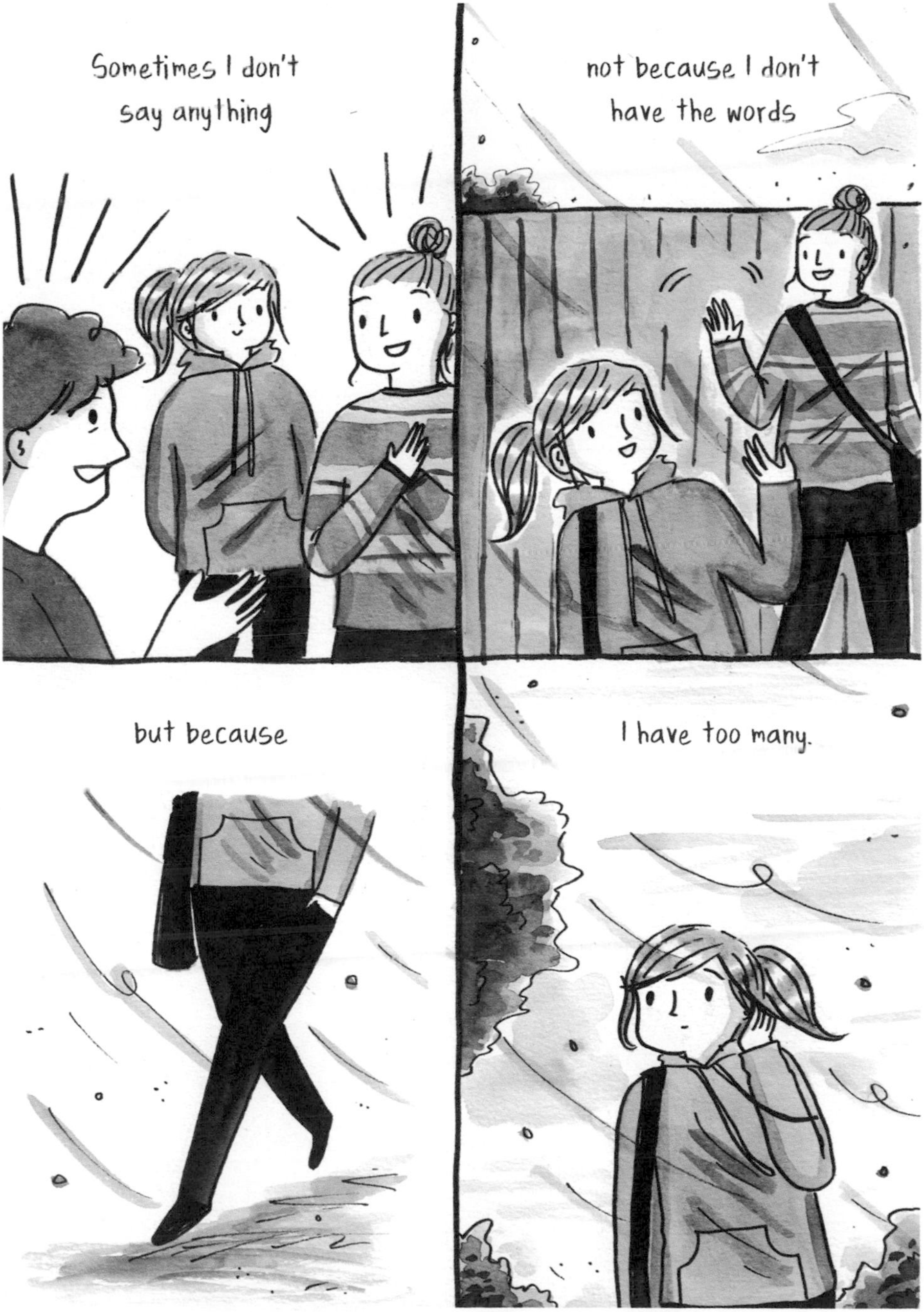
Sometimes I don't say anything
not because I don't have the words
but because
I have too many.

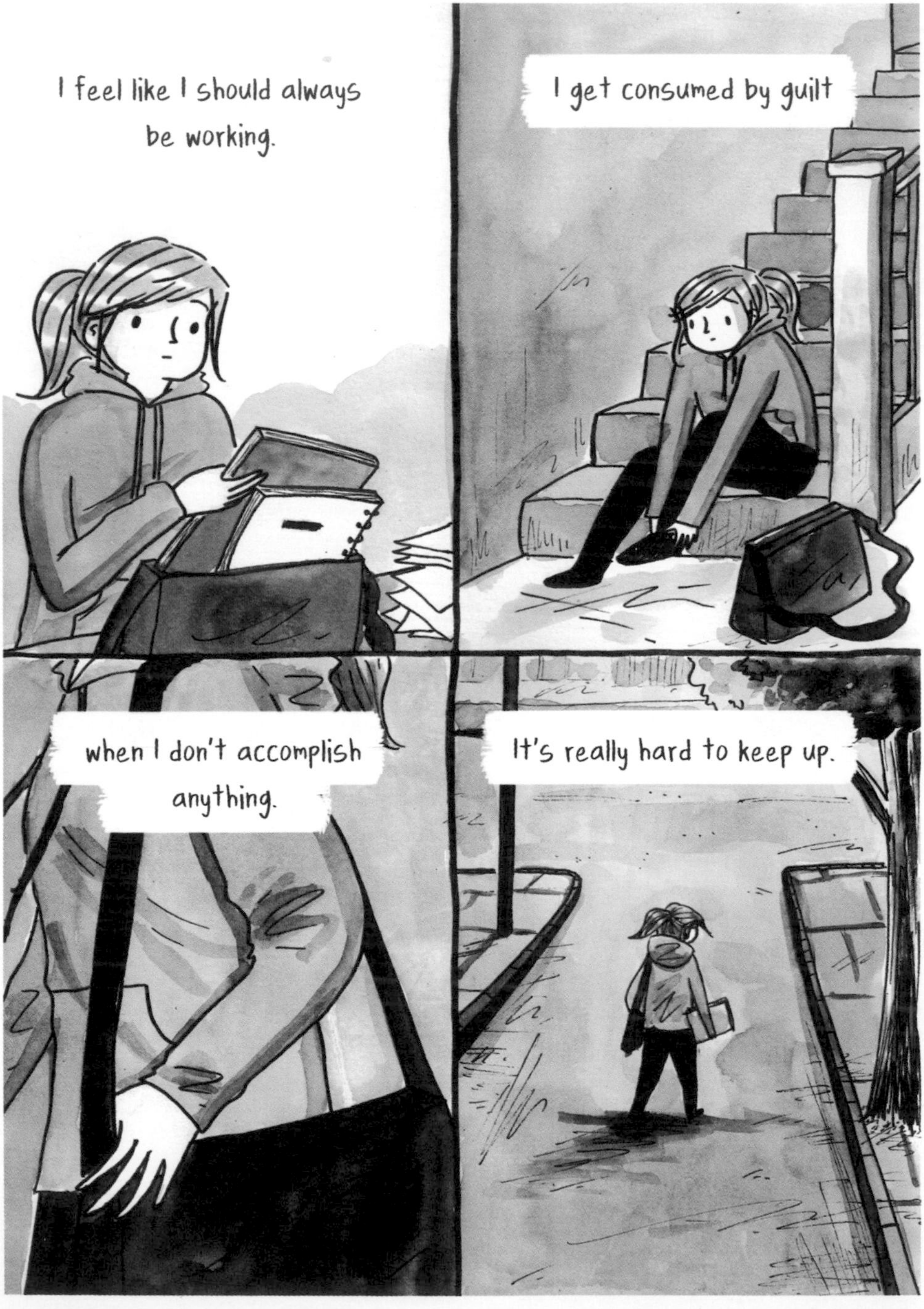
I feel like I should always be working.
I get consumed by guilt
when I don't accomplish anything.
It's really hard to keep up.

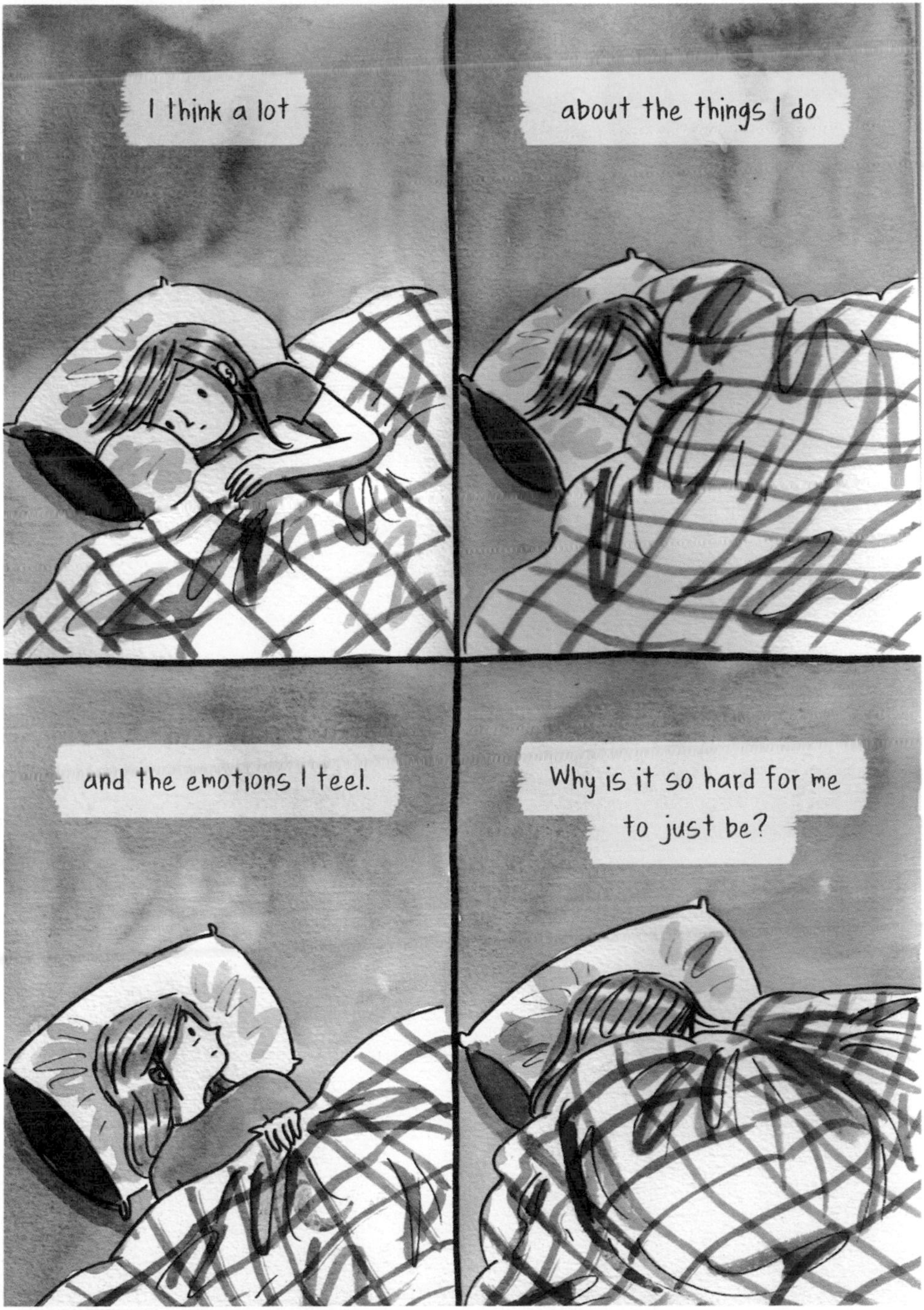
I think a lot
about the things I do
and the emotions I feel.
Why is it so hard for me to just be?

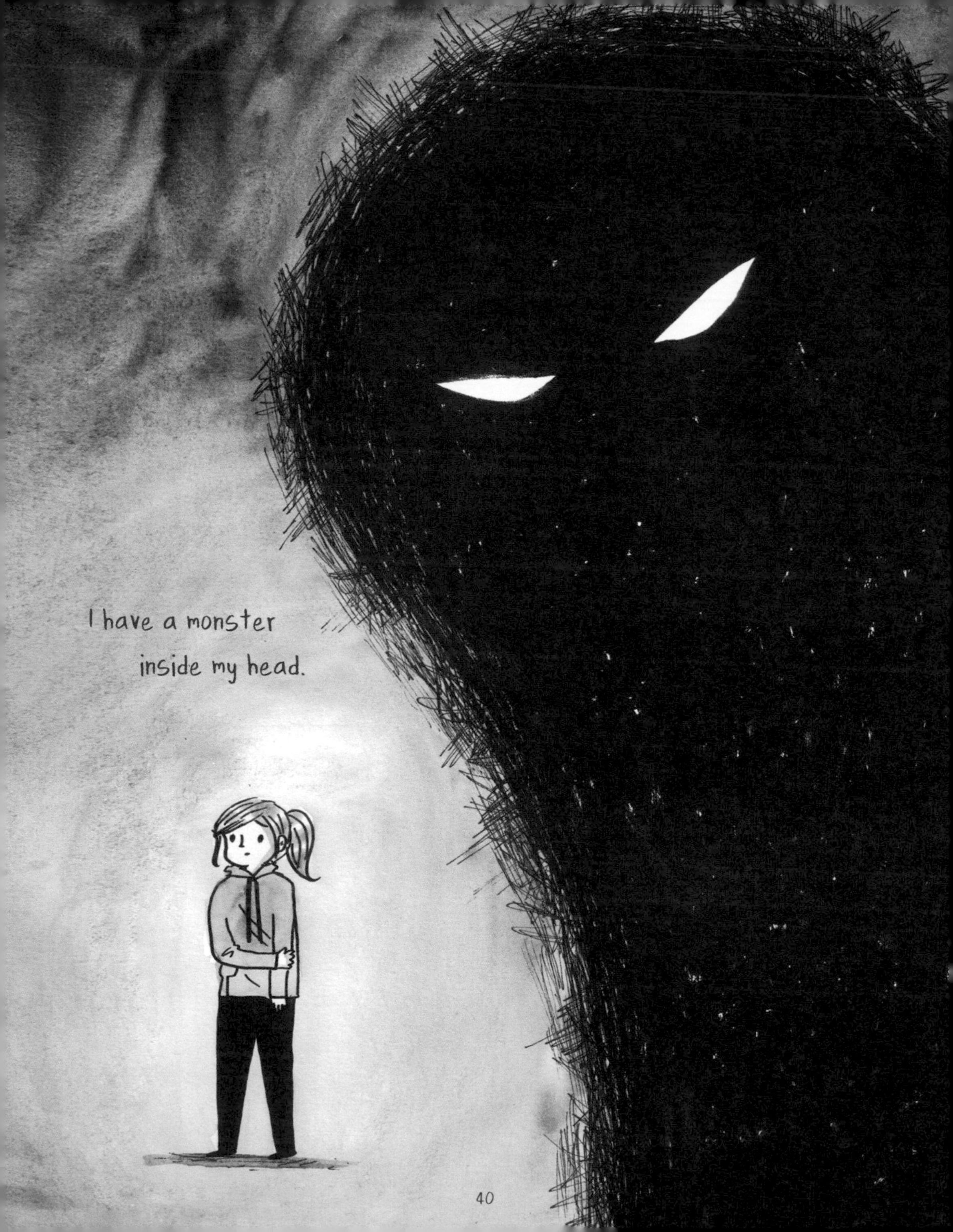
I have a monster
inside my head.

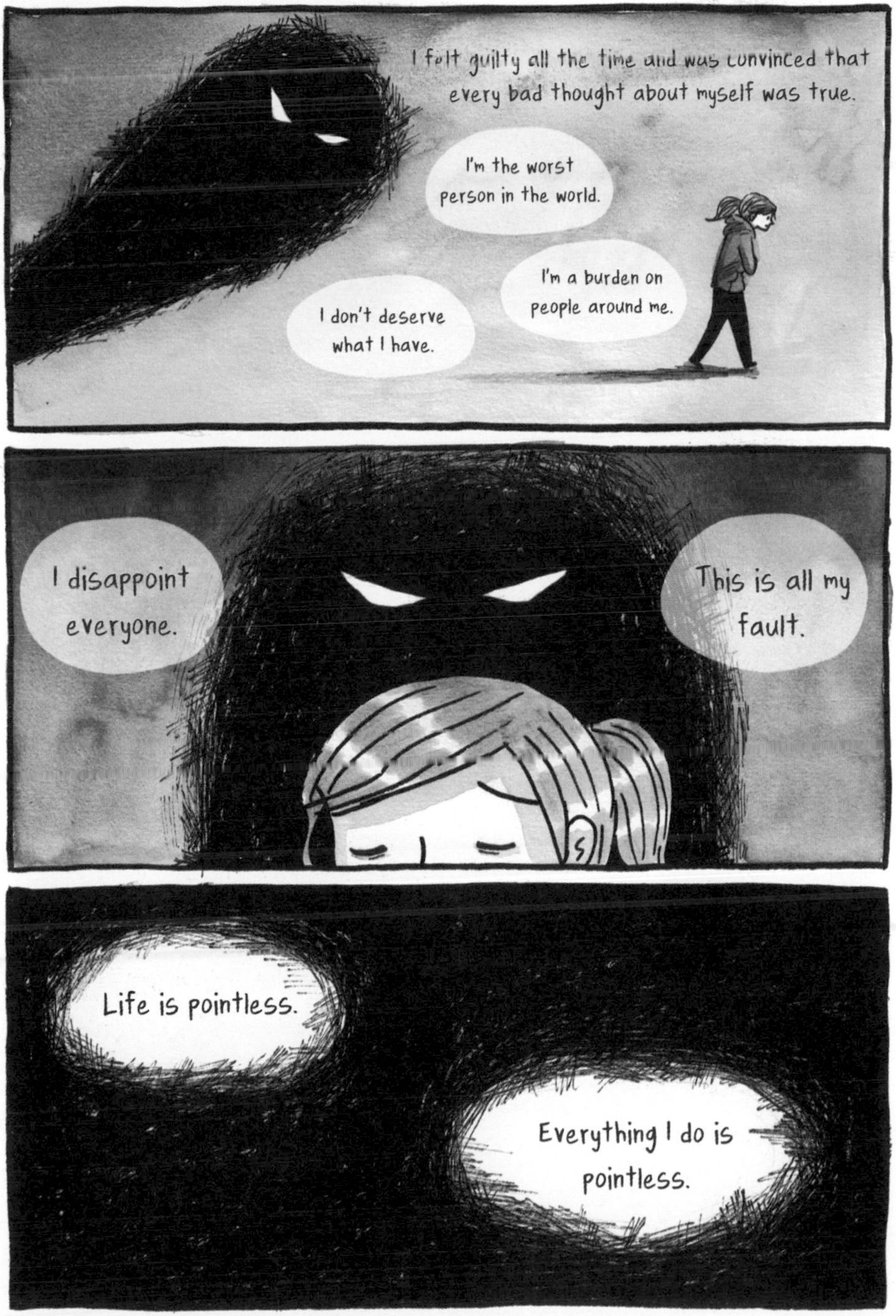
I felt guilty all the time and was convinced that every bad thought about myself was true.
I'm the worst person in the world.
I'm a burden on people around me.
I don't deserve what I have.
I disappoint everyone.
This is all my fault.
Life is pointless.
Everything I do is pointless.

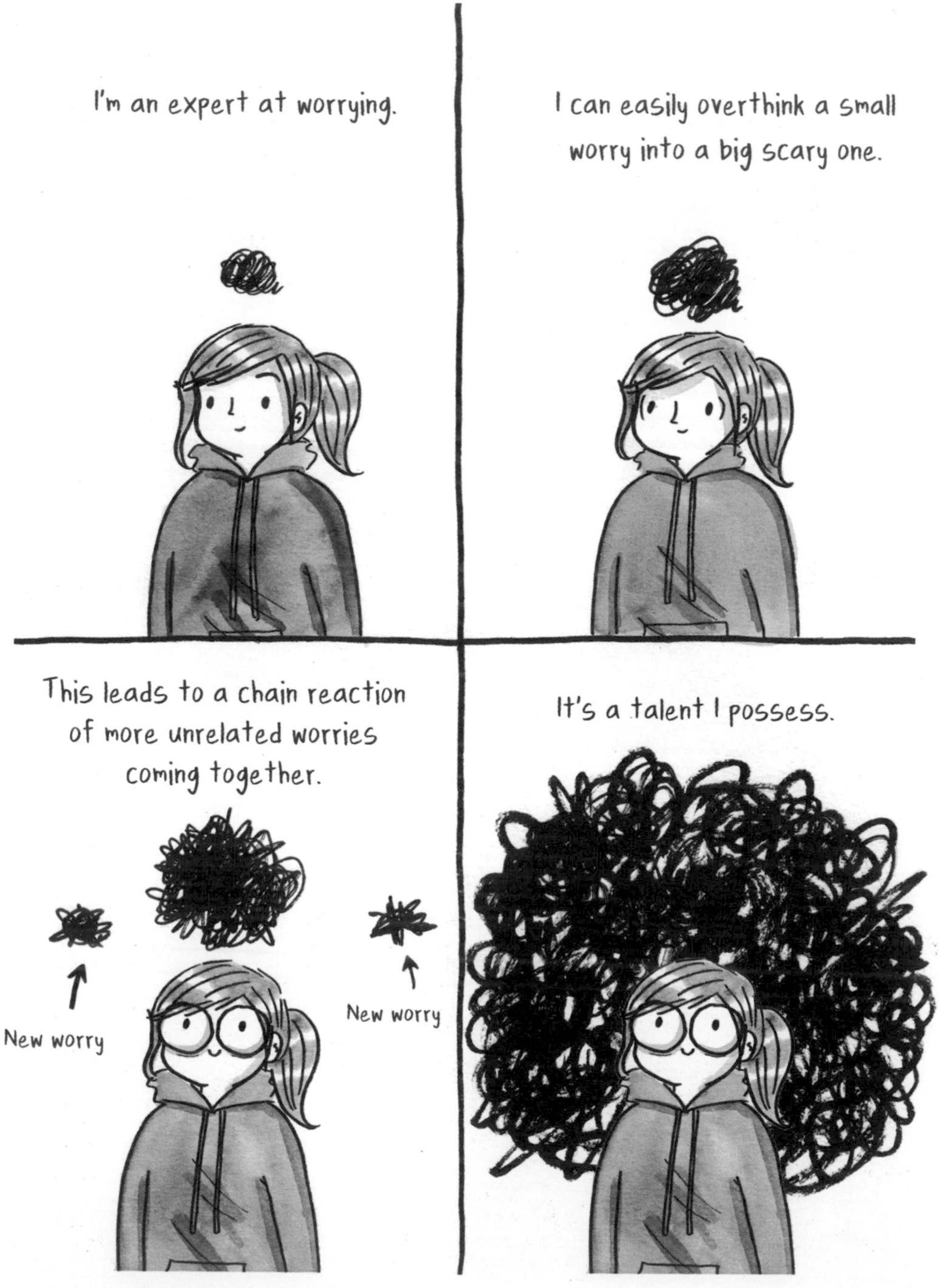
I'm an expert at worrying.
I can easily overthink a small worry into a big scary one.
This leads to a chain reaction of more unrelated worries coming together.
New worry
New worry
It's a talent I possess.

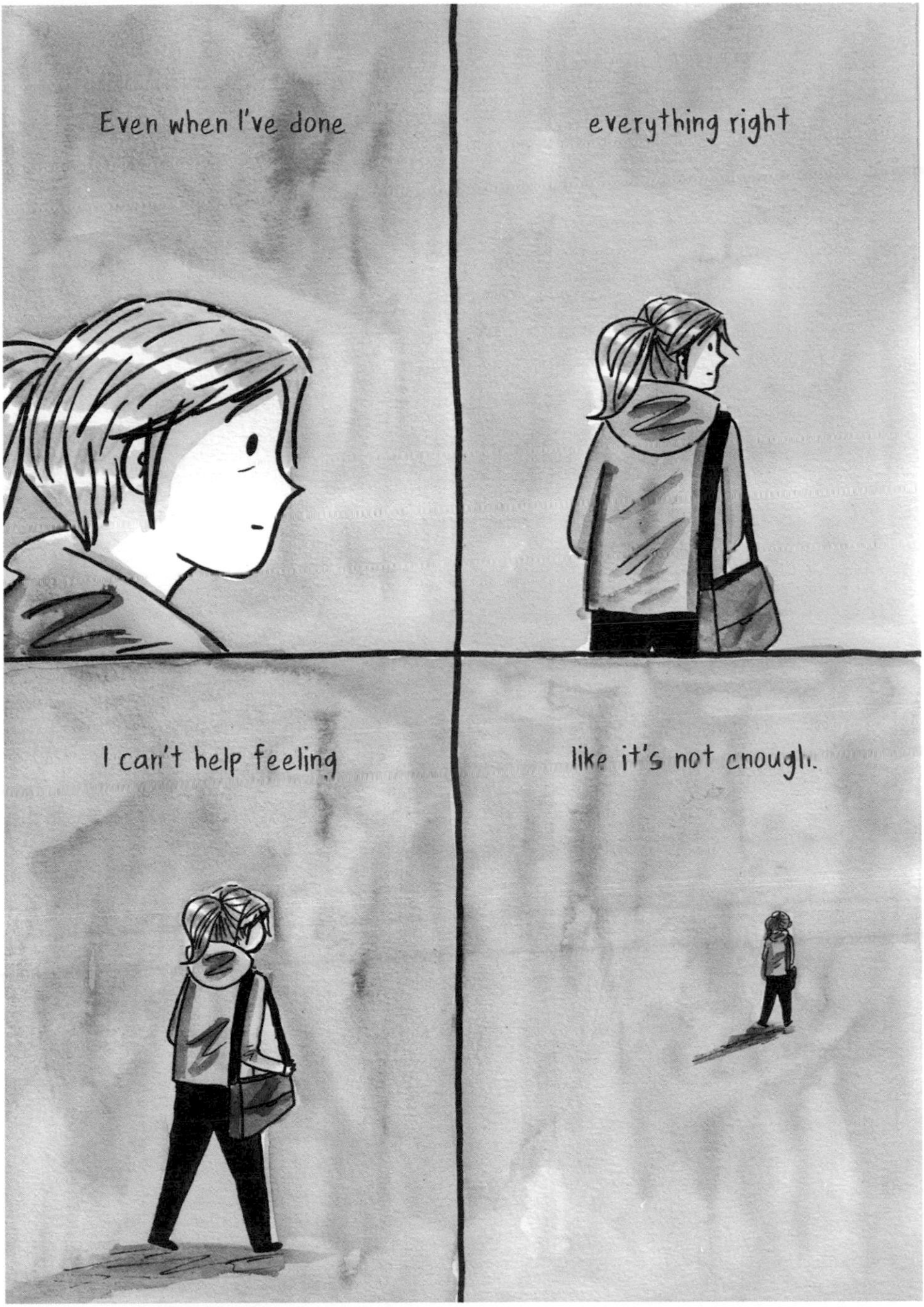
Even when I've done
everything right
I can't help feeling
like it's not enough.

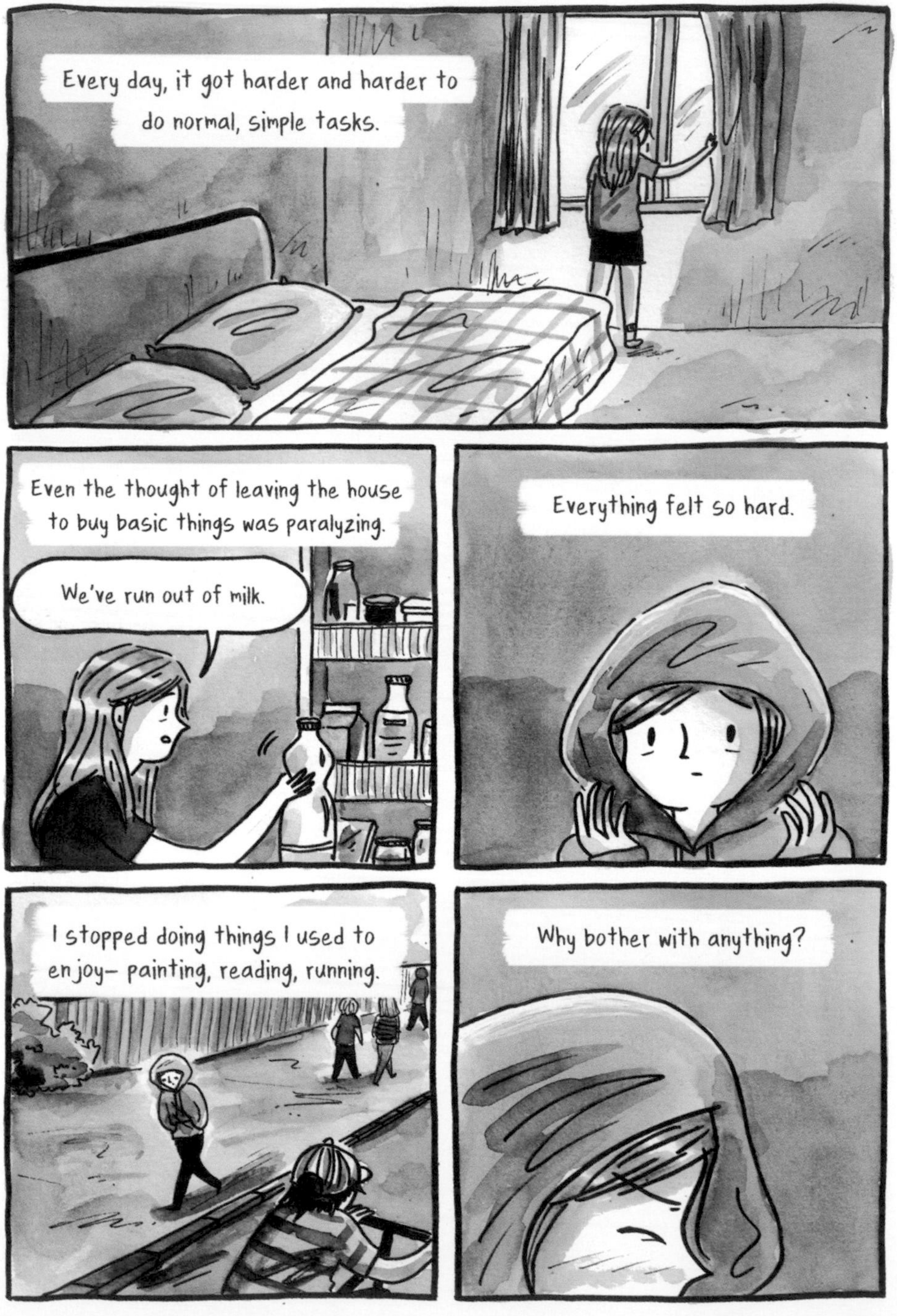
Every day, it got harder and harder to do normal, simple tasks.
Even the thought of leaving the house to buy basic things was paralyzing.
We've run out of milk.
Everything felt so hard.
I stopped doing things I used to enjoy– painting, reading, running.
Why bother with anything?

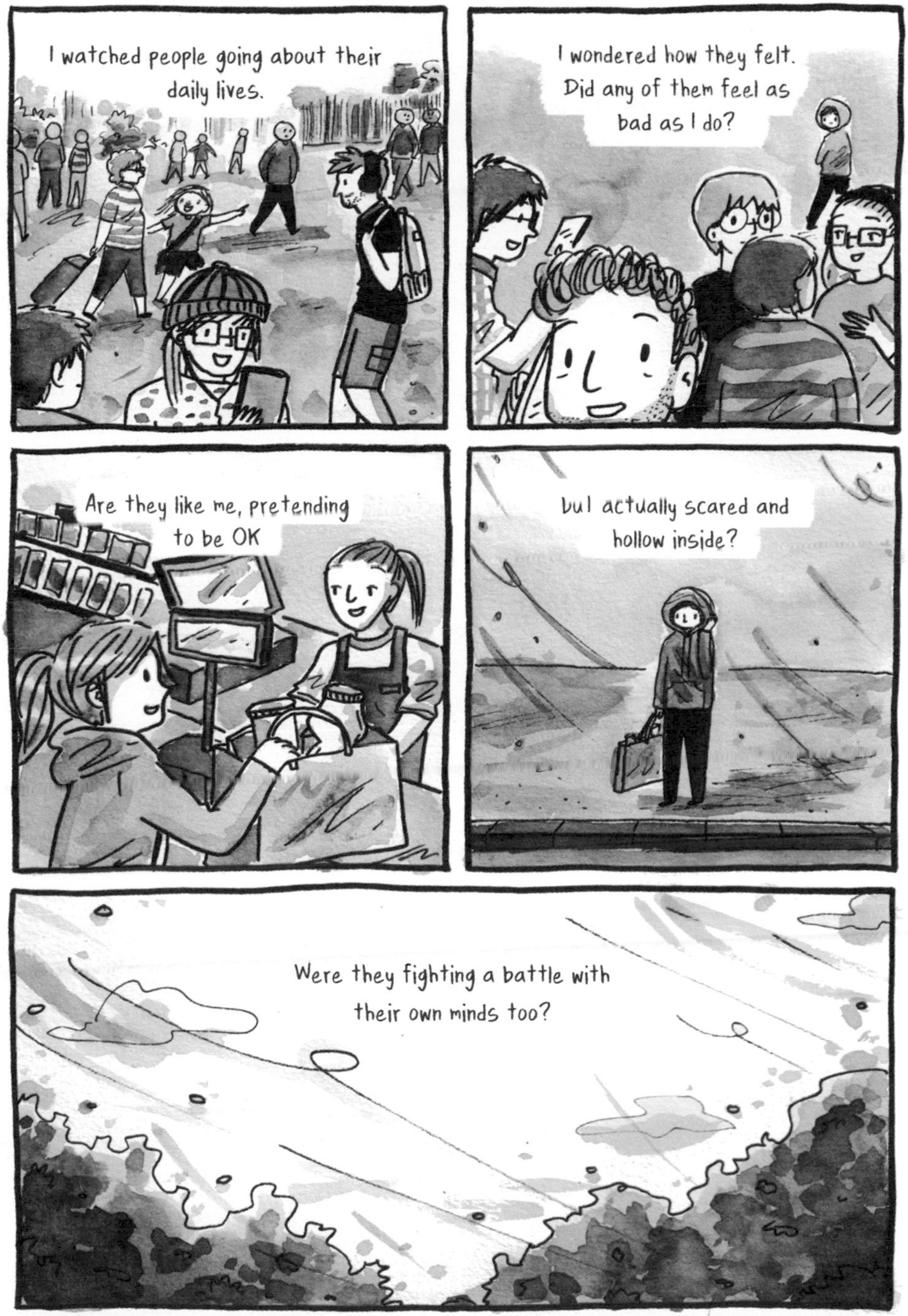
I watched people going about their daily lives.
I wondered how they felt. Did any of them feel as bad as I do?
Are they like me, pretending to be OK
but actually scared and hollow inside?
Were they fighting a battle with their own minds too?

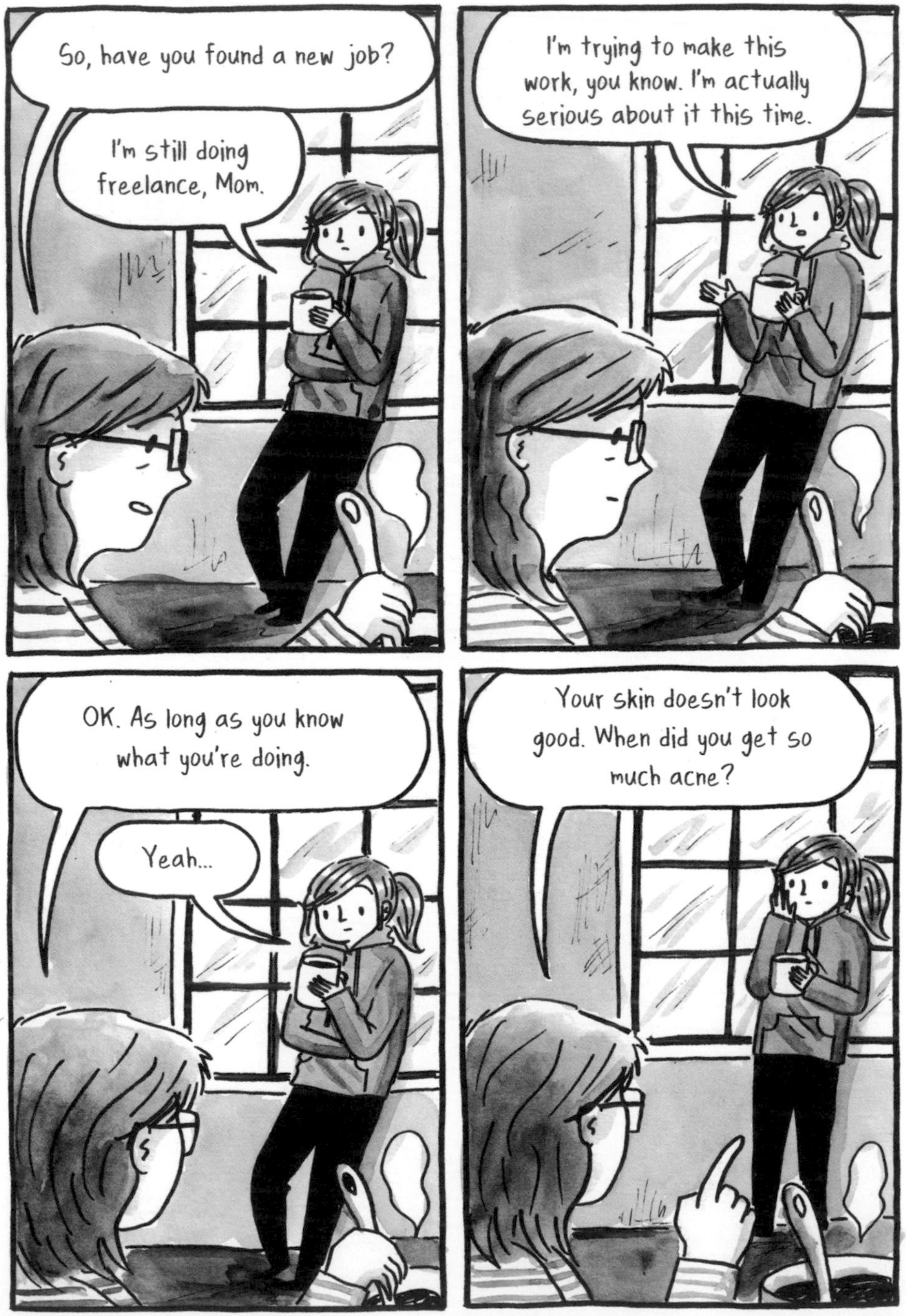
So, have you found a new job?
I'm still doing freelance, Mom.
I'm trying to make this work, you know. I'm actually serious about it this time.
OK. As long as you know what you're doing.
Yeah...
Your skin doesn't look good. When did you get so much acne?

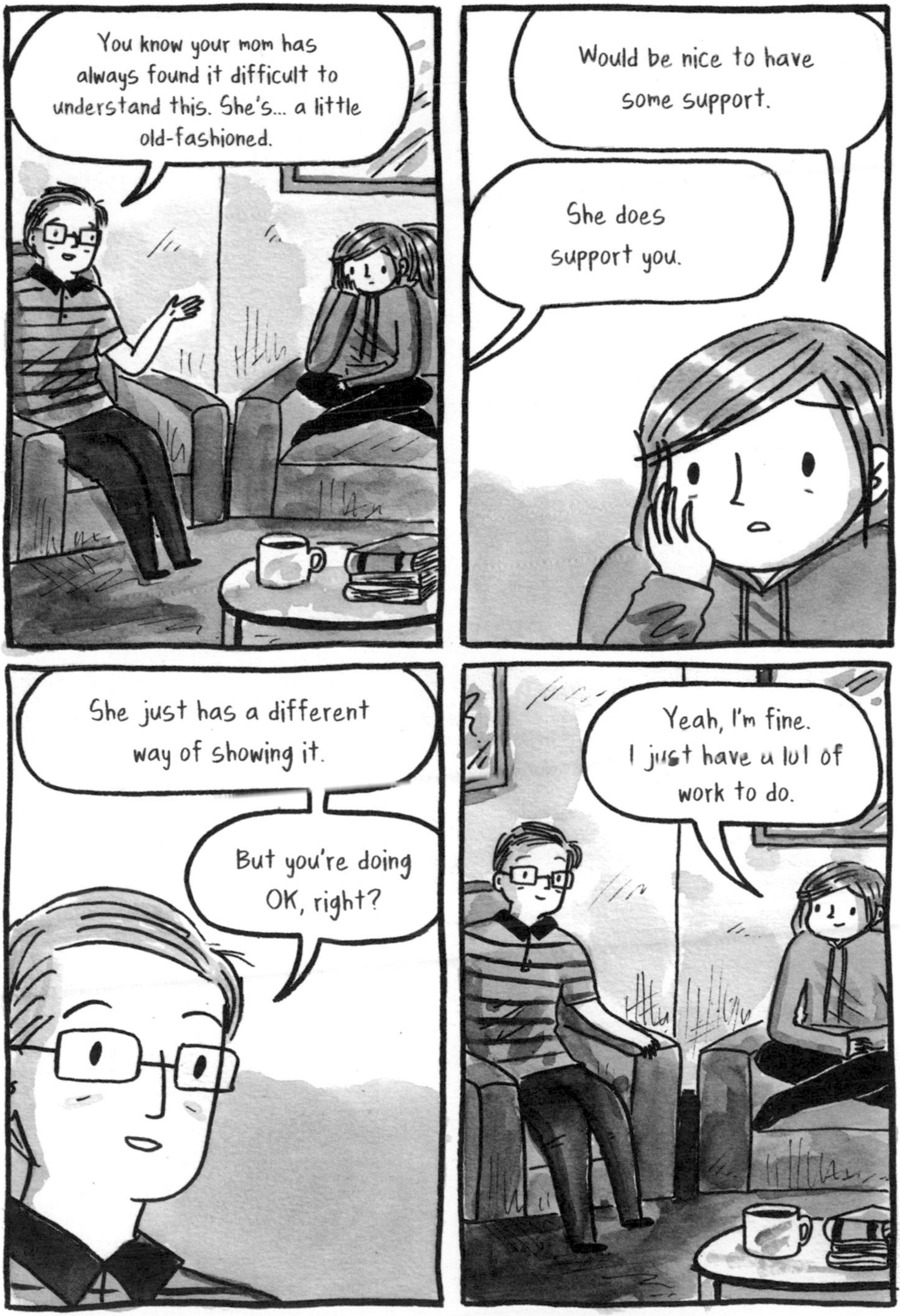
You know your mom has always found it difficult to understand this. She's... a little old-fashioned.
Would be nice to have some support.
She does support you.
She just has a different way of showing it.
But you're doing OK, right?
Yeah, I'm fine. I just have a lot of work to do.

Don't you dare cry.

Not now.

Don't show any weakness.

It will mean you've given up and everything is ruined.

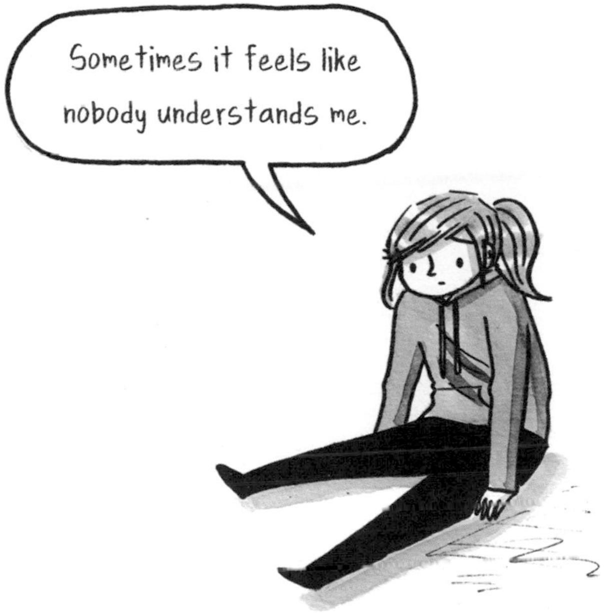
Sometimes it feels like nobody understands me.

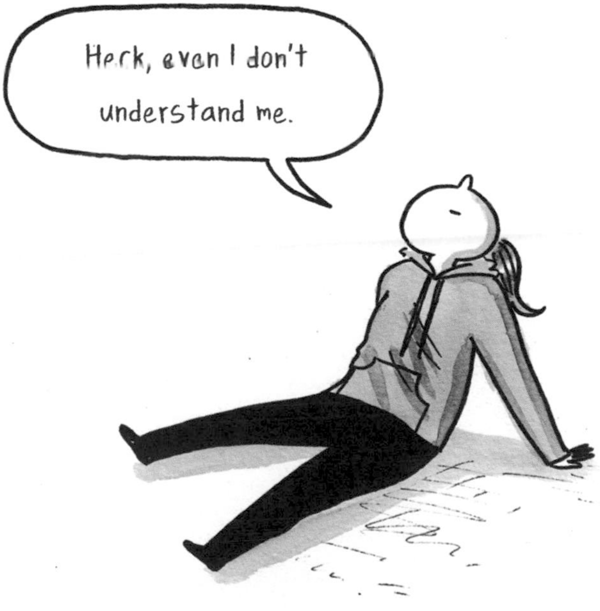
Heck, even I don't understand me.

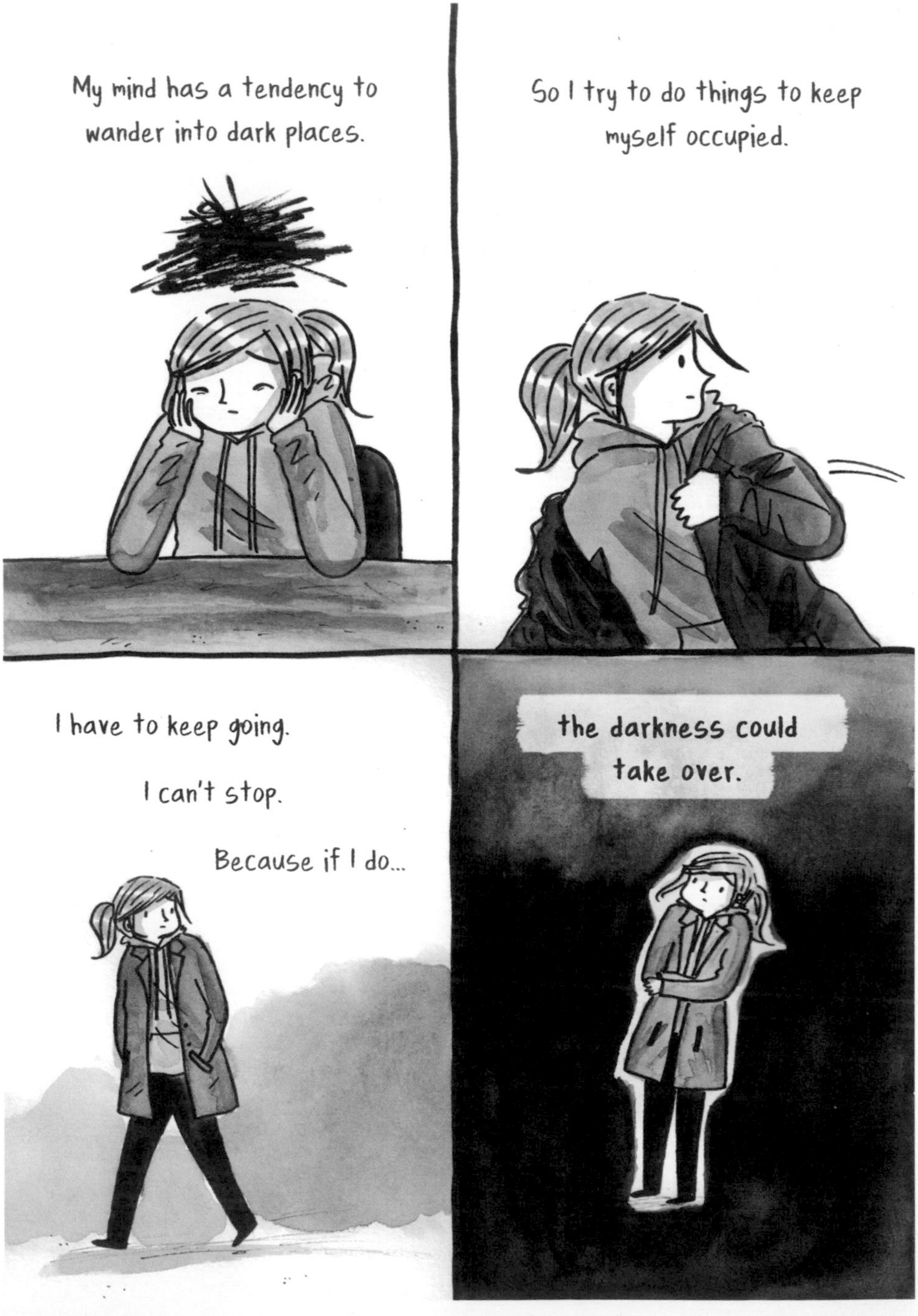
My mind has a tendency to wander into dark places.
So I try to do things to keep myself occupied.
I have to keep going.
I can't stop.
Because if I do...
the darkness could take over.

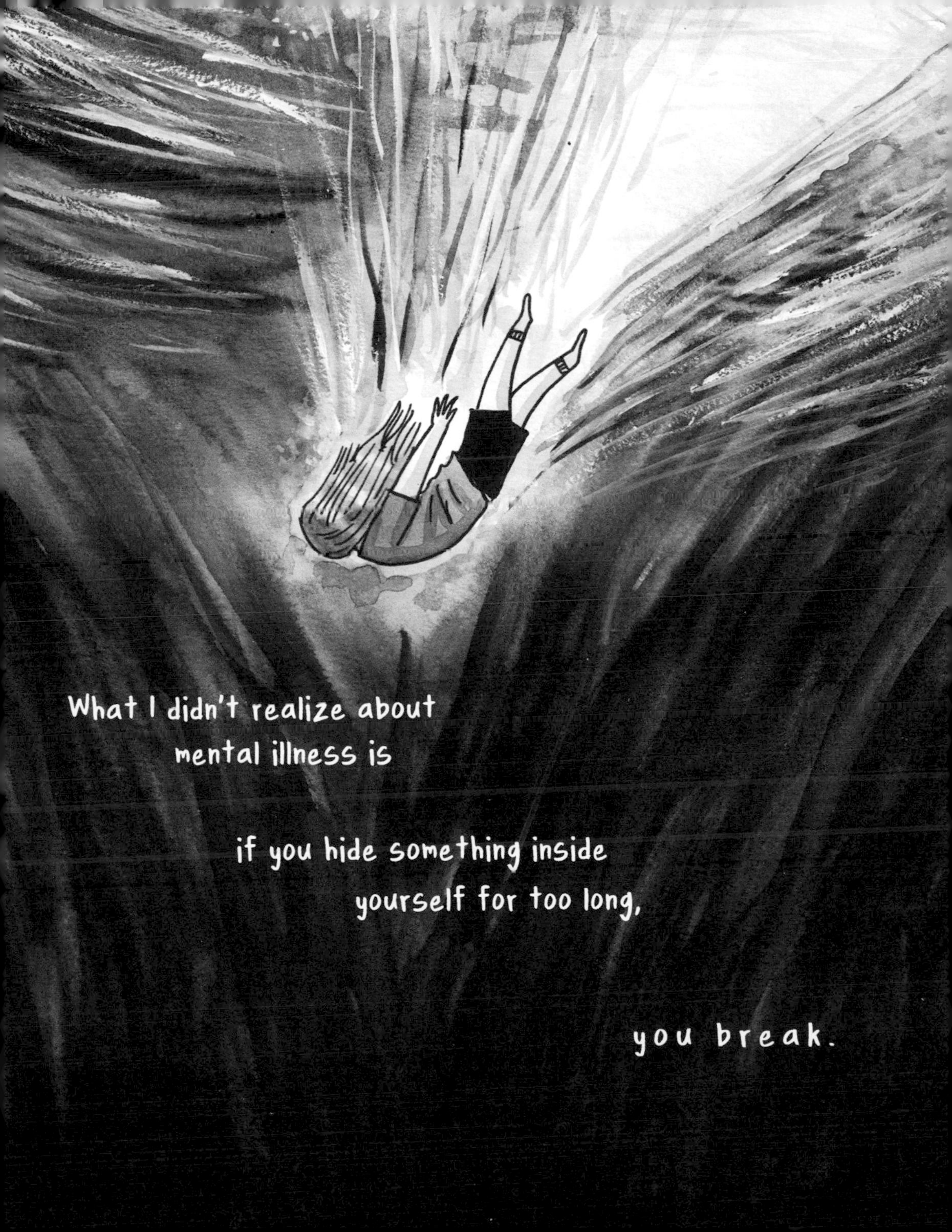
What I didn't realize about
mental illness is
if you hide something inside
yourself for too long,
you break.

At night, I lay awake
even though I was
completely exhausted.

When I did fall asleep,
I didn't want to
wake up.

And when I did, I wished I had
never woken up.

I just wanted to
disappear forever.

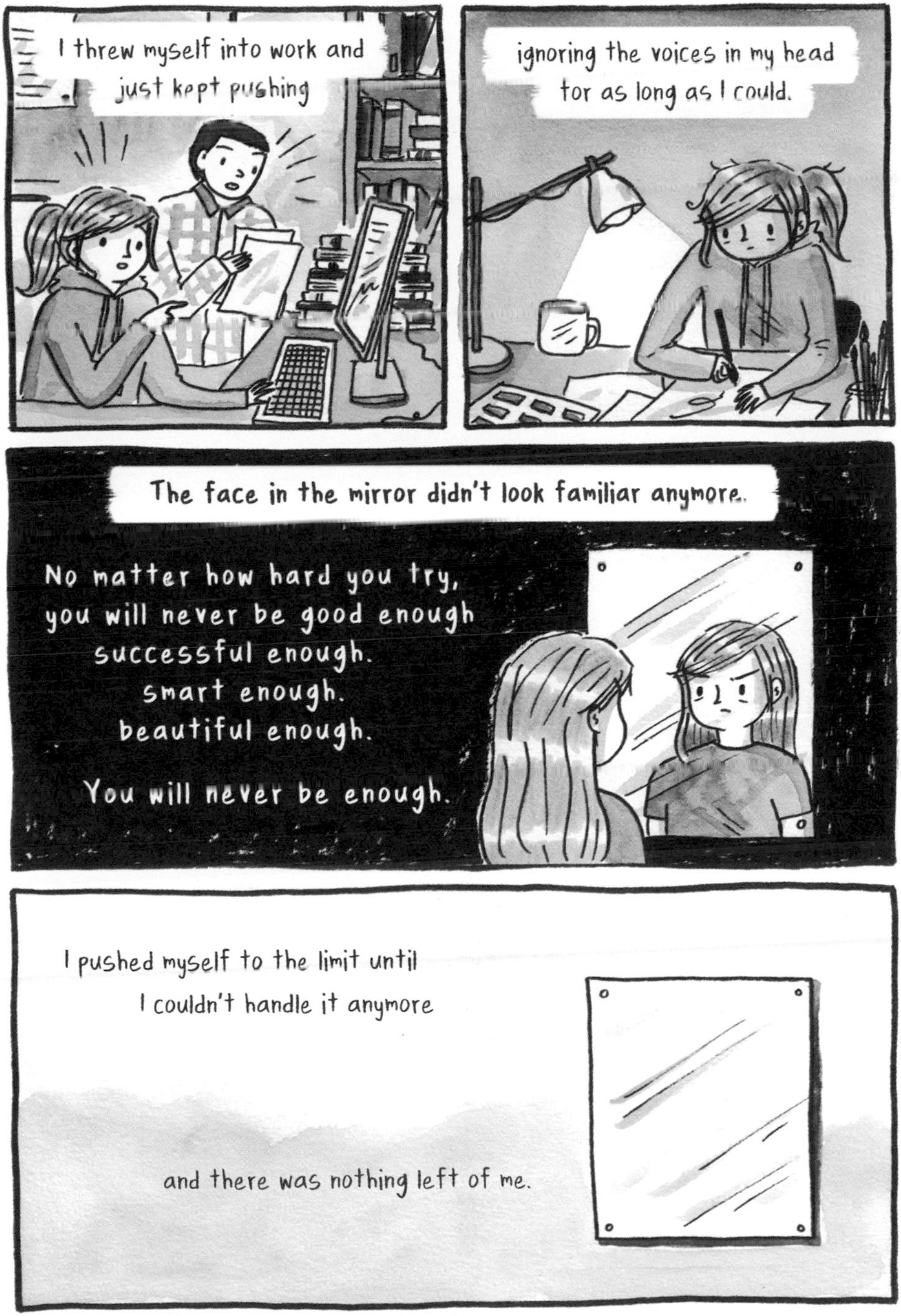
I threw myself into work and just kept pushing
ignoring the voices in my head for as long as I could.
The face in the mirror didn't look familiar anymore.
No matter how hard you try,
you will never be good enough
successful enough.
smart enough.
beautiful enough.
You will never be enough.
I pushed myself to the limit until
I couldn't handle it anymore
and there was nothing left of me.

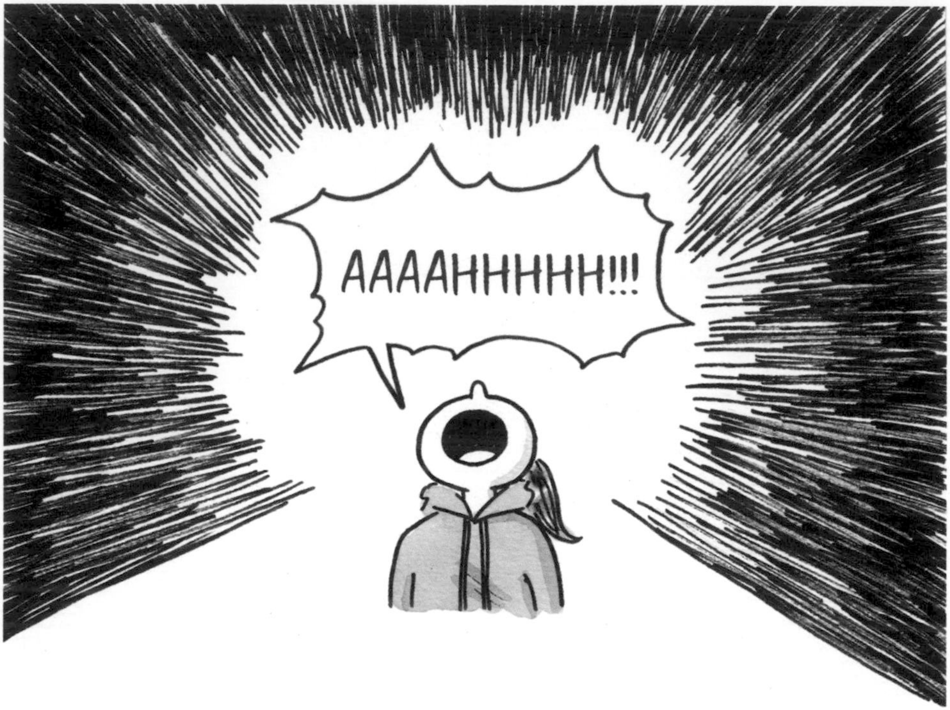
AAAAHHHHH!!!

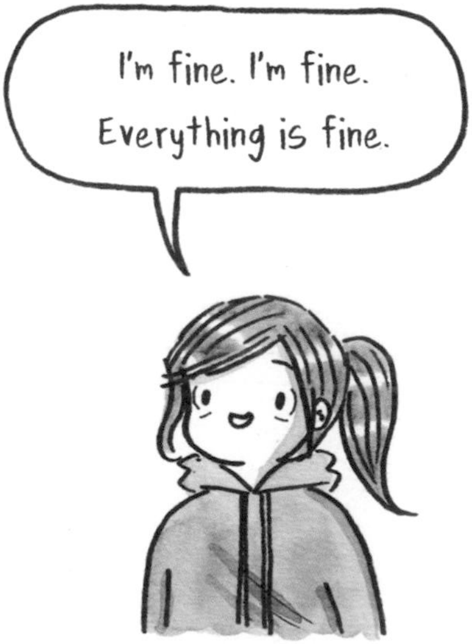
I'm fine. I'm fine.
Everything is fine.

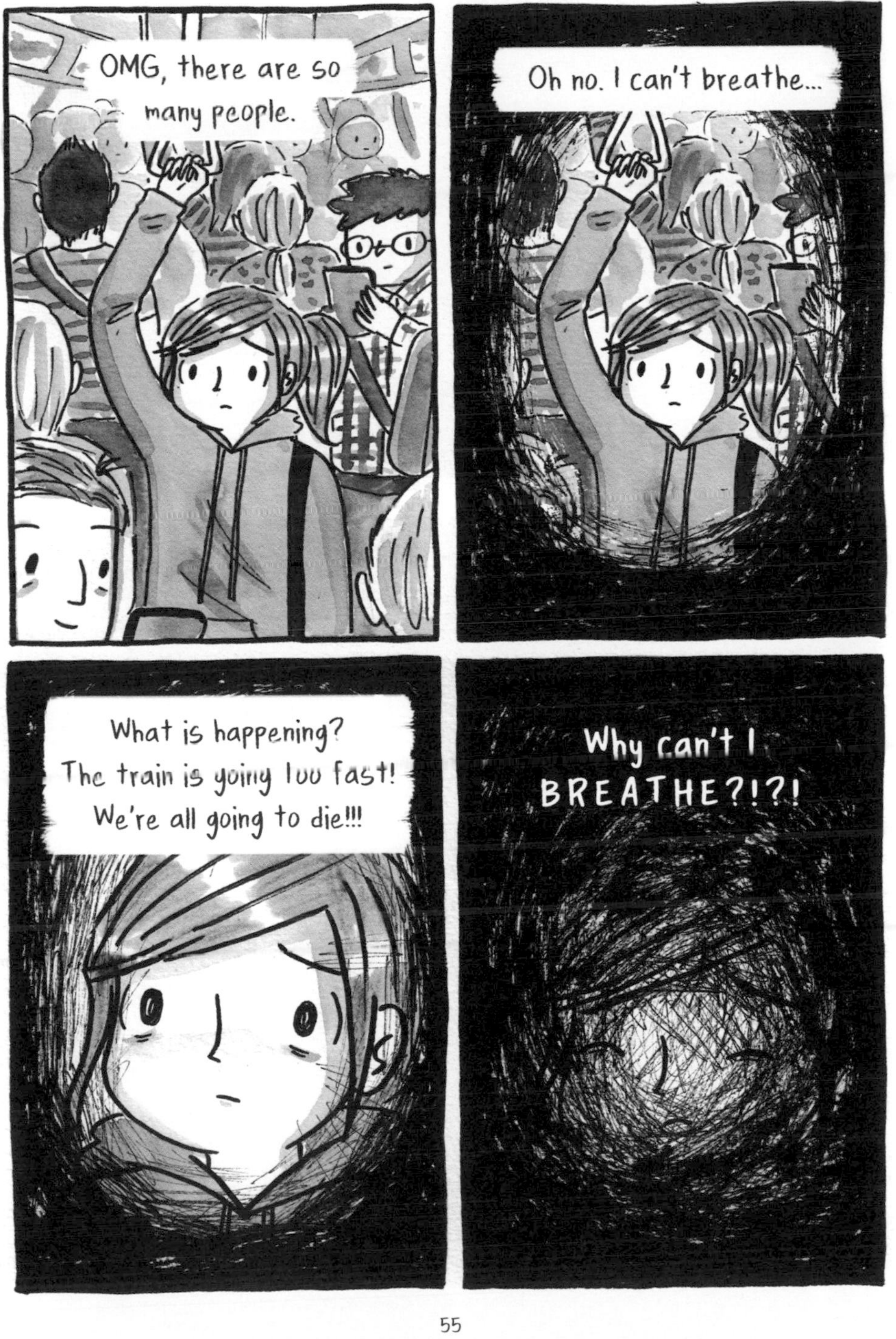
OMG, there are so many people.
Oh no. I can't breathe...
What is happening? The train is going too fast! We're all going to die!!!
Why can't I BREATHE?!?!

A panic attack felt like...

Everything was too loud.

A hundred thoughts
flooding into my head
at the same time.

My heart was racing and
my chest tightened as
I found it harder
and harder
to breathe.

Being paralyzed
by irrational
fear and
paranoia.

My mind was
spiraling out
of control.

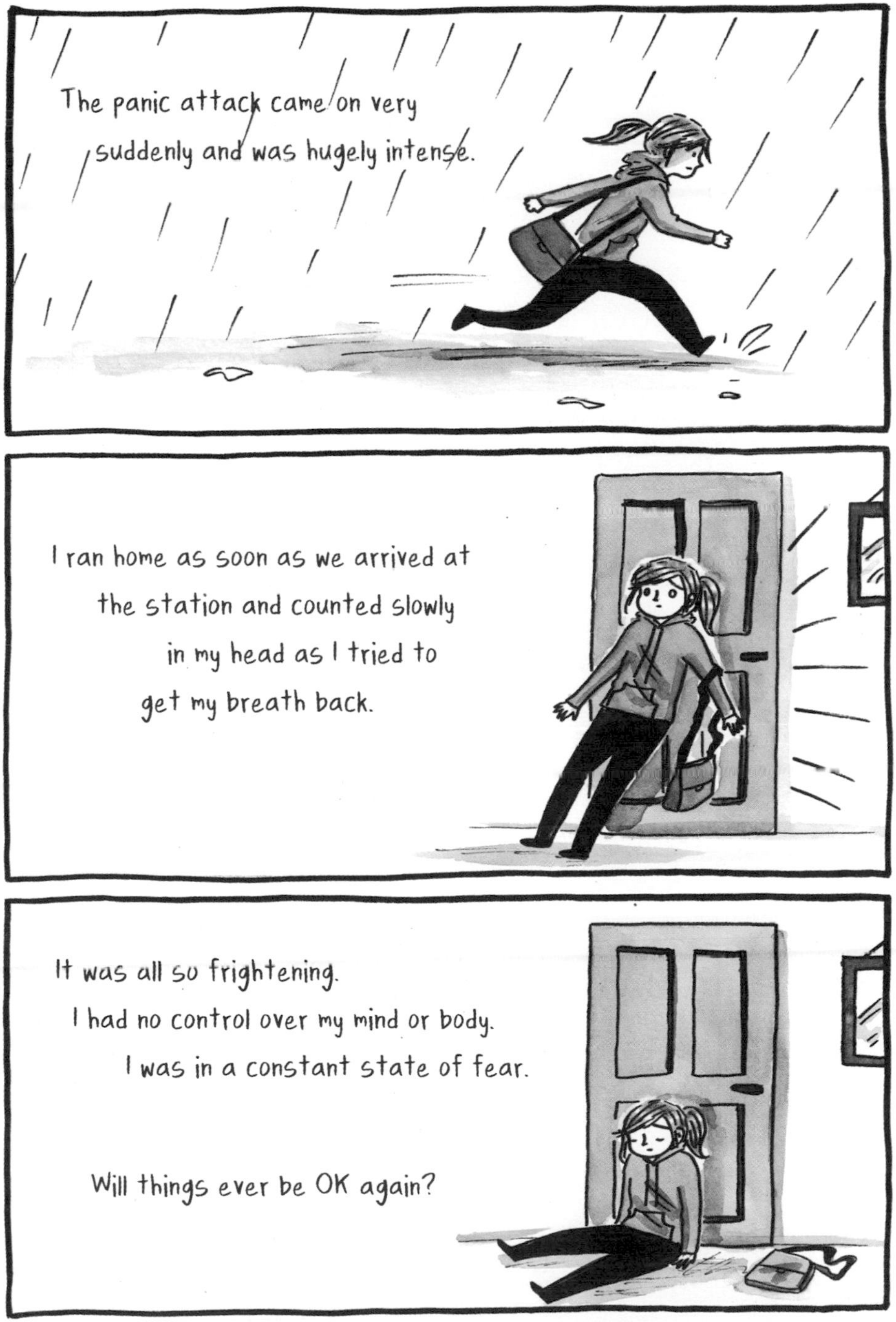
The panic attack came on very suddenly and was hugely intense.
I ran home as soon as we arrived at the station and counted slowly in my head as I tried to get my breath back.
It was all so frightening.
I had no control over my mind or body.
I was in a constant state of fear.
Will things ever be OK again?

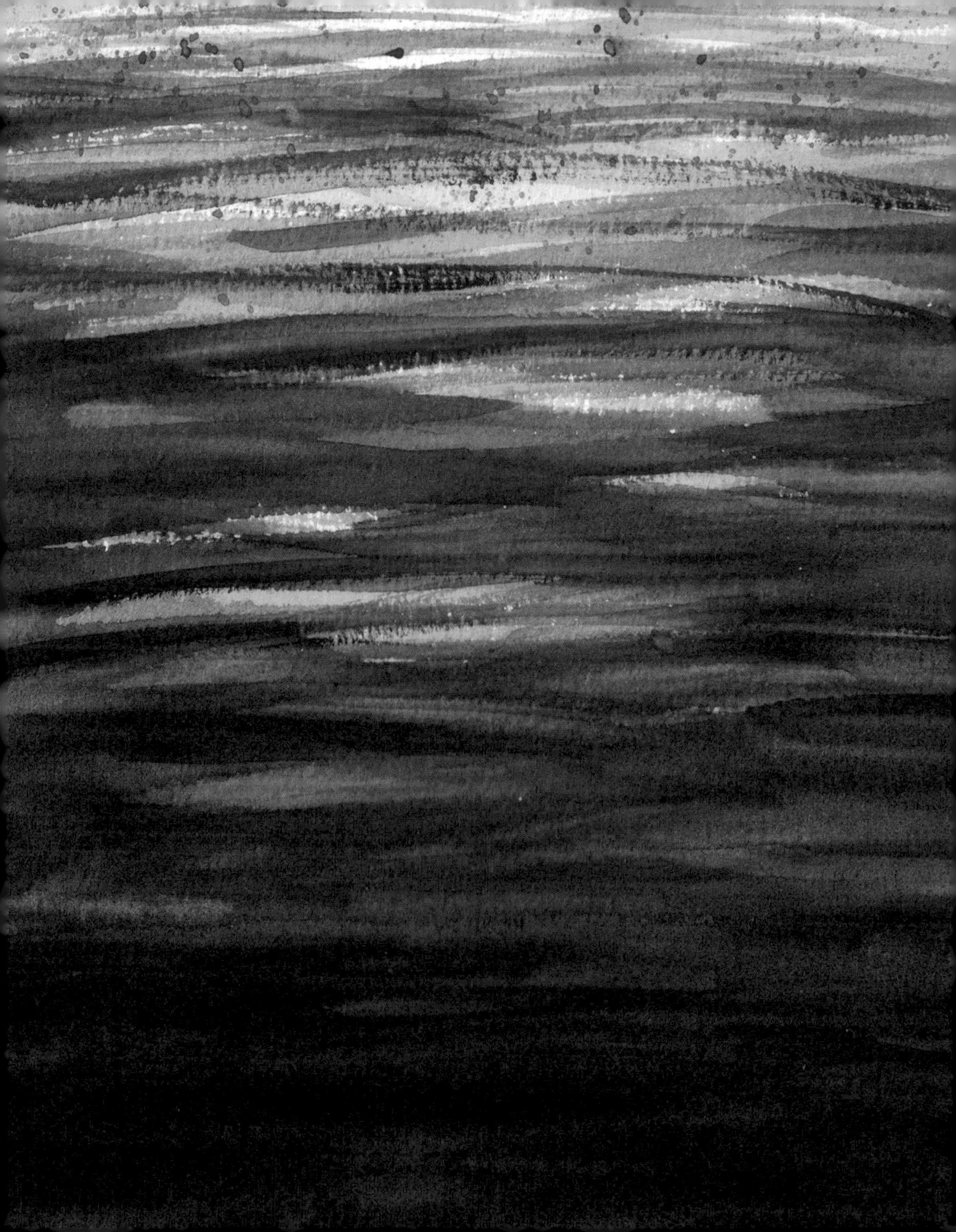

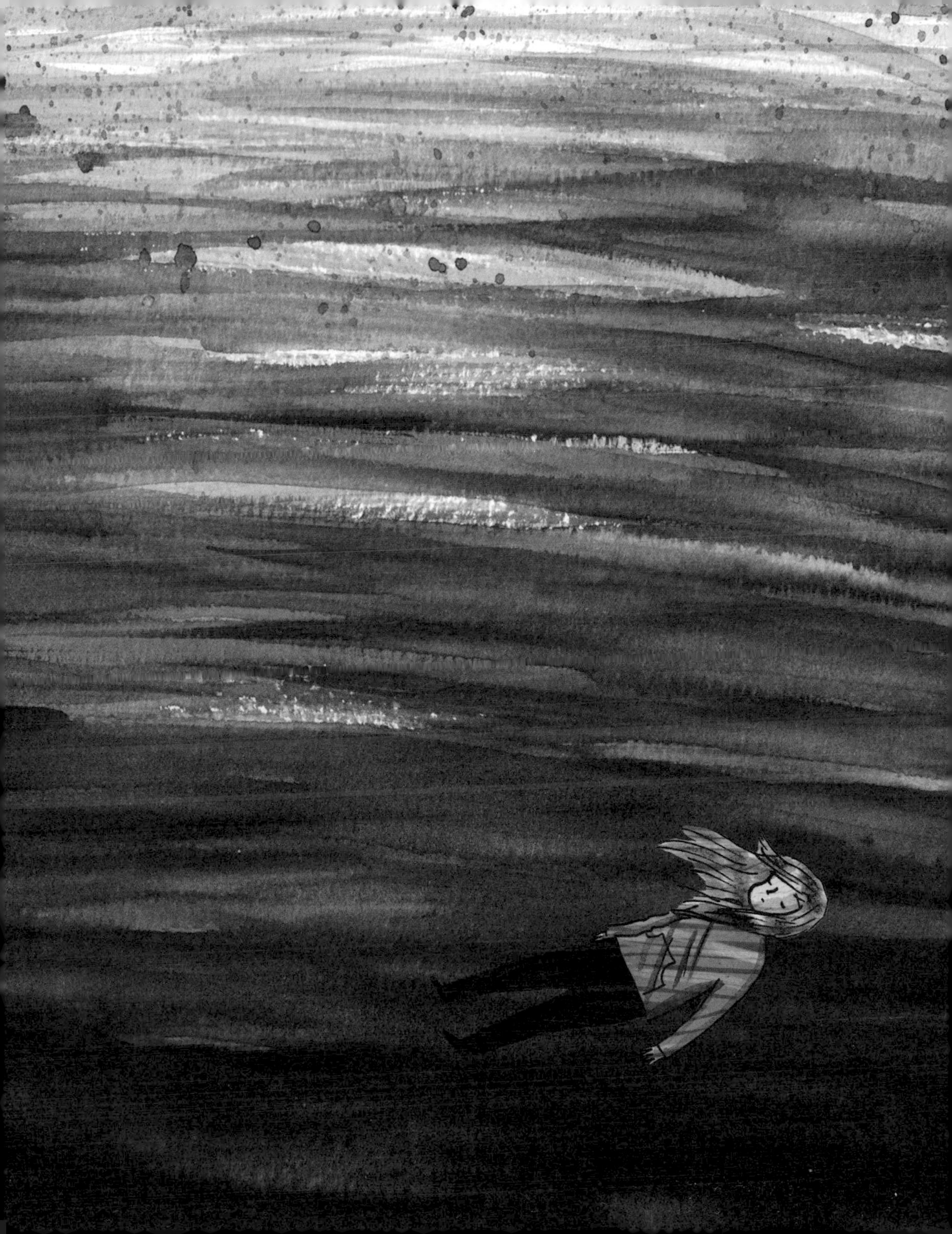

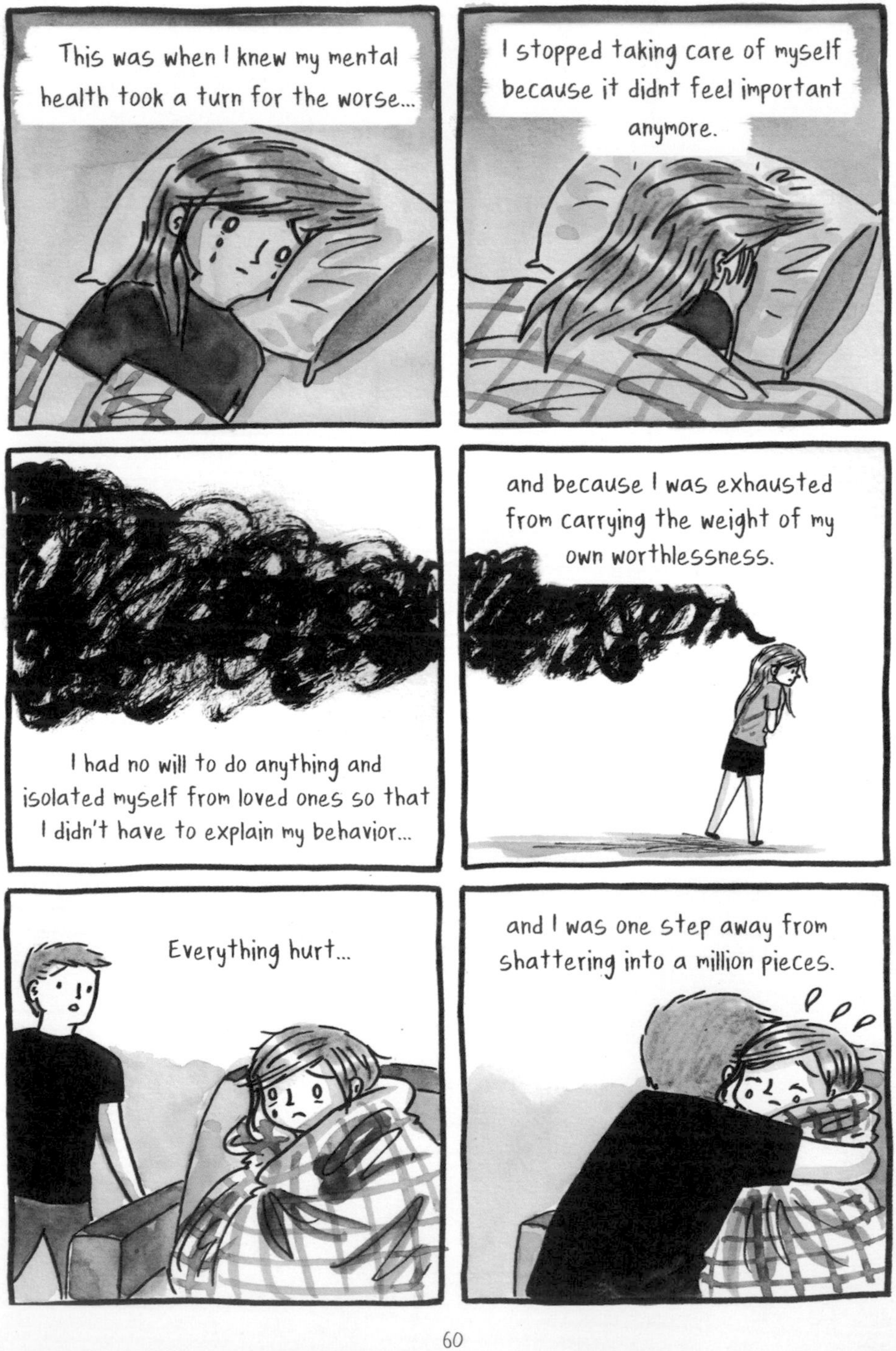
This was when I knew my mental health took a turn for the worse...
I stopped taking care of myself because it didnt feel important anymore.
I had no will to do anything and isolated myself from loved ones so that I didn't have to explain my behavior...
and because I was exhausted from carrying the weight of my own worthlessness.
Everything hurt...
and I was one step away from shattering into a million pieces.

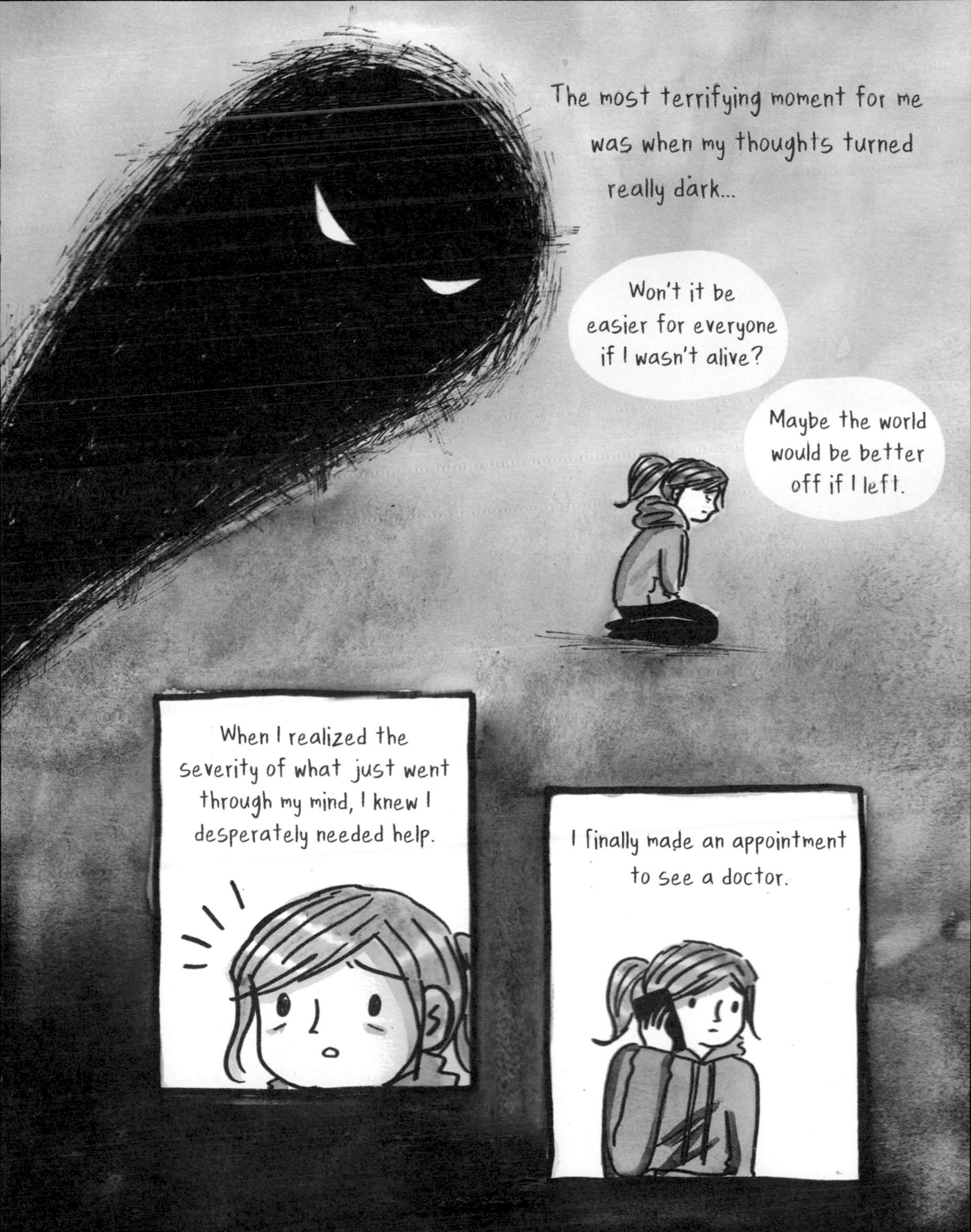
The most terrifying moment for me was when my thoughts turned really dark...
Won't it be easier for everyone if I wasn't alive?
Maybe the world would be better off if I left.
When I realized the severity of what just went through my mind, I knew I desperately needed help.
I finally made an appointment to see a doctor.

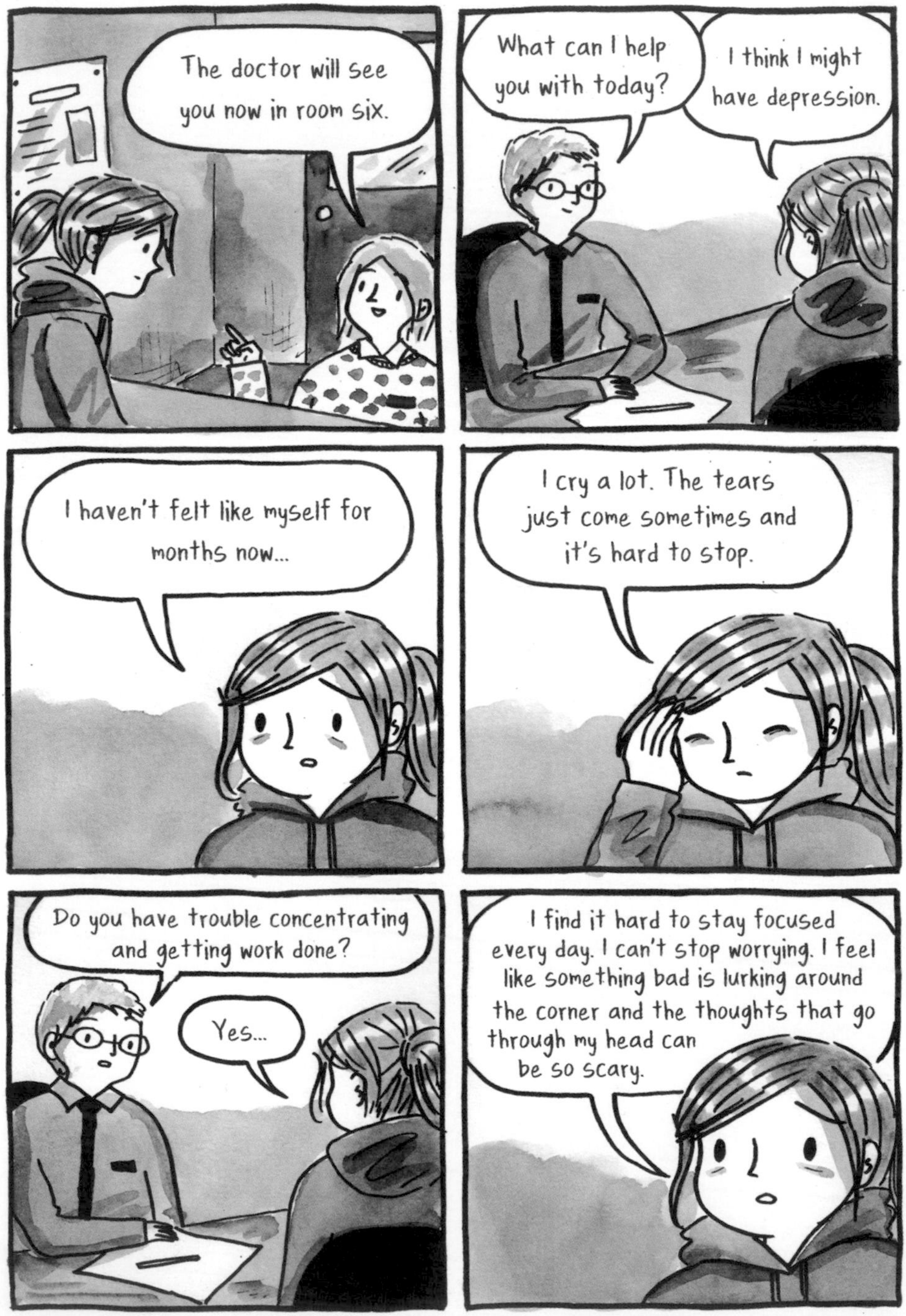

The doctor will see you now in room six.
What can I help you with today?
I think I might have depression.
I haven't felt like myself for months now...
I cry a lot. The tears just come sometimes and it's hard to stop.
Do you have trouble concentrating and getting work done?
Yes...
I find it hard to stay focused every day. I can't stop worrying. I feel like something bad is lurking around the corner and the thoughts that go through my head can be so scary.

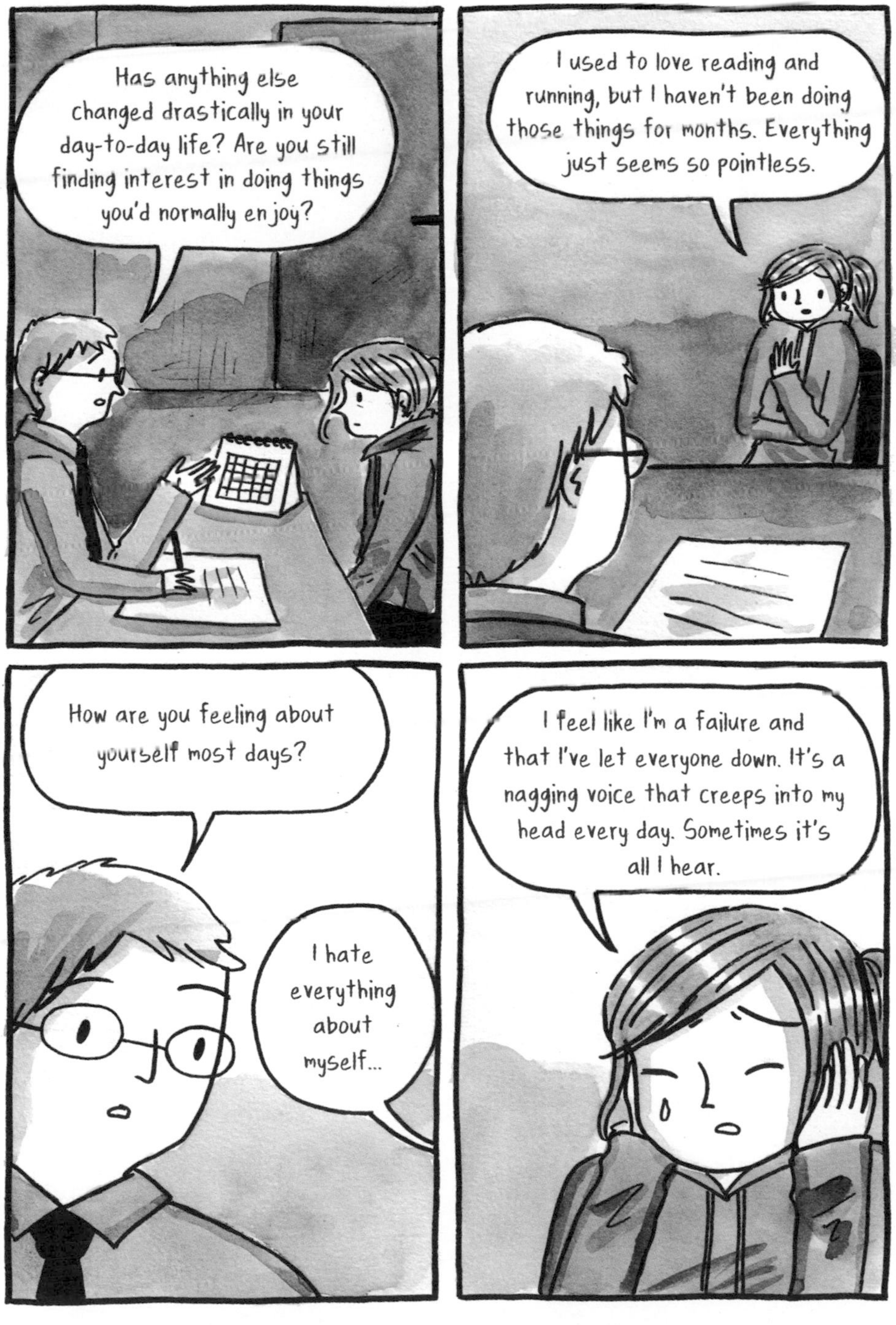
Has anything else changed drastically in your day-to-day life? Are you still finding interest in doing things you'd normally enjoy?
I used to love reading and running, but I haven't been doing those things for months. Everything just seems so pointless.
How are you feeling about yourself most days?
I hate everything about myself...
I feel like I'm a failure and that I've let everyone down. It's a nagging voice that creeps into my head every day. Sometimes it's all I hear.

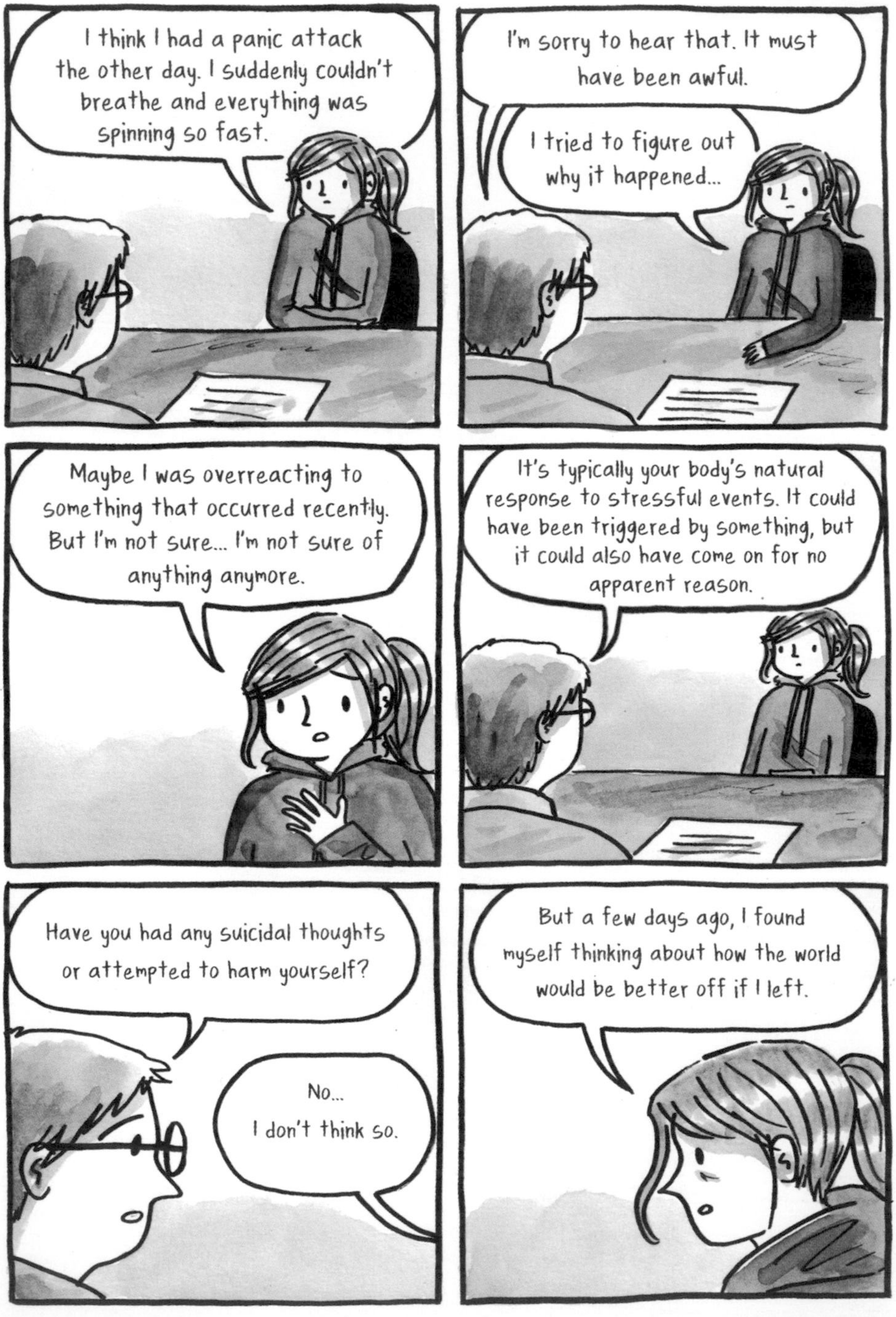
I think I had a panic attack the other day. I suddenly couldn't breathe and everything was spinning so fast.
I'm sorry to hear that. It must have been awful.
I tried to figure out why it happened...
Maybe I was overreacting to something that occurred recently. But I'm not sure... I'm not sure of anything anymore.
It's typically your body's natural response to stressful events. It could have been triggered by something, but it could also have come on for no apparent reason.
Have you had any suicidal thoughts or attempted to harm yourself?
No... I don't think so.
But a few days ago, I found myself thinking about how the world would be better off if I left.

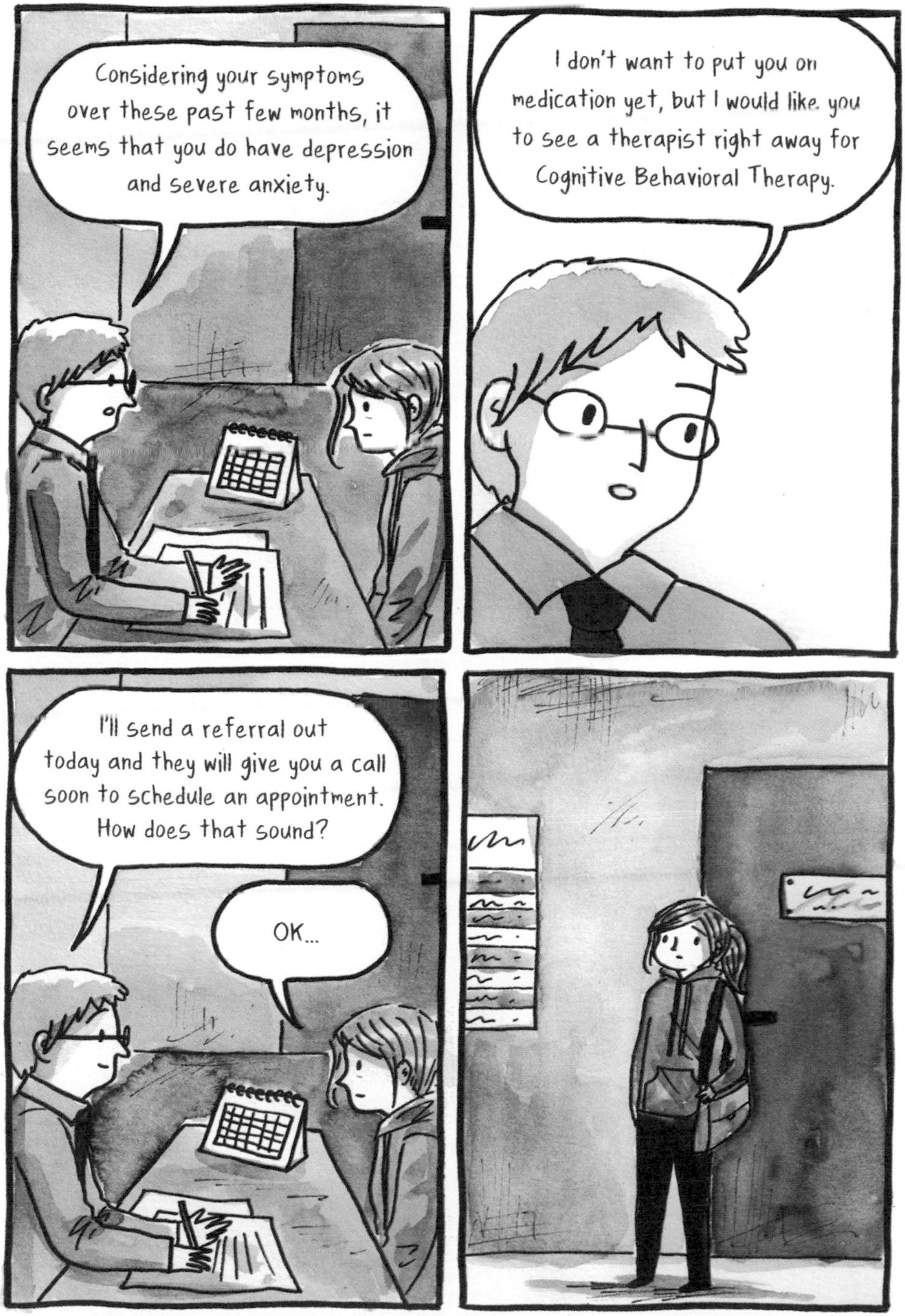
Considering your symptoms over these past few months, it seems that you do have depression and severe anxiety.
I don't want to put you on medication yet, but I would like you to see a therapist right away for Cognitive Behavioral Therapy.
I'll send a referral out today and they will give you a call soon to schedule an appointment. How does that sound?
OK...

I was finally serious about asking for help about my mental health.
It felt liberating. The diagnosis was a huge relief.
But I also knew it meant that I had to start working hard on getting better...

Perhaps the hardest thing we ever do is admit we need help.

To put our pride and denial aside and allow ourselves to be vulnerable.

Asking for help was the most courageous thing I ever did.

It meant that I refused to give up and I wanted to give myself a chance to heal.

When you're depressed you feel all alone. You internalize
everything because of the stigma surrounding mental illness.

You're scared people will judge
you and alienate you.

You feel a huge overbearing
pressure to pretend that

everything is OK.

That's probably the most difficult thing
when you're depressed— to have to keep
acting completely normal...

when every part of you
feels broken.

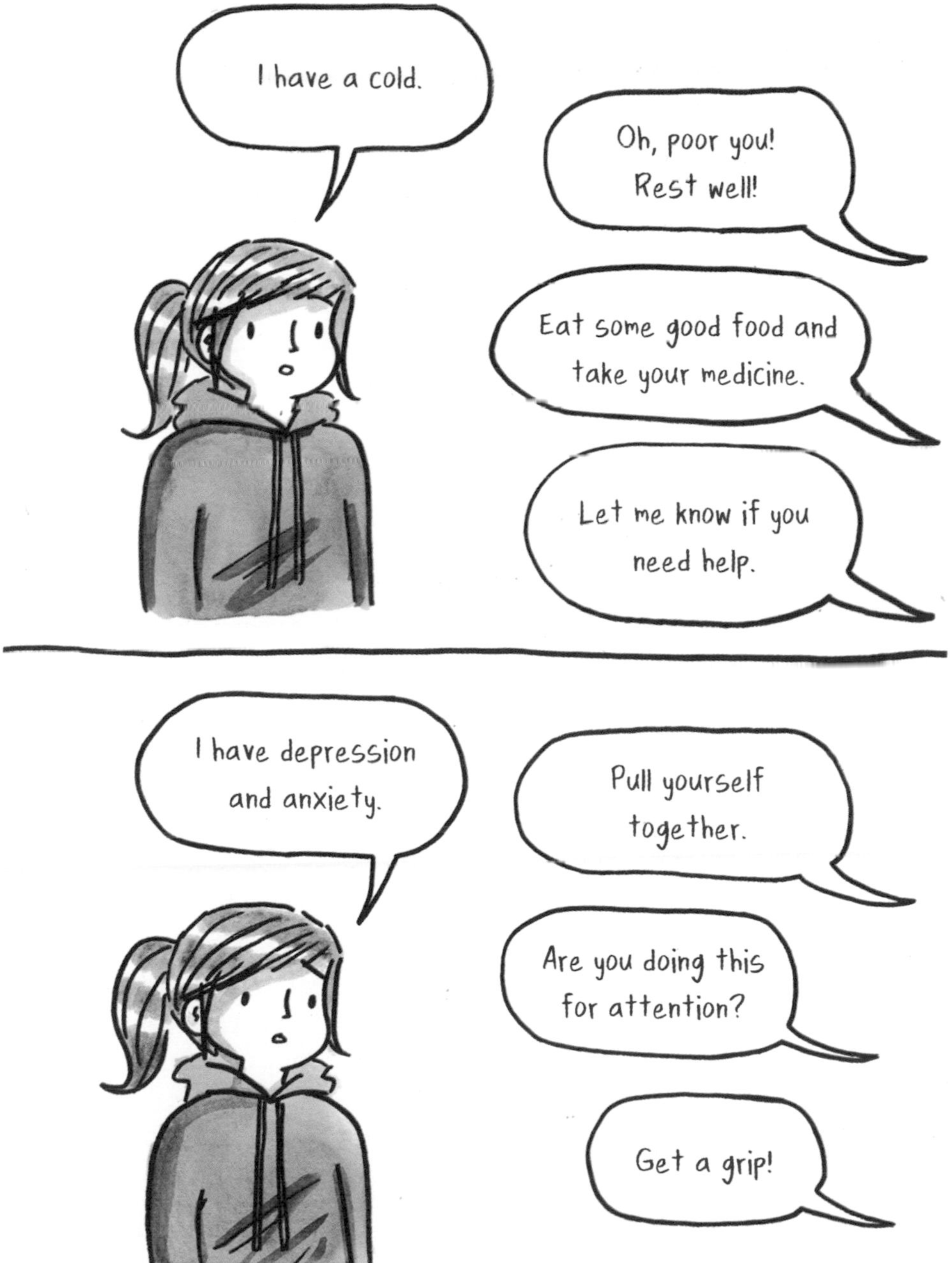
I have a cold.
Oh, poor you! Rest well!
Eat some good food and take your medicine.
Let me know if you need help.
I have depression and anxiety.
Pull yourself together.
Are you doing this for attention?
Get a grip!

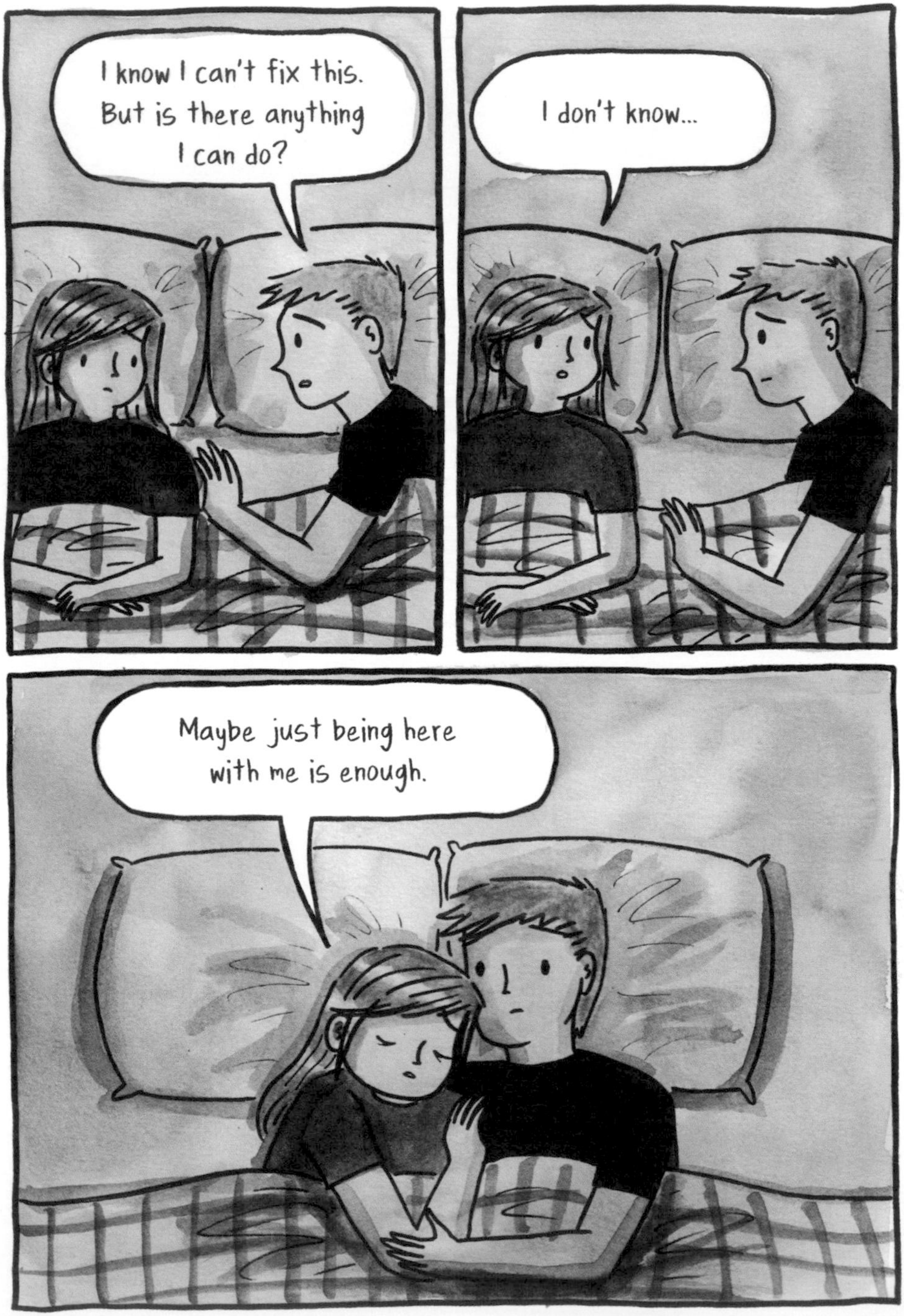
I know I can't fix this. But is there anything I can do?
I don't know...
Maybe just being here with me is enough.

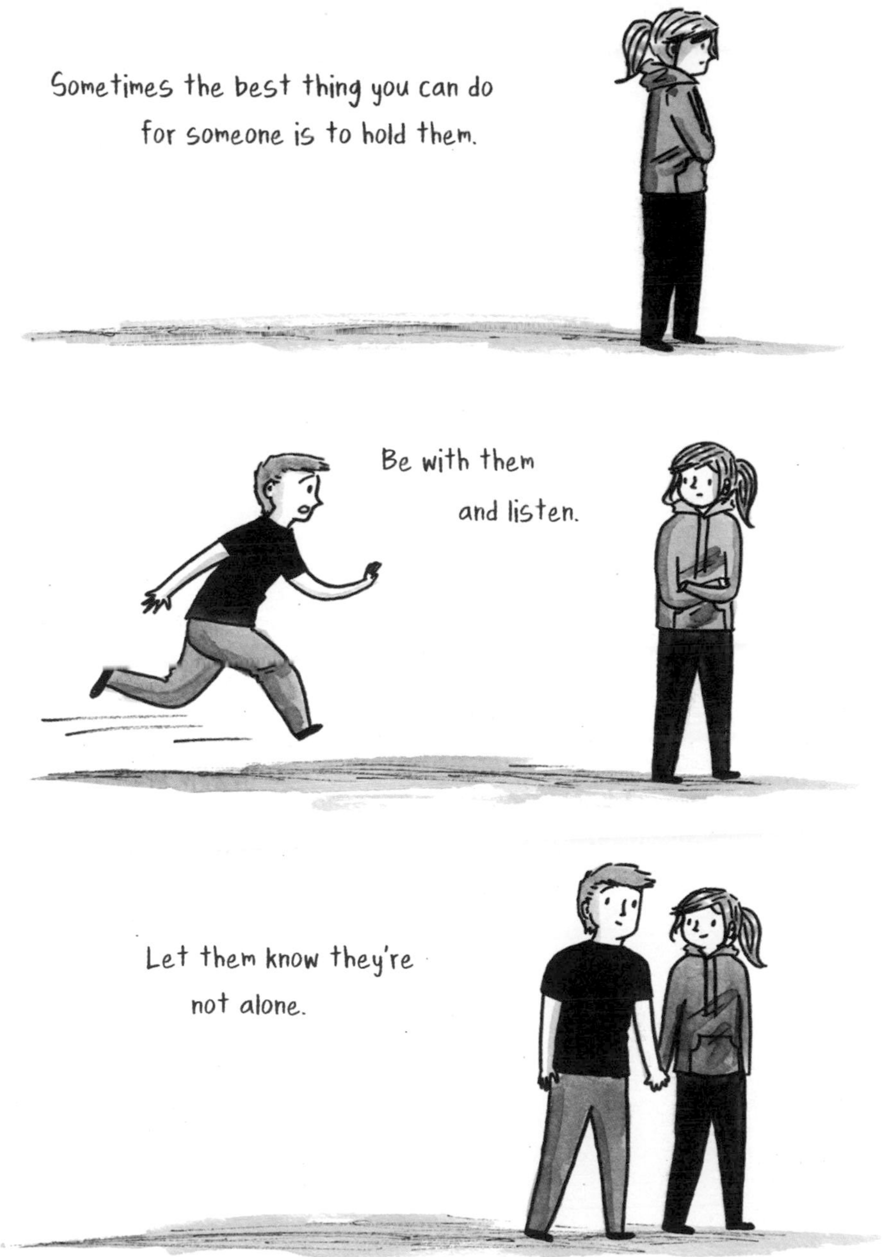
Sometimes the best thing you can do
for someone is to hold them.
Be with them
and listen.
Let them know they're
not alone.

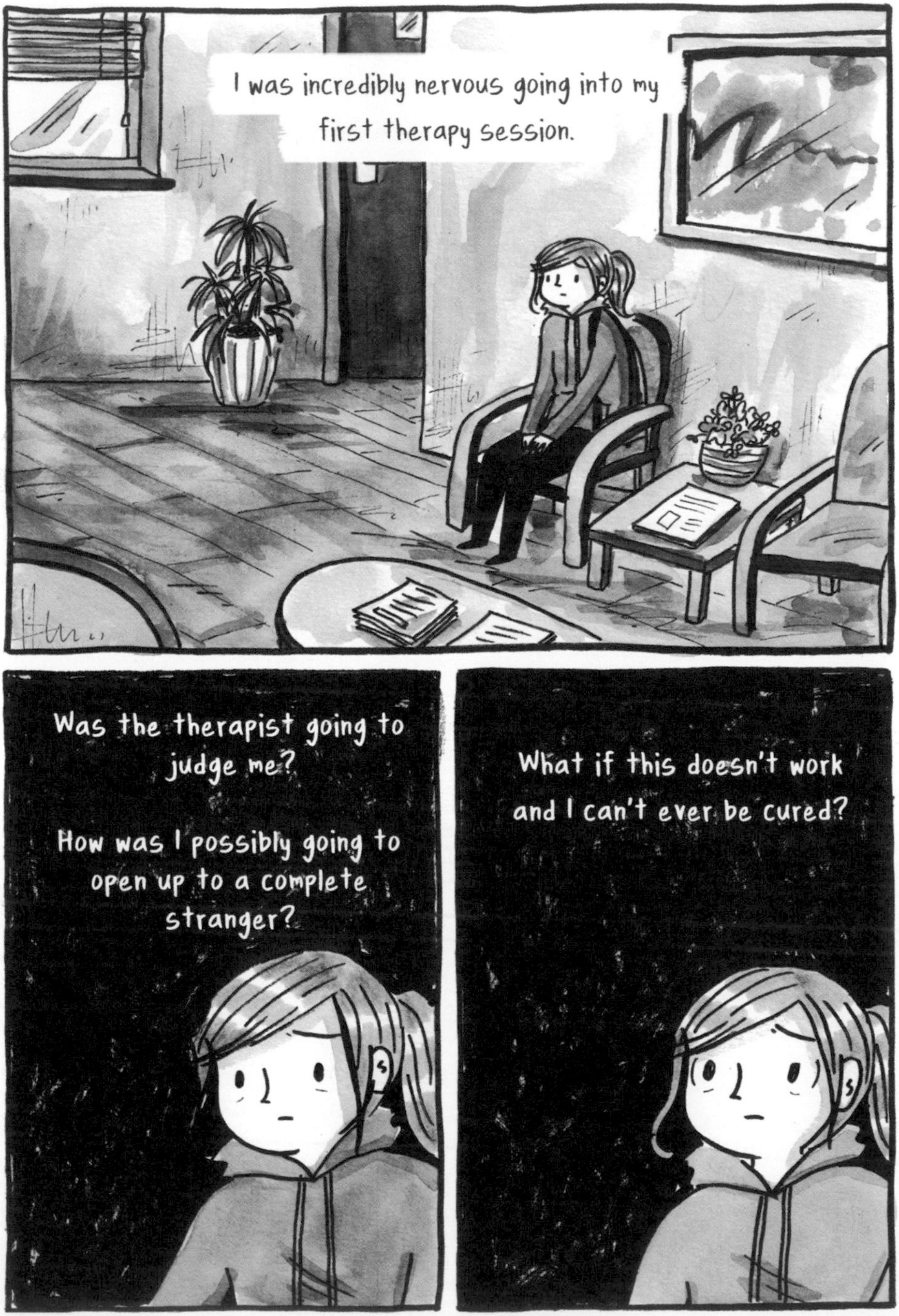
I was incredibly nervous going into my first therapy session.
Was the therapist going to judge me?
How was I possibly going to open up to a complete stranger?
What if this doesn't work and I can't ever be cured?

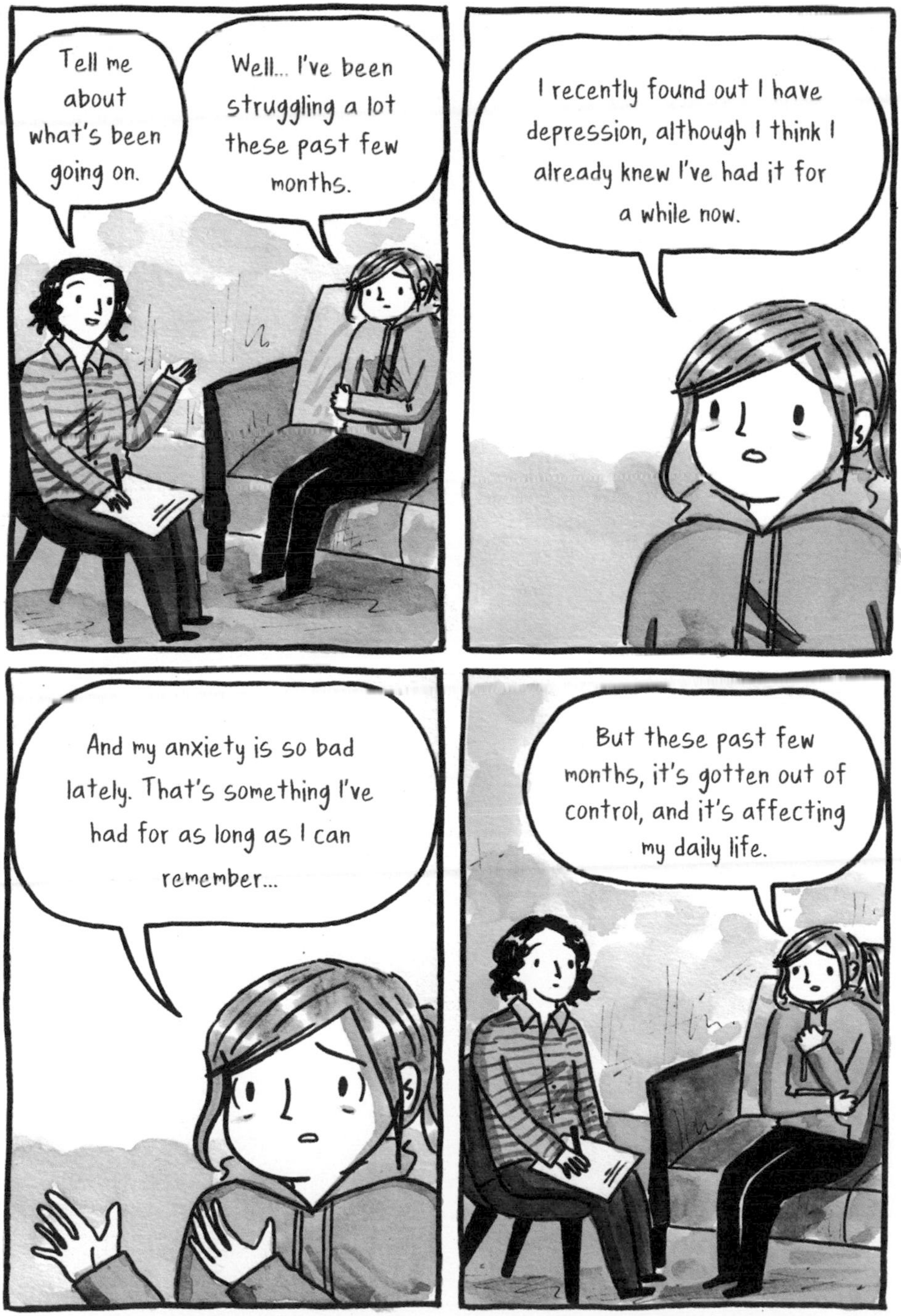
Tell me about what's been going on.
Well... I've been struggling a lot these past few months.
I recently found out I have depression, although I think I already knew I've had it for a while now.
And my anxiety is so bad lately. That's something I've had for as long as I can remember...
But these past few months, it's gotten out of control, and it's affecting my daily life.

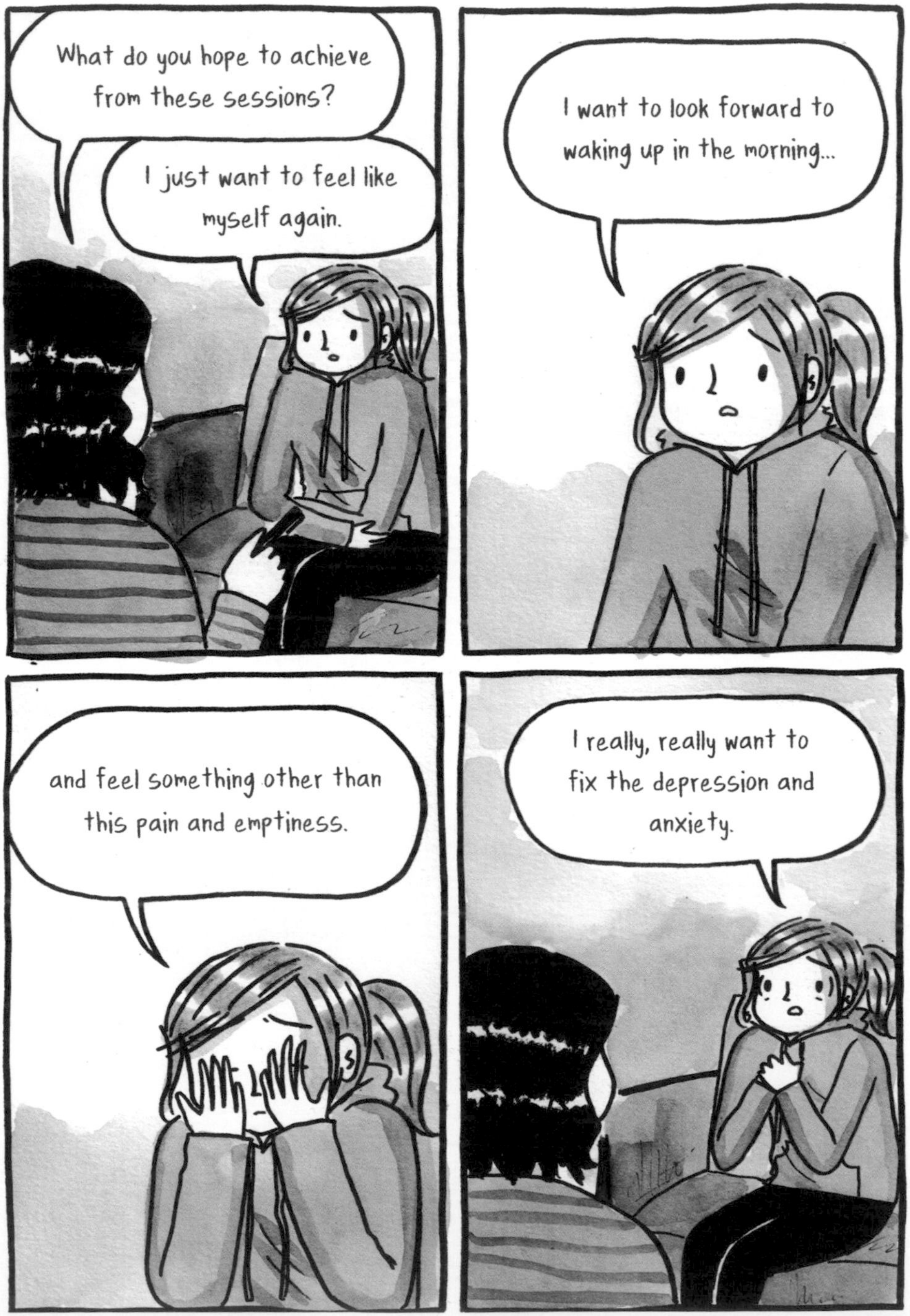
What do you hope to achieve from these sessions?
I just want to feel like myself again.
I want to look forward to waking up in the morning...
and feel something other than this pain and emptiness.
I really, really want to fix the depression and anxiety.

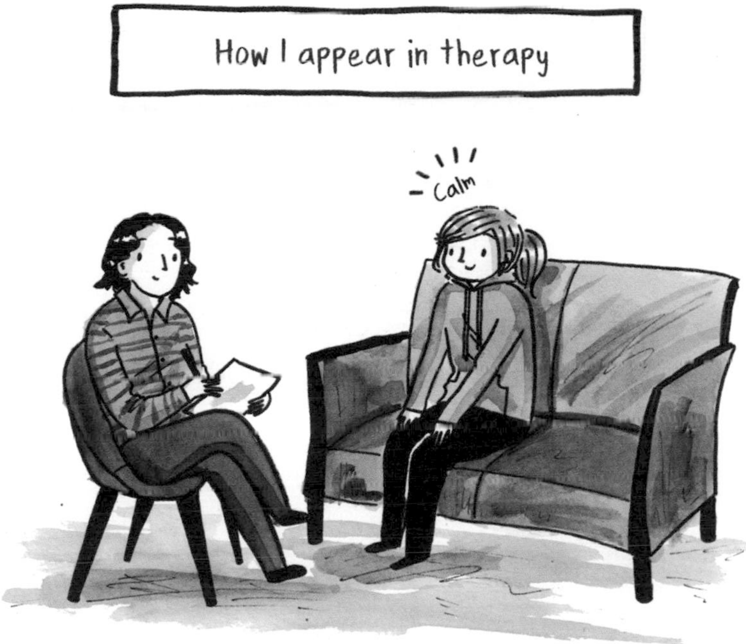
How I appear in therapy
Calm

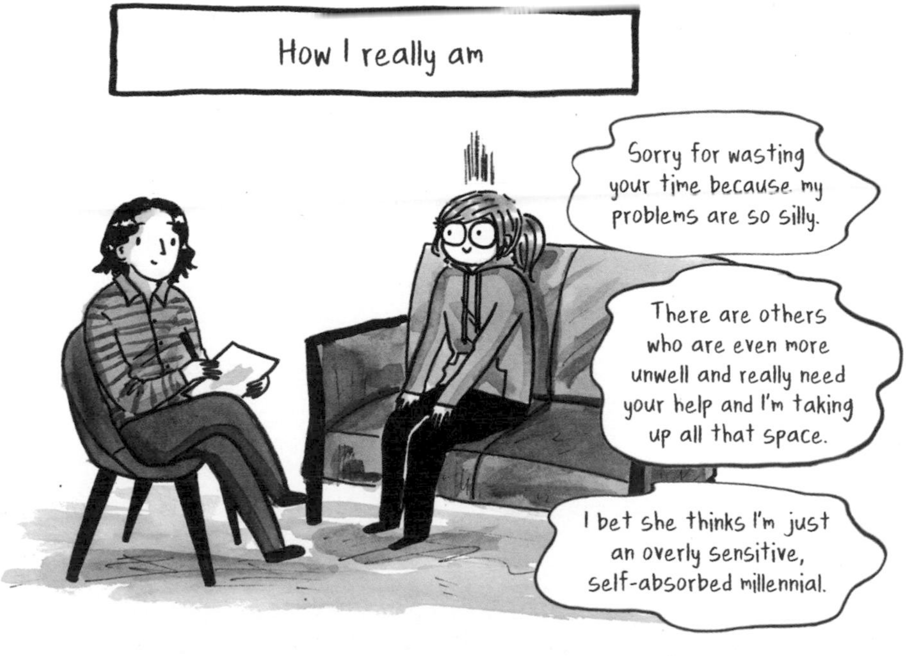
How I really am
Sorry for wasting your time because my problems are so silly.
There are others who are even more unwell and really need your help and I'm taking up all that space.
I bet she thinks I'm just an overly sensitive, self-absorbed millennial.

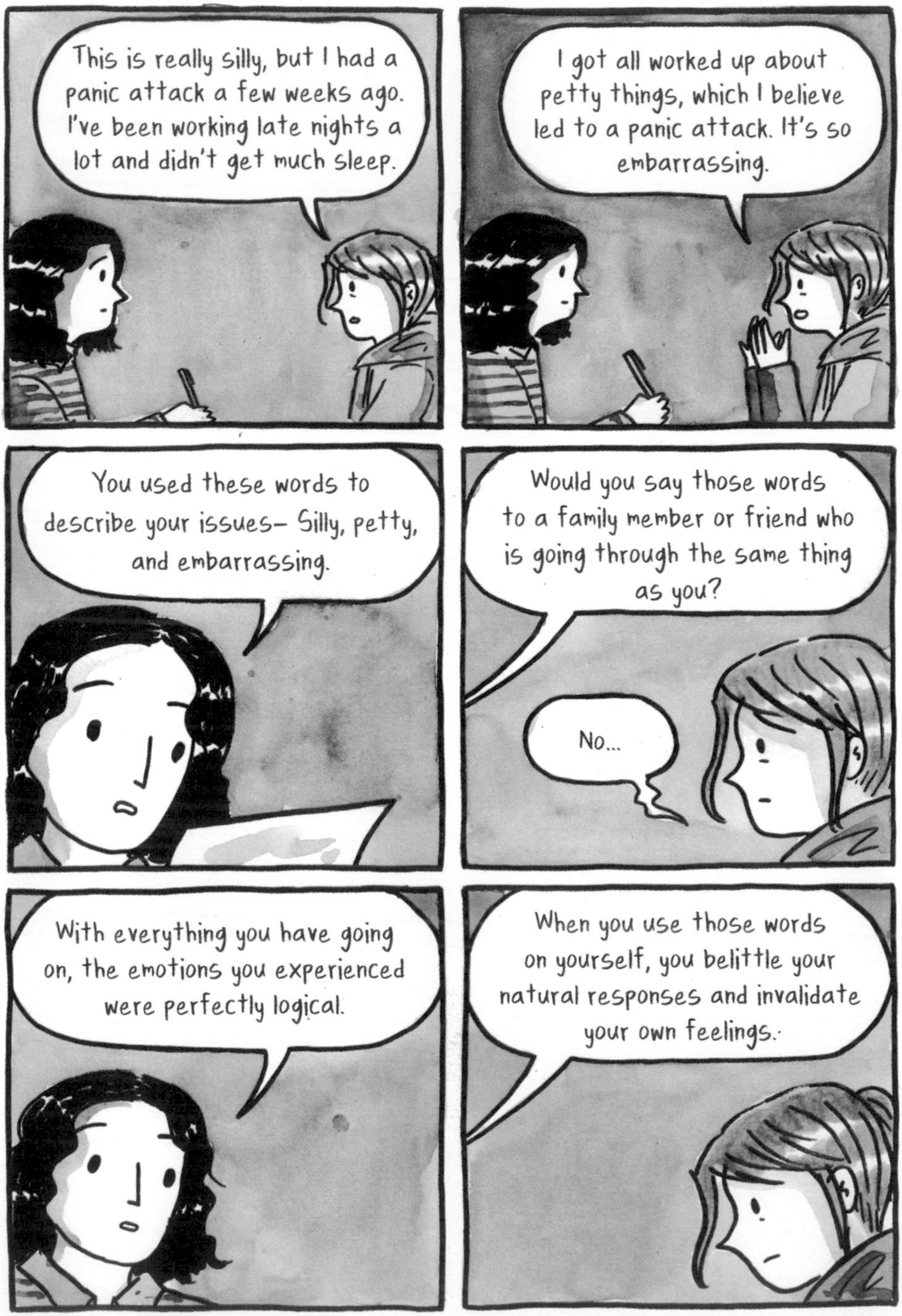
This is really silly, but I had a panic attack a few weeks ago. I've been working late nights a lot and didn't get much sleep.
I got all worked up about petty things, which I believe led to a panic attack. It's so embarrassing.
You used these words to describe your issues– Silly, petty, and embarrassing.
Would you say those words to a family member or friend who is going through the same thing as you?
No...
With everything you have going on, the emotions you experienced were perfectly logical.
When you use those words on yourself, you belittle your natural responses and invalidate your own feelings.

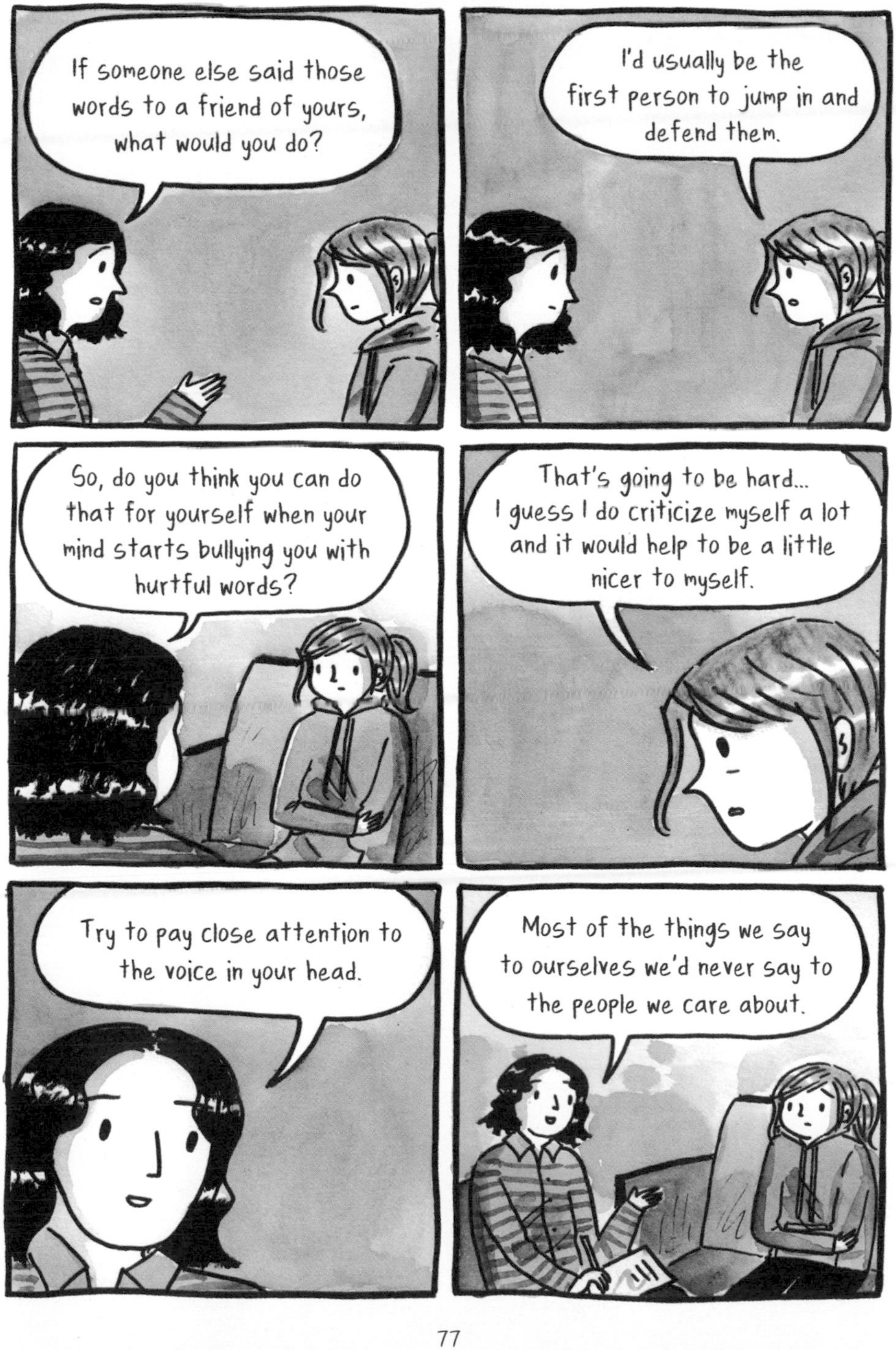
If someone else said those words to a friend of yours, what would you do?
I'd usually be the first person to jump in and defend them.
So, do you think you can do that for yourself when your mind starts bullying you with hurtful words?
That's going to be hard... I guess I do criticize myself a lot and it would help to be a little nicer to myself.
Try to pay close attention to the voice in your head.
Most of the things we say to ourselves we'd never say to the people we care about.

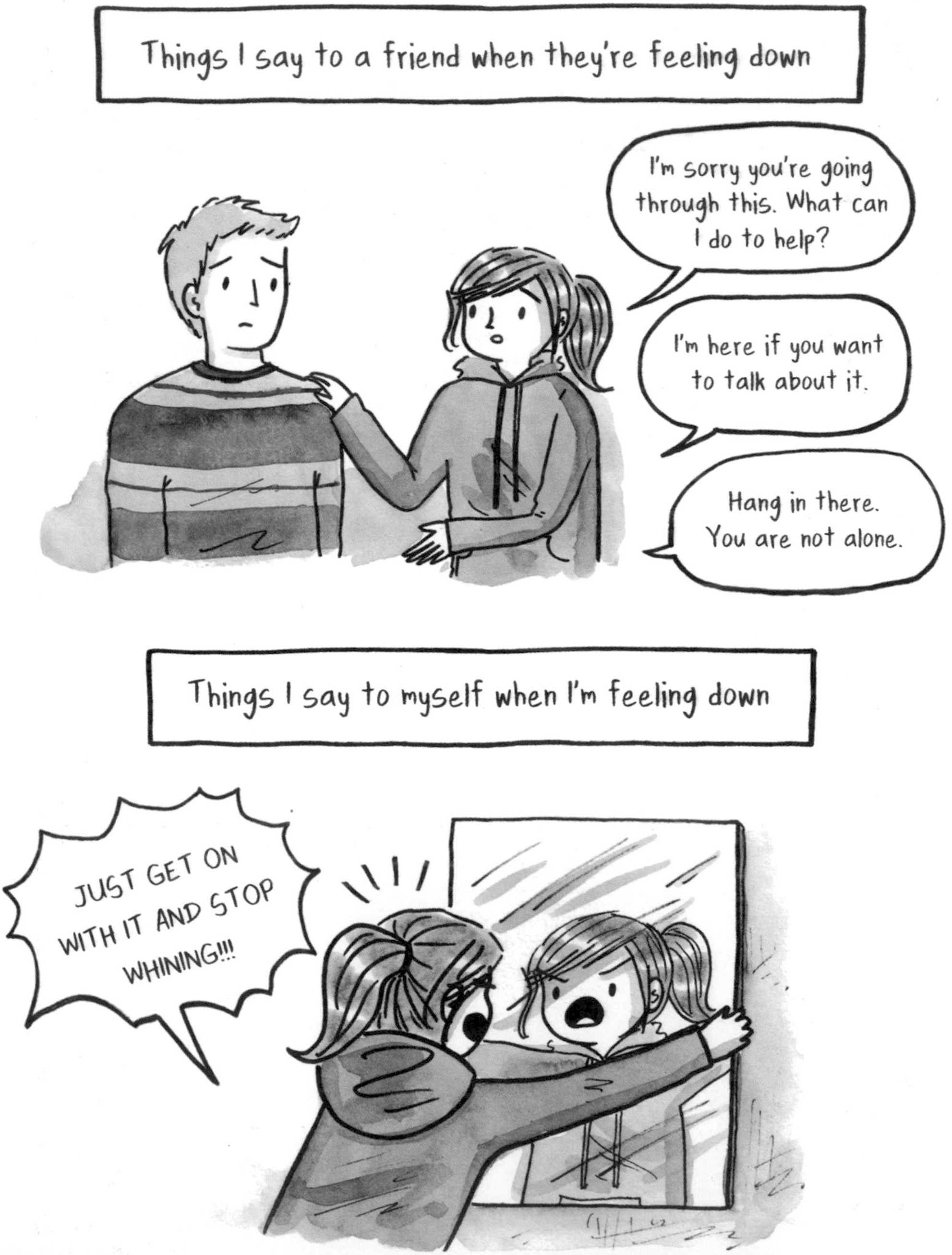
Things I say to a friend when they're feeling down
I'm sorry you're going through this. What can I do to help?
I'm here if you want to talk about it.
Hang in there. You are not alone.
Things I say to myself when I'm feeling down
JUST GET ON WITH IT AND STOP WHINING!!!

Depression lies. But when you're in the thick of it, it feels very real.

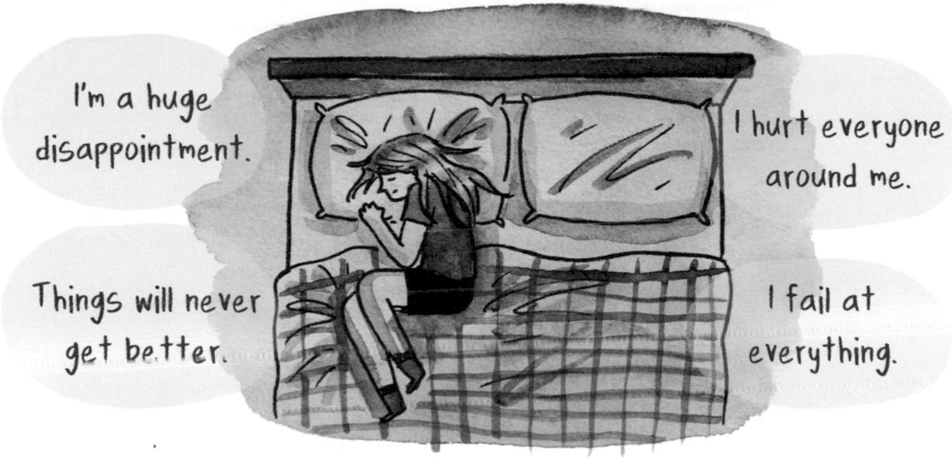
I'm a huge disappointment.
I hurt everyone around me.
Things will never get better.
I fail at everything.

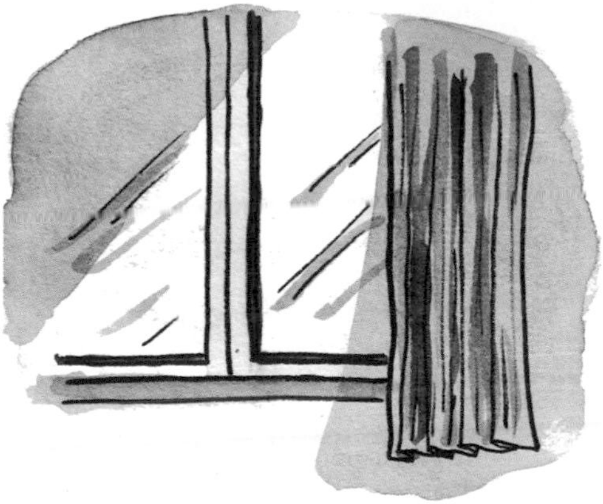

When your inner voice starts getting harsh and demeaning, take a step back.

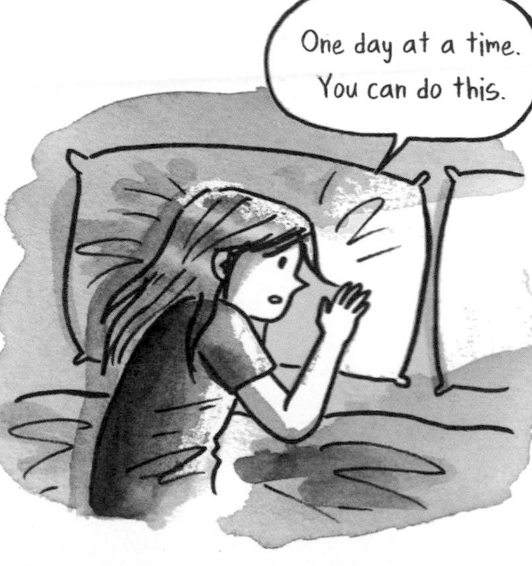
One day at a time. You can do this.

Talk to yourself the way you would talk to someone you care about.

Be your own friend.

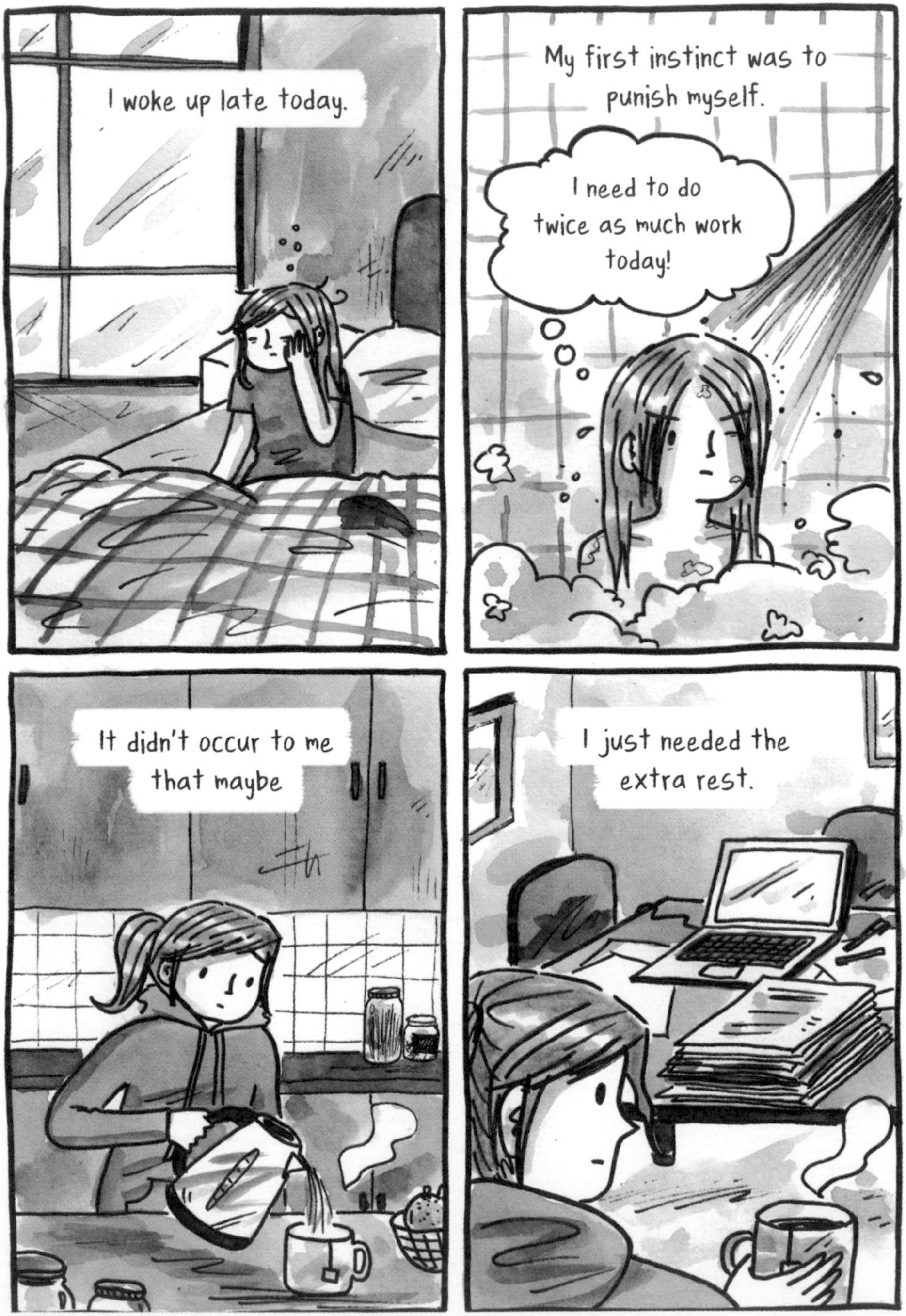
I woke up late today.
My first instinct was to punish myself.
I need to do twice as much work today!
It didn't occur to me that maybe
I just needed the extra rest.

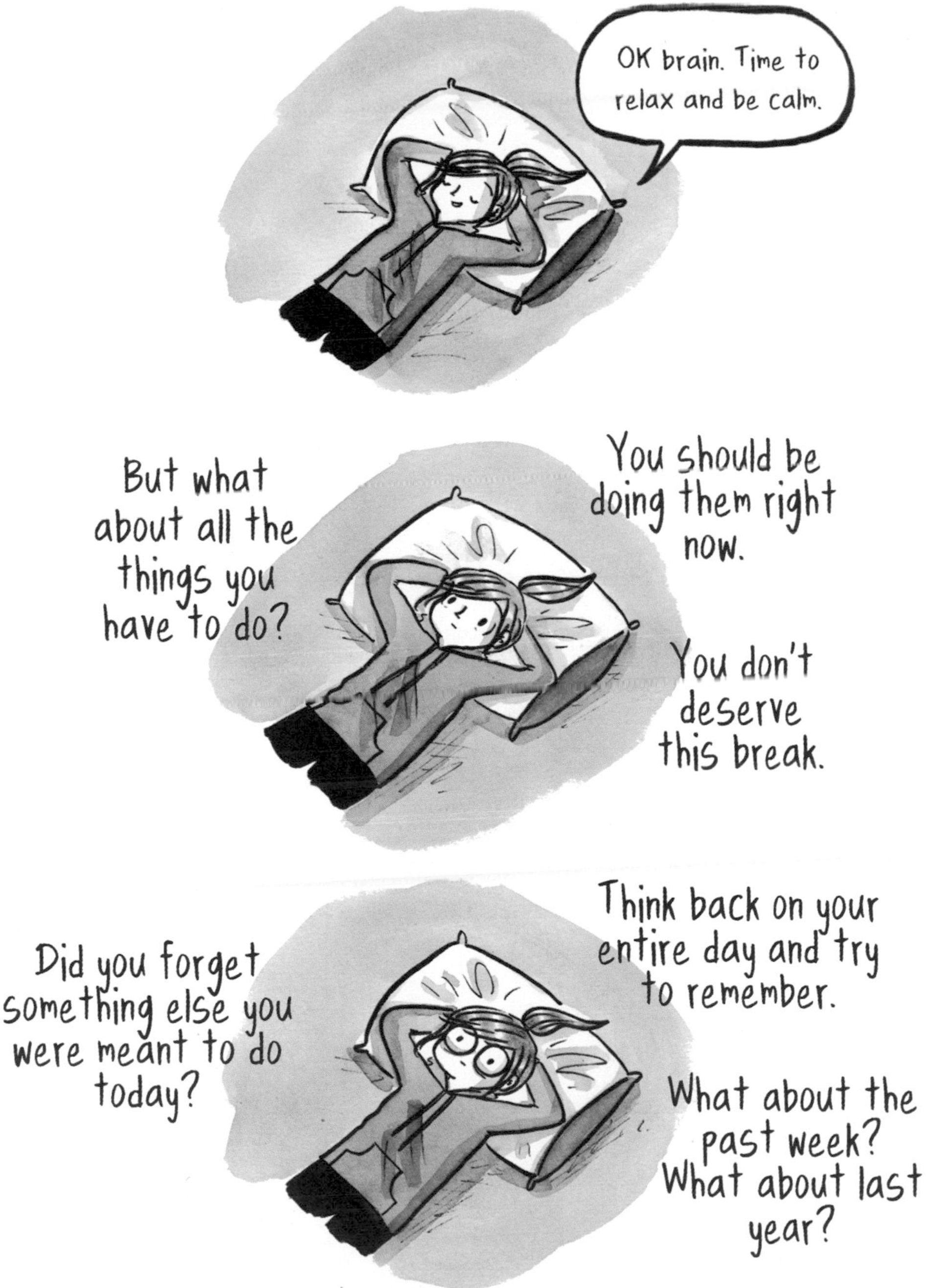
OK brain. Time to relax and be calm.
But what about all the things you have to do?
You should be doing them right now.
You don't deserve this break.
Did you forget something else you were meant to do today?
Think back on your entire day and try to remember.
What about the past week? What about last year?

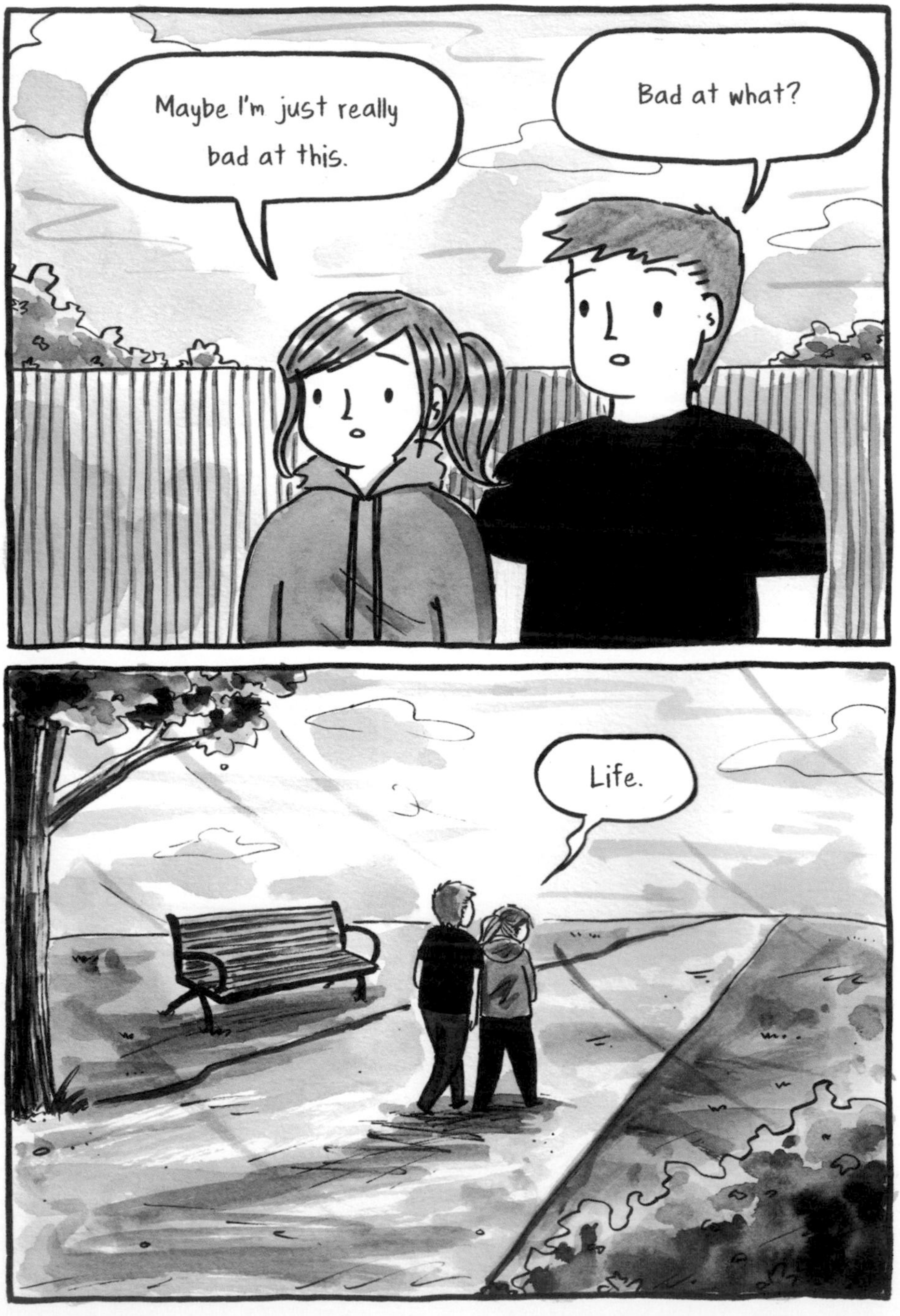
Maybe I'm just really bad at this.
Bad at what?
Life.

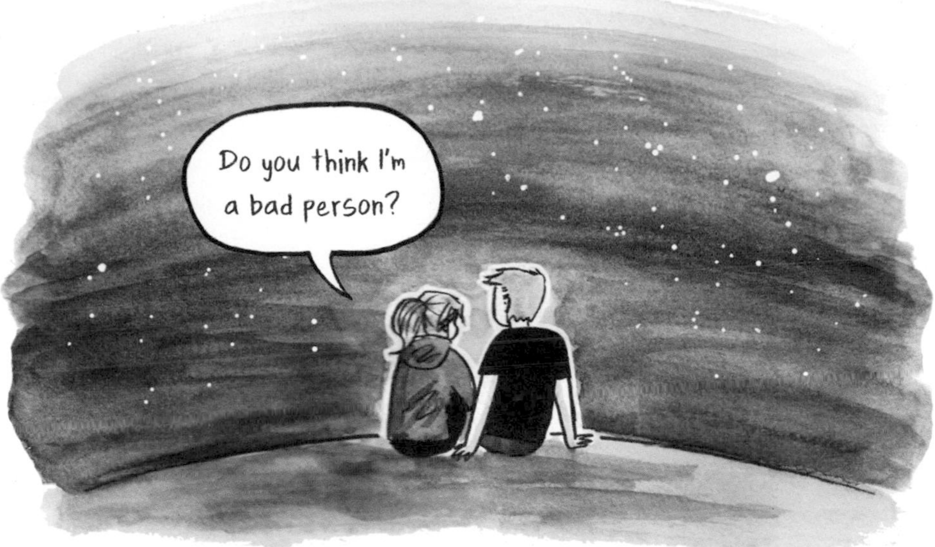
Do you think I'm a bad person?

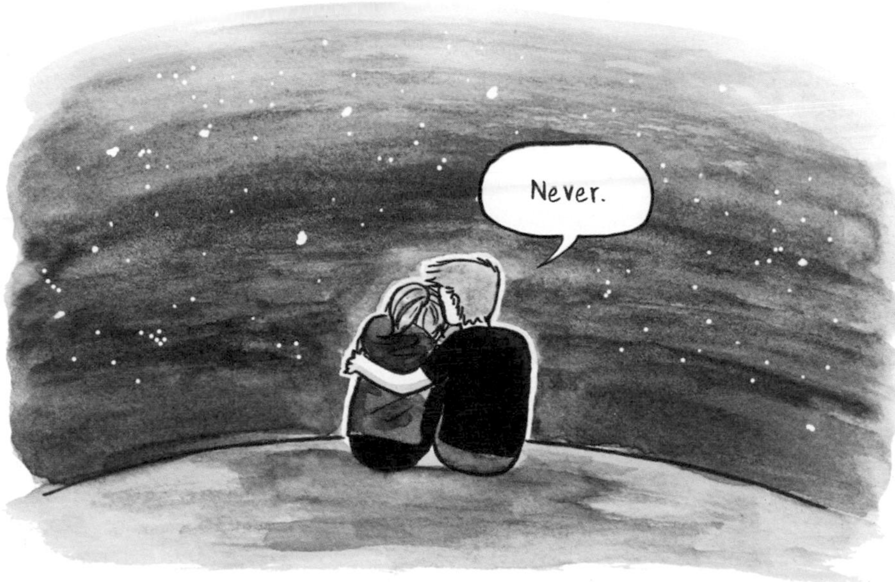
Never.

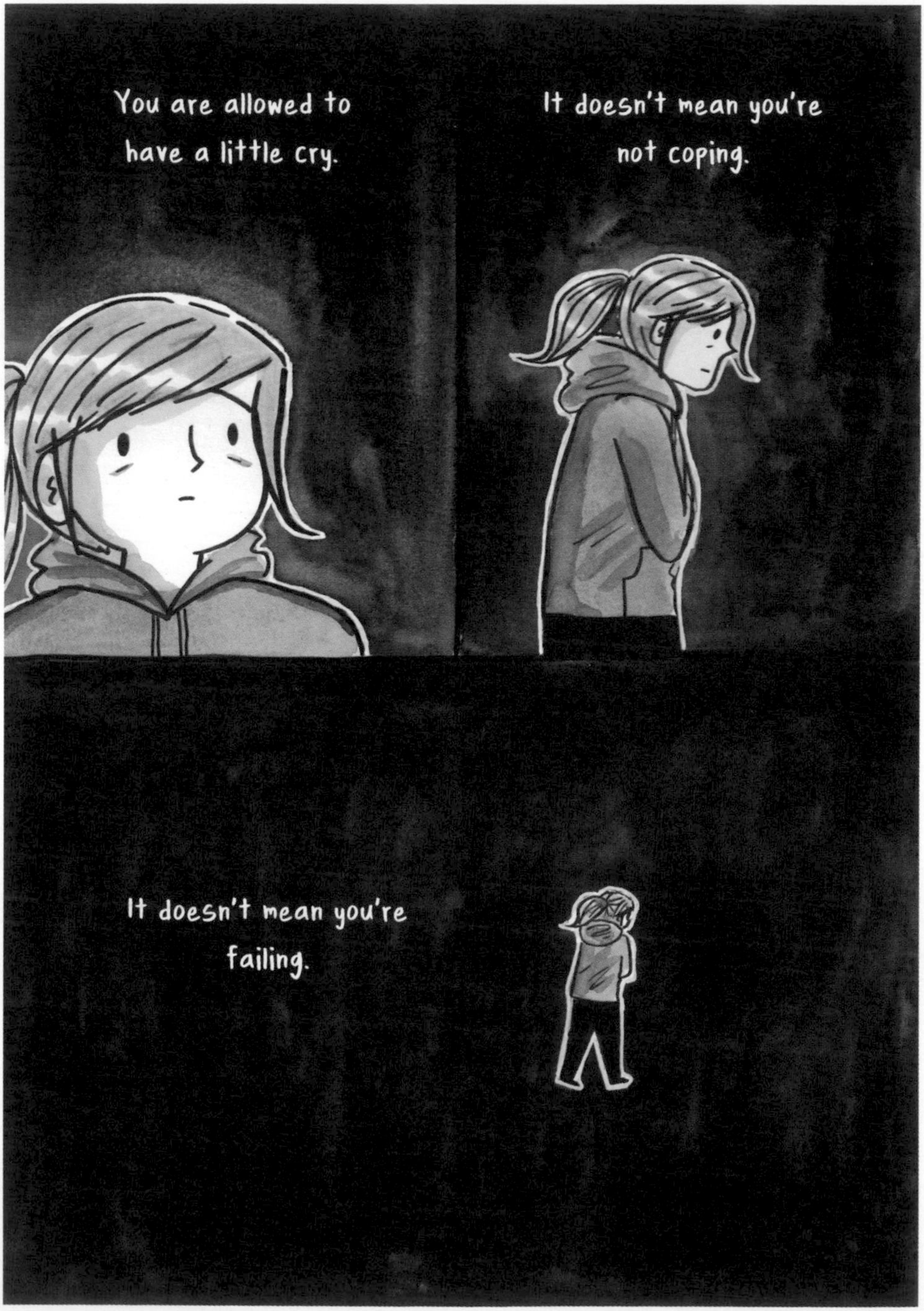
You are allowed to have a little cry.
It doesn't mean you're not coping.
It doesn't mean you're failing.

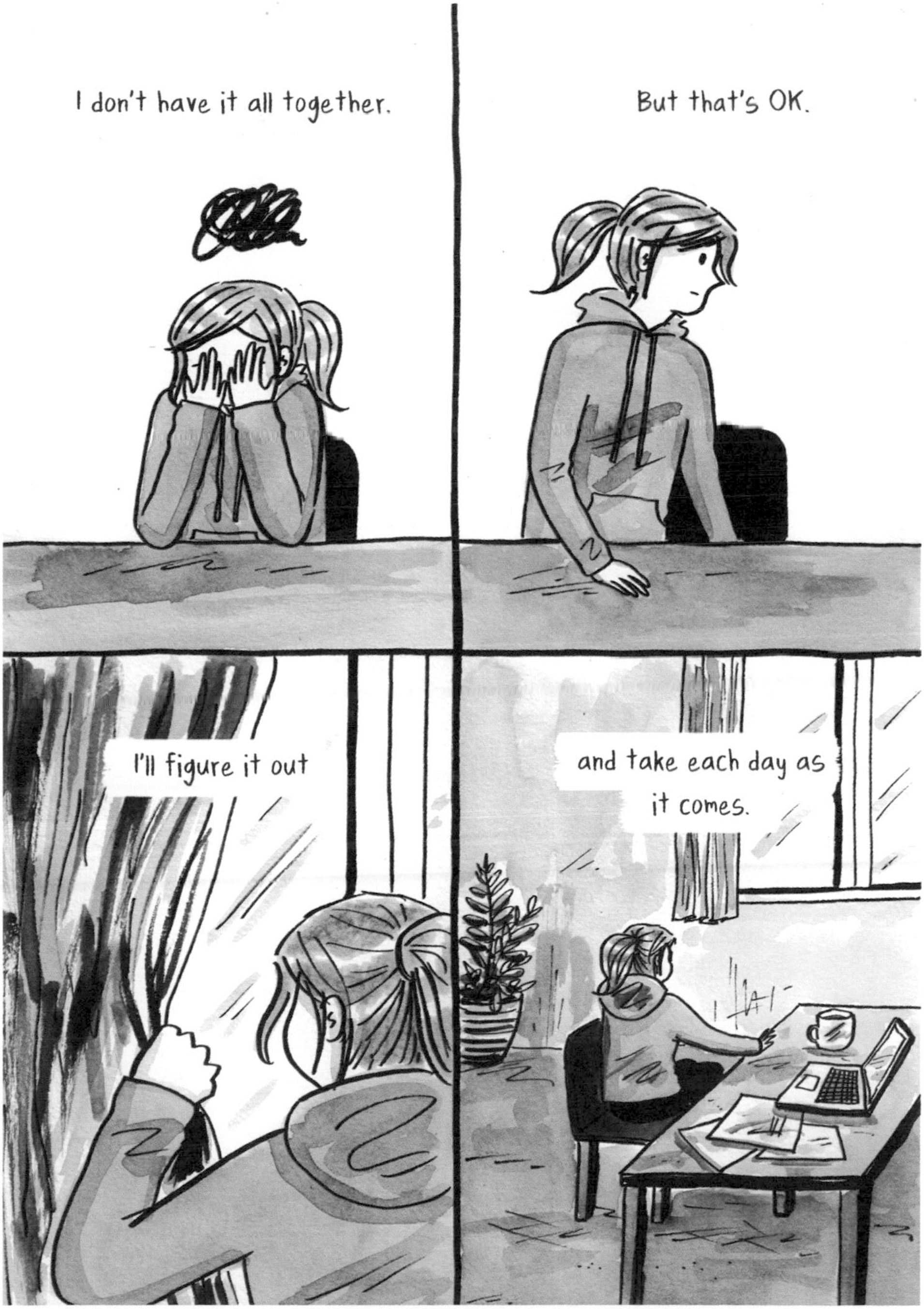
I don't have it all together.
But that's OK.
I'll figure it out
and take each day as it comes.

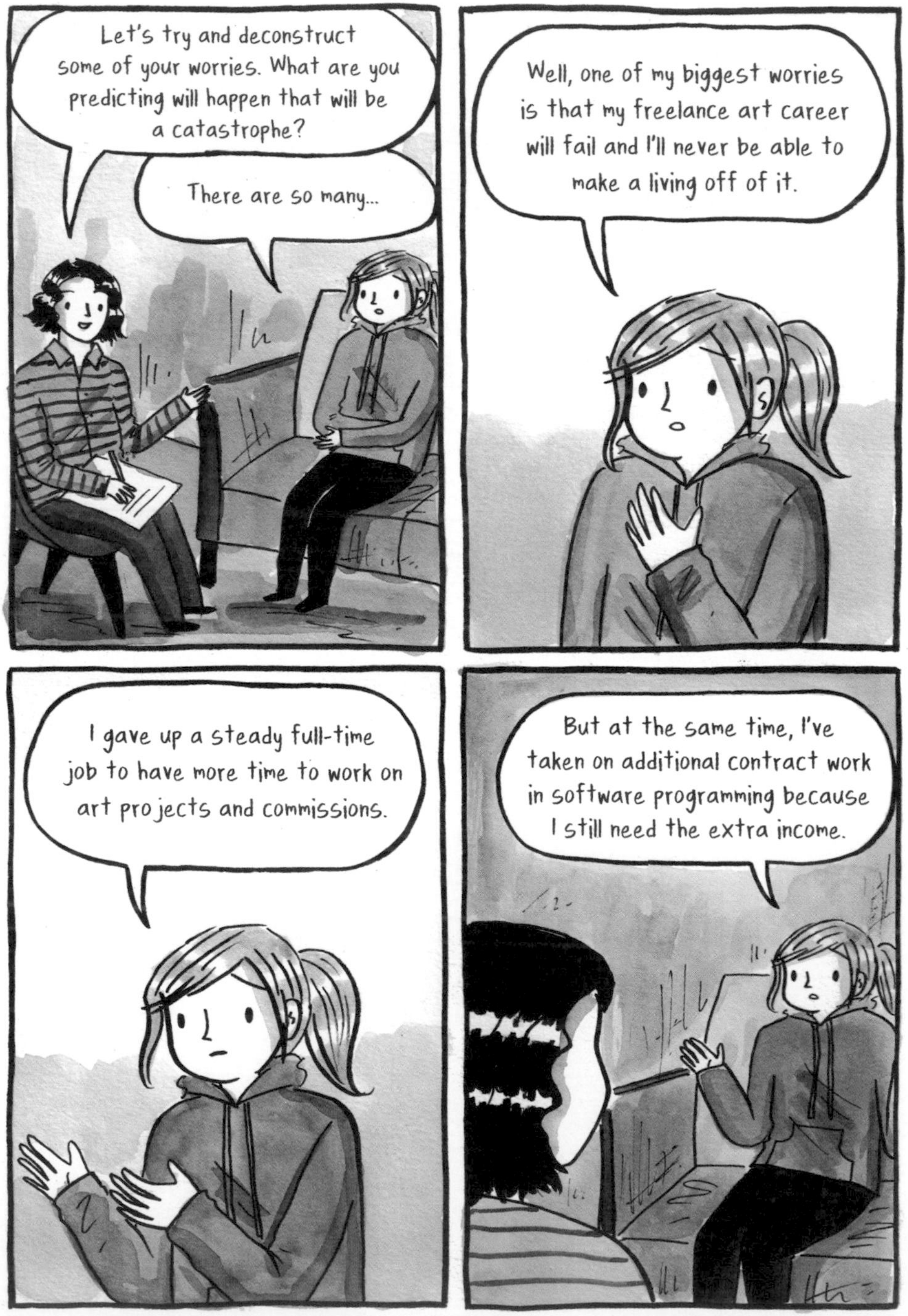
Let's try and deconstruct some of your worries. What are you predicting will happen that will be a catastrophe?
There are so many...
Well, one of my biggest worries is that my freelance art career will fail and I'll never be able to make a living off of it.
I gave up a steady full-time job to have more time to work on art projects and commissions.
But at the same time, I've taken on additional contract work in software programming because I still need the extra income.

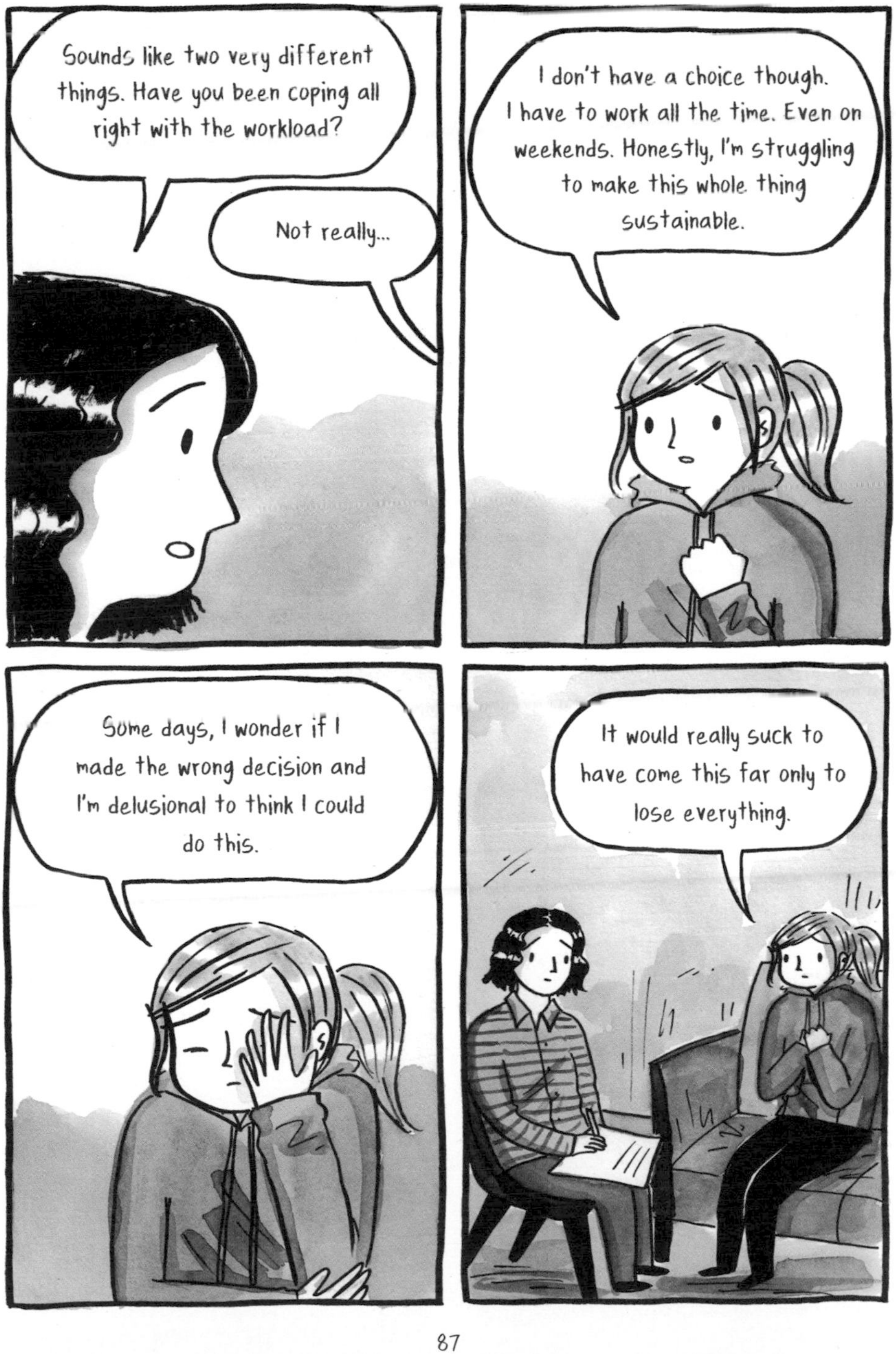
Sounds like two very different things. Have you been coping all right with the workload?
Not really...
I don't have a choice though. I have to work all the time. Even on weekends. Honestly, I'm struggling to make this whole thing sustainable.
Some days, I wonder if I made the wrong decision and I'm delusional to think I could do this.
It would really suck to have come this far only to lose everything.

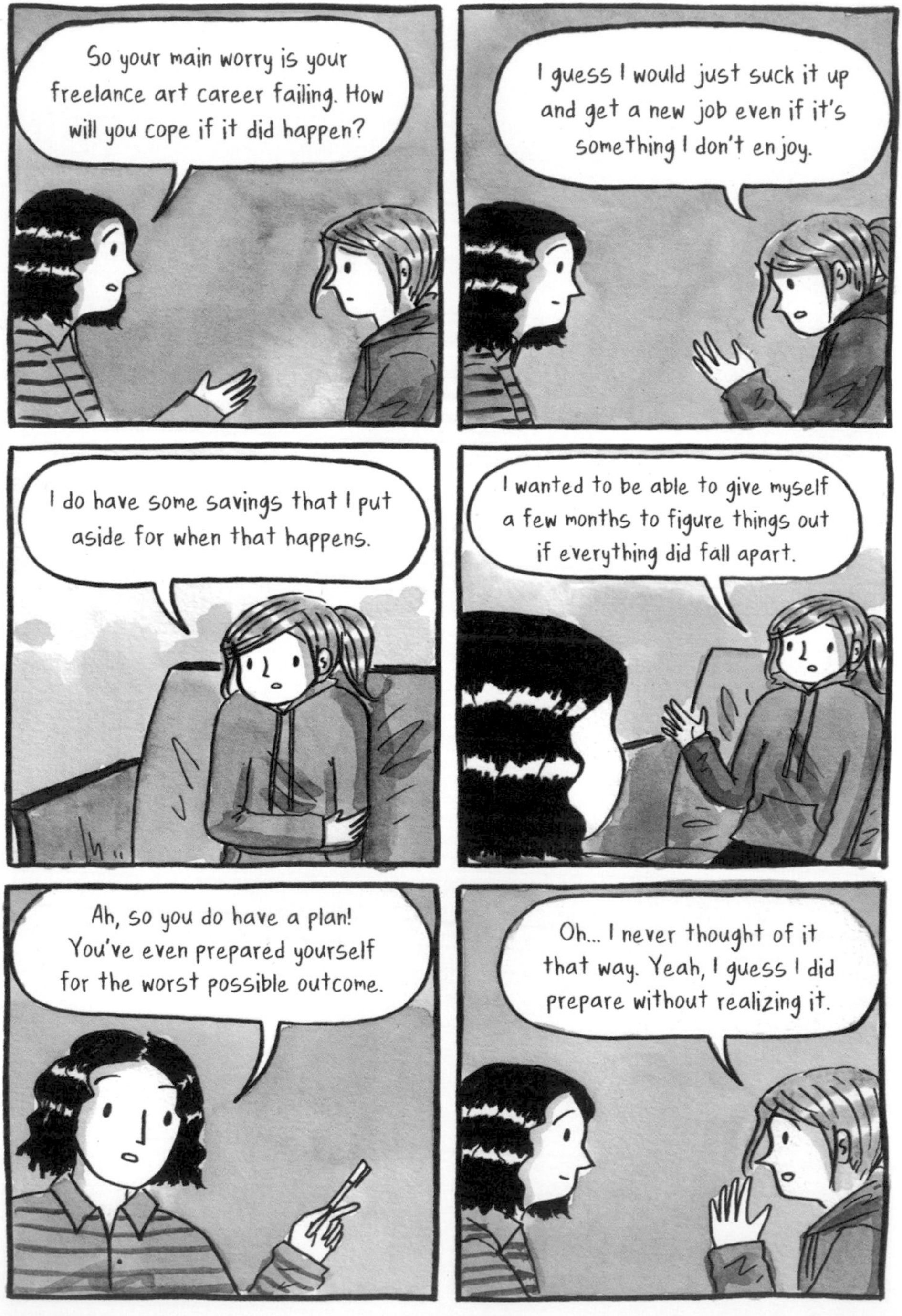
So your main worry is your freelance art career failing. How will you cope if it did happen?
I guess I would just suck it up and get a new job even if it's something I don't enjoy.
I do have some savings that I put aside for when that happens.
I wanted to be able to give myself a few months to figure things out if everything did fall apart.
Ah, so you do have a plan! You've even prepared yourself for the worst possible outcome.
Oh... I never thought of it that way. Yeah, I guess I did prepare without realizing it.

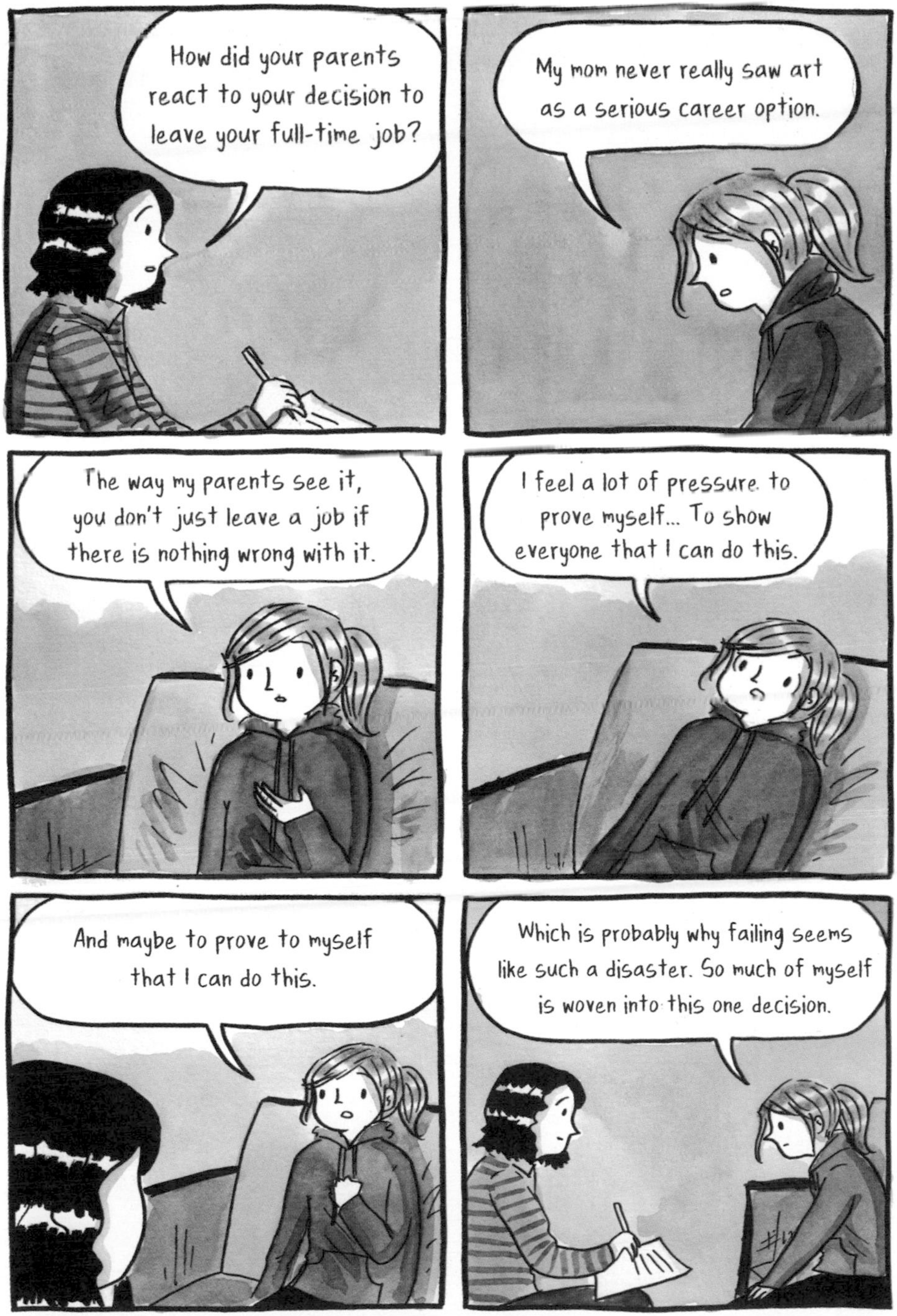
How did your parents react to your decision to leave your full-time job?
My mom never really saw art as a serious career option.
The way my parents see it, you don't just leave a job if there is nothing wrong with it.
I feel a lot of pressure to prove myself... To show everyone that I can do this.
And maybe to prove to myself that I can do this.
Which is probably why failing seems like such a disaster. So much of myself is woven into this one decision.

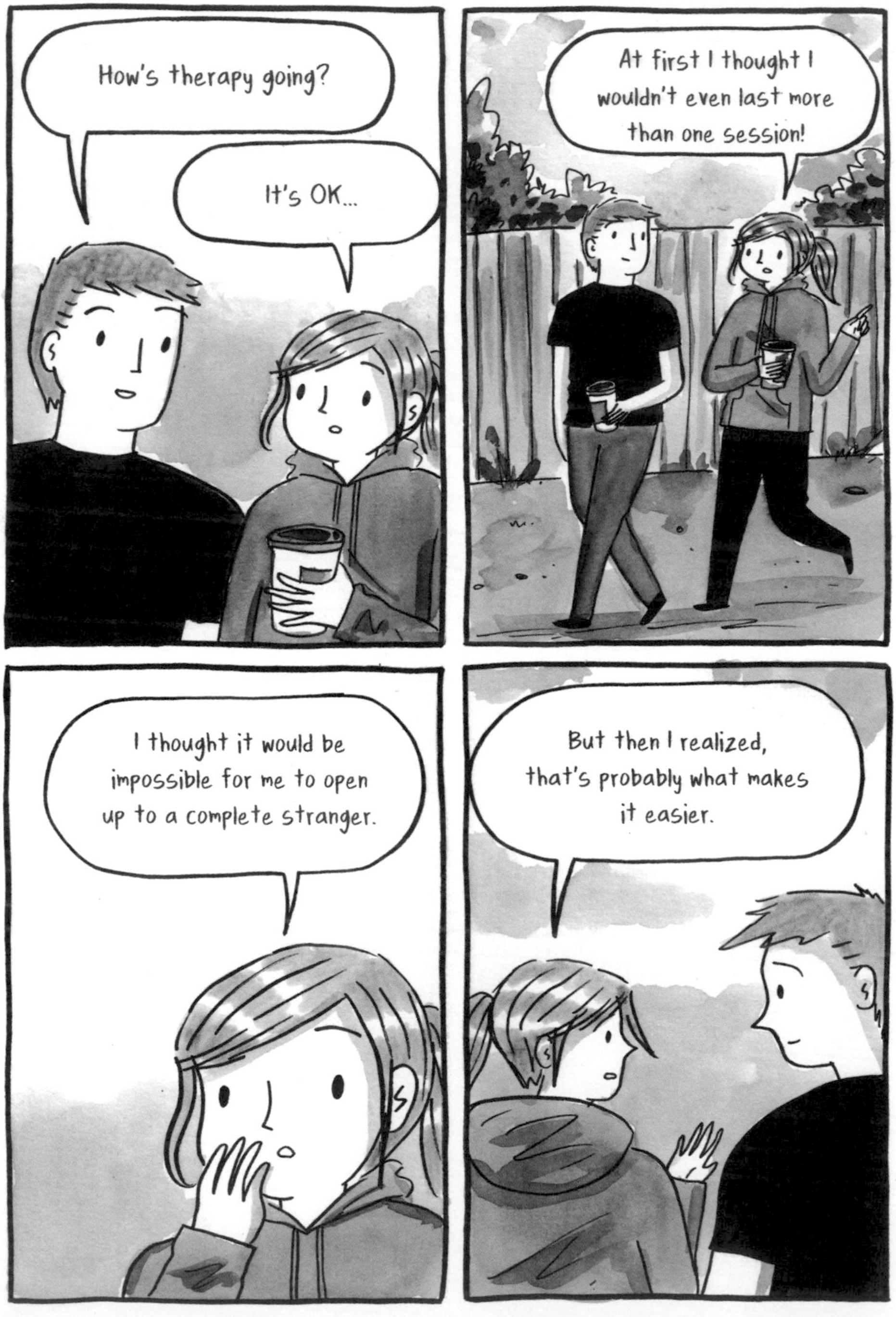
How's therapy going?
It's OK...
At first I thought I wouldn't even last more than one session!
I thought it would be impossible for me to open up to a complete stranger.
But then I realized, that's probably what makes it easier.

Just getting to talk about the things in your head that you'd never say out loud is so important.

To reveal my deepest, darkest thoughts and emotions is like venturing into the unknown.

It's pretty scary to do it alone.

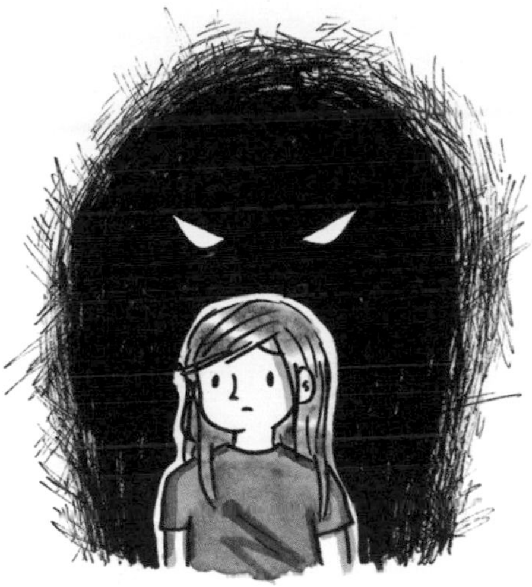

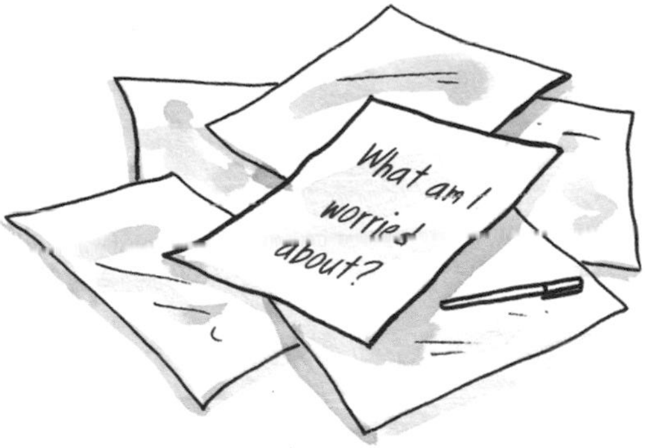
What am I worried about?

Going to therapy means that I had someone to show me different perspectives and encourage better thinking habits in the long run.

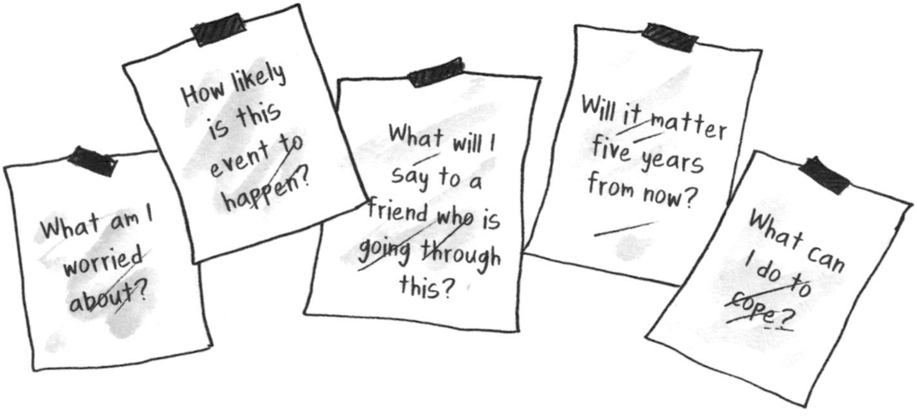
What am I worried about?
How likely is this event to happen?
What will I say to a friend who is going through this?
Will it matter five years from now?
What can I do to cope?

I can be really hard on myself.

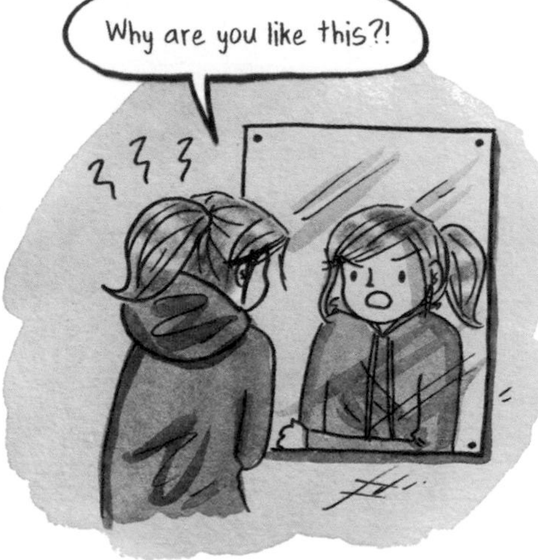
Why are you like this?!

But I'm still learning.

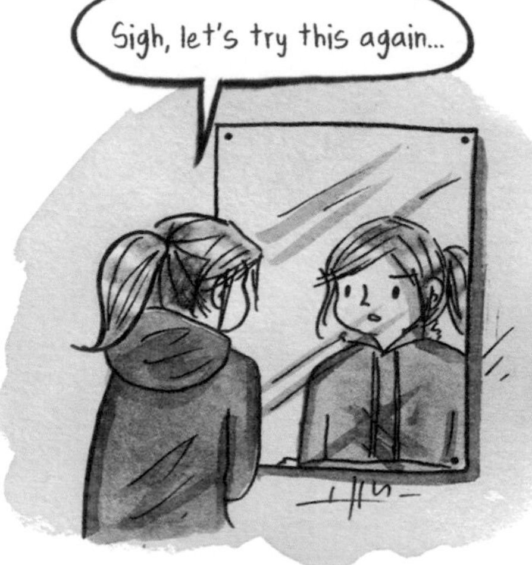
Sigh, let's try this again...

I'm trying my best.

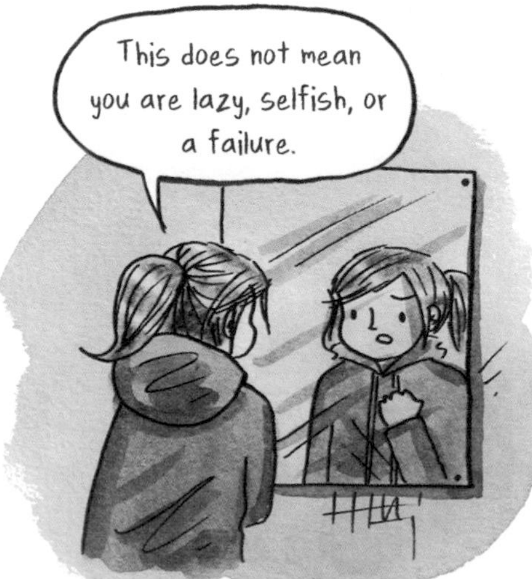
This does not mean you are lazy, selfish, or a failure.

And that's what matters.

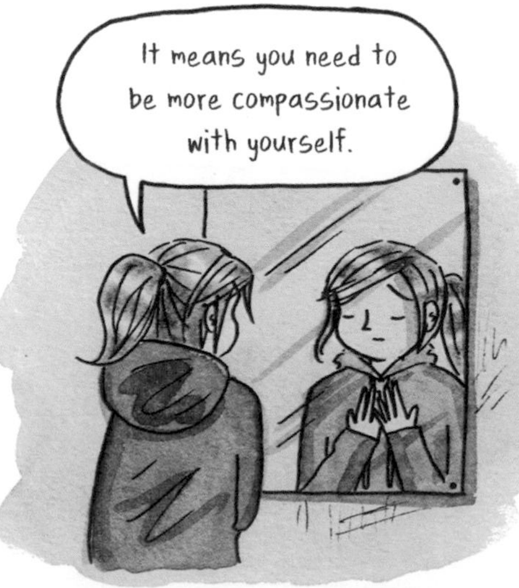
It means you need to be more compassionate with yourself.

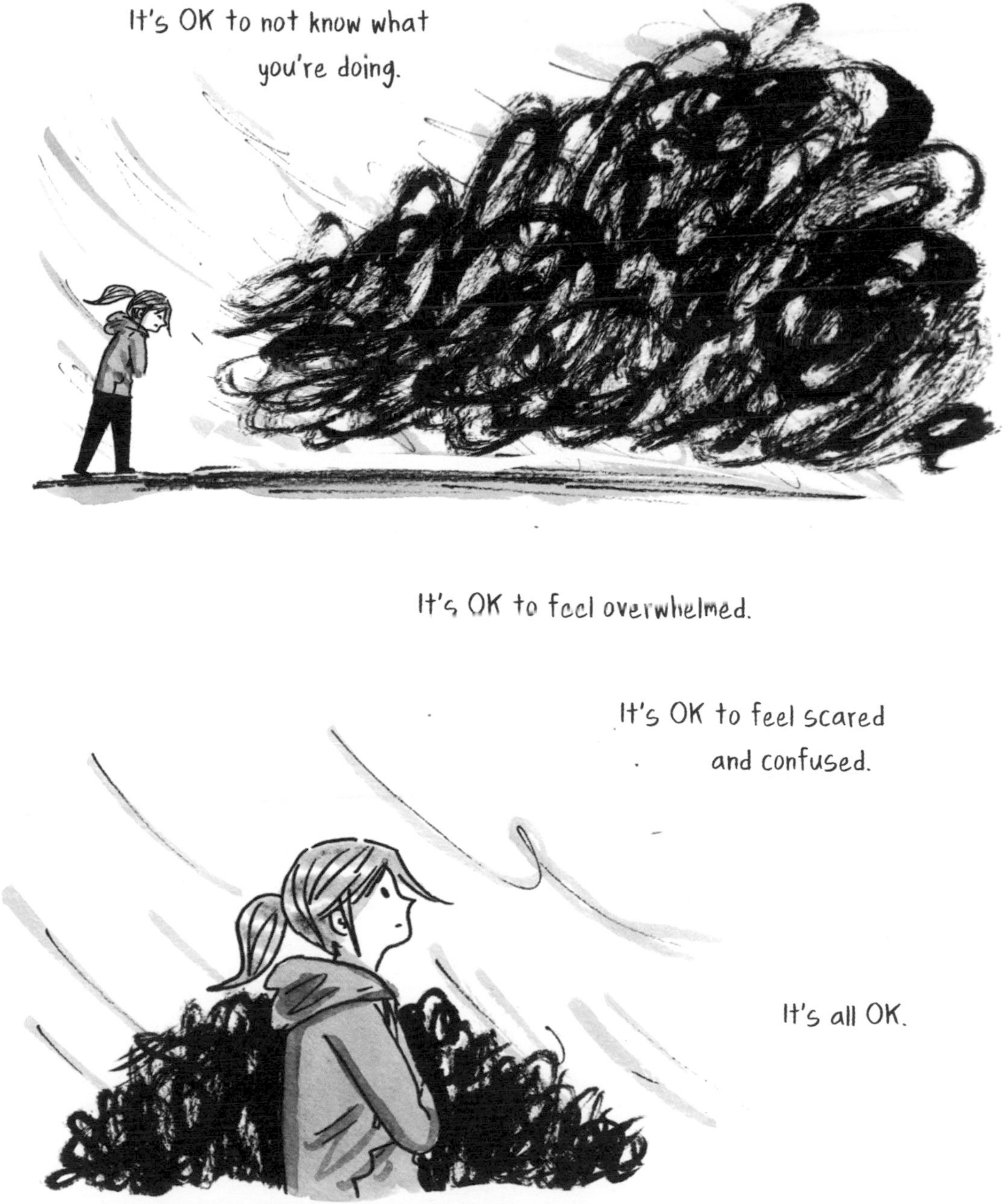
It's OK to not know what you're doing.
It's OK to feel overwhelmed.
It's OK to feel scared and confused.
It's all OK.

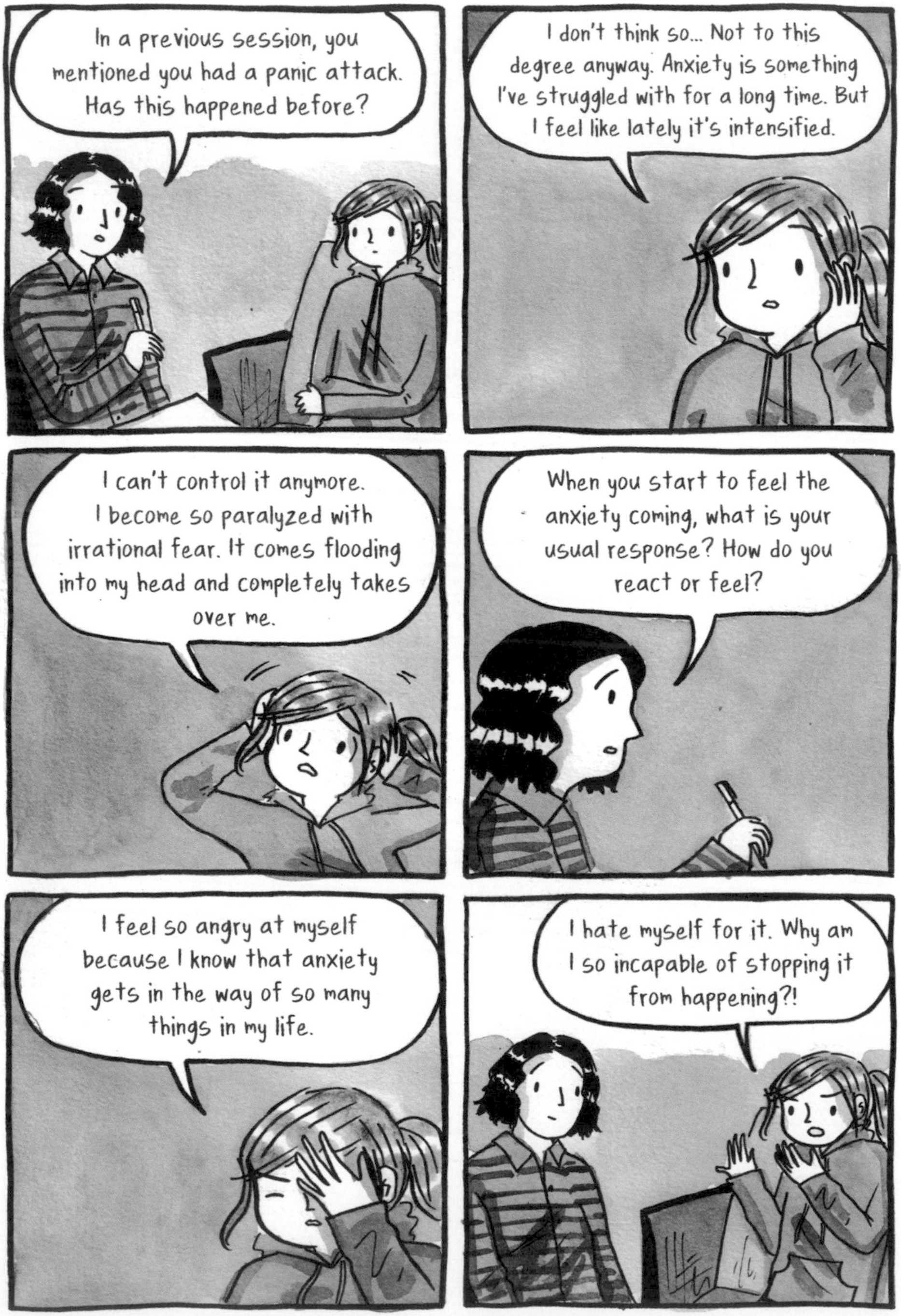
In a previous session, you mentioned you had a panic attack. Has this happened before?
I don't think so... Not to this degree anyway. Anxiety is something I've struggled with for a long time. But I feel like lately it's intensified.
I can't control it anymore. I become so paralyzed with irrational fear. It comes flooding into my head and completely takes over me.
When you start to feel the anxiety coming, what is your usual response? How do you react or feel?
I feel so angry at myself because I know that anxiety gets in the way of so many things in my life.
I hate myself for it. Why am I so incapable of stopping it from happening?!

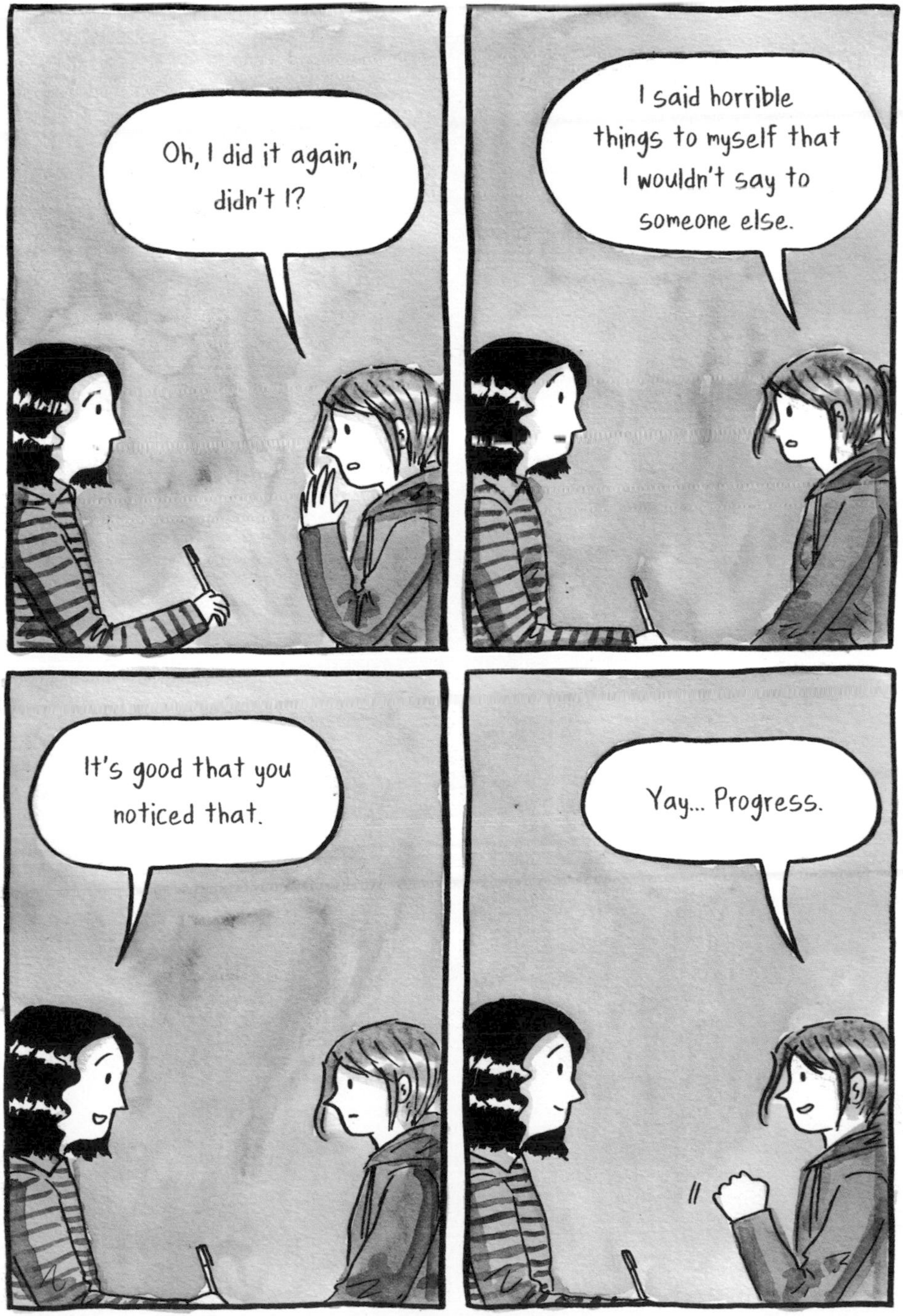
Oh, I did it again, didn't I?
I said horrible things to myself that I wouldn't say to someone else.
It's good that you noticed that.
Yay... Progress.

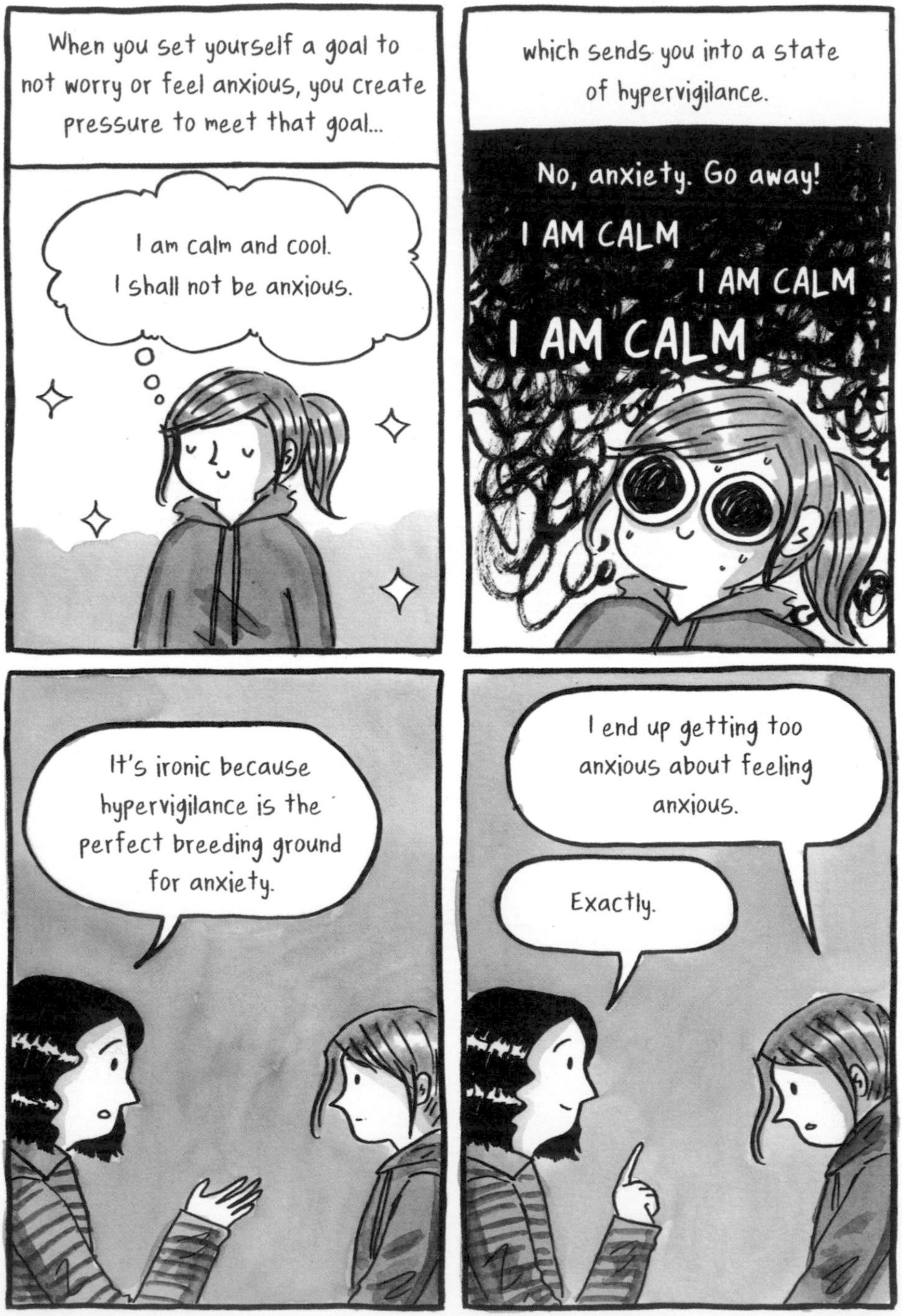
When you set yourself a goal to not worry or feel anxious, you create pressure to meet that goal...
I am calm and cool. I shall not be anxious.
which sends you into a state of hypervigilance.
No, anxiety. Go away!
I AM CALM
I AM CALM
I AM CALM
It's ironic because hypervigilance is the perfect breeding ground for anxiety.
I end up getting too anxious about feeling anxious.
Exactly.

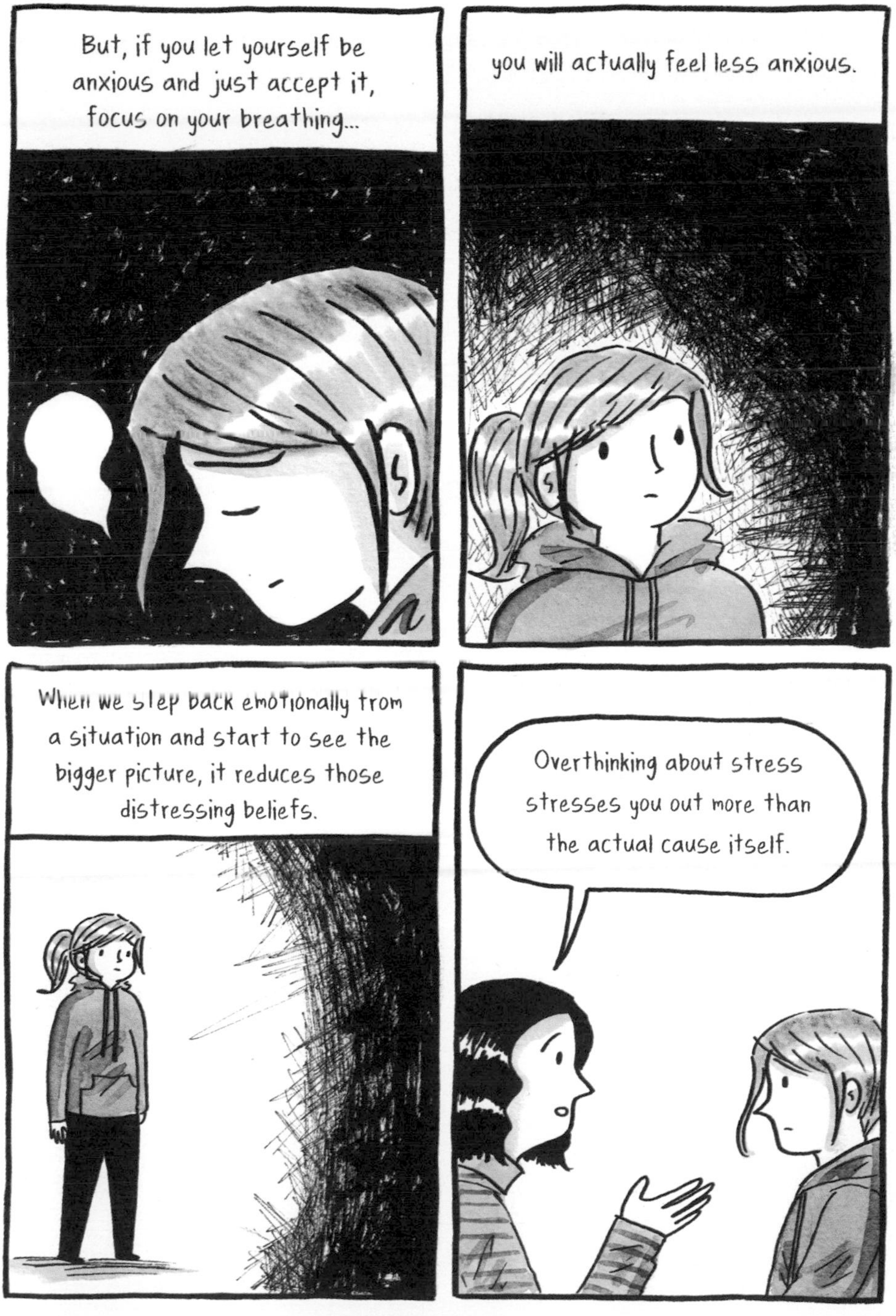
But, if you let yourself be anxious and just accept it, focus on your breathing...
you will actually feel less anxious.
When we step back emotionally from a situation and start to see the bigger picture, it reduces those distressing beliefs.
Overthinking about stress stresses you out more than the actual cause itself.

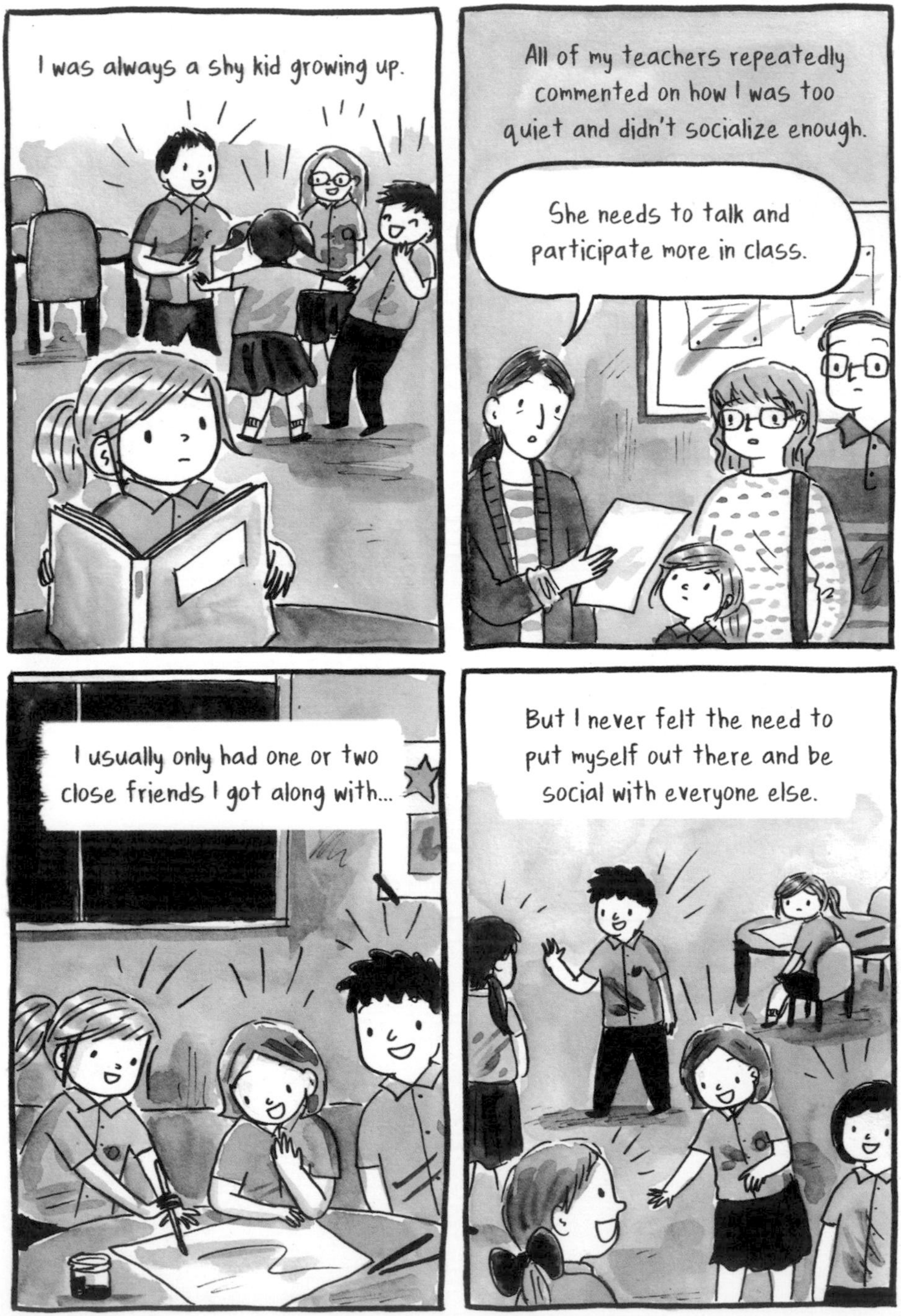
I was always a shy kid growing up.
All of my teachers repeatedly commented on how I was too quiet and didn't socialize enough.
She needs to talk and participate more in class.
I usually only had one or two close friends I got along with...
But I never felt the need to put myself out there and be social with everyone else.

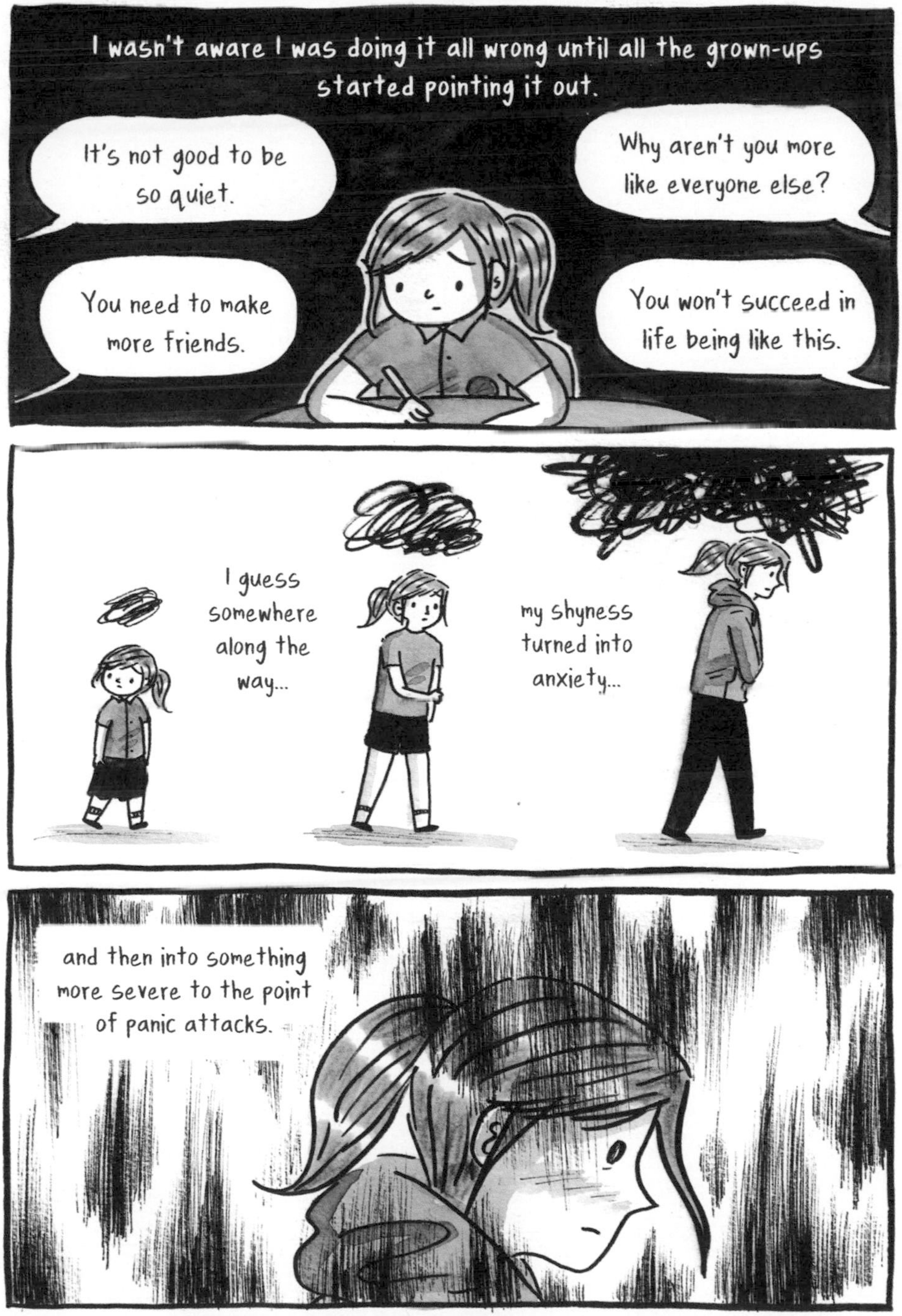
I wasn't aware I was doing it all wrong until all the grown-ups started pointing it out.
It's not good to be so quiet.
Why aren't you more like everyone else?
You need to make more friends.
You won't succeed in life being like this.
I guess somewhere along the way...
my shyness turned into anxiety...
and then into something more severe to the point of panic attacks.

Sometimes, coping with difficult things is giving the problem some space in your life and not locked away inside.

Allow yourself to be with your emotions and let it all exist.

Cry, feel anger, sit in despair.

They will eventually pass.

You are allowed to feel the things you feel

and those feelings matter.

Remember that not all thoughts are true.
Just because you believe in them now, doesn't mean they are facts.

While you can't always control your thoughts and feelings,
you can choose how you respond to them.

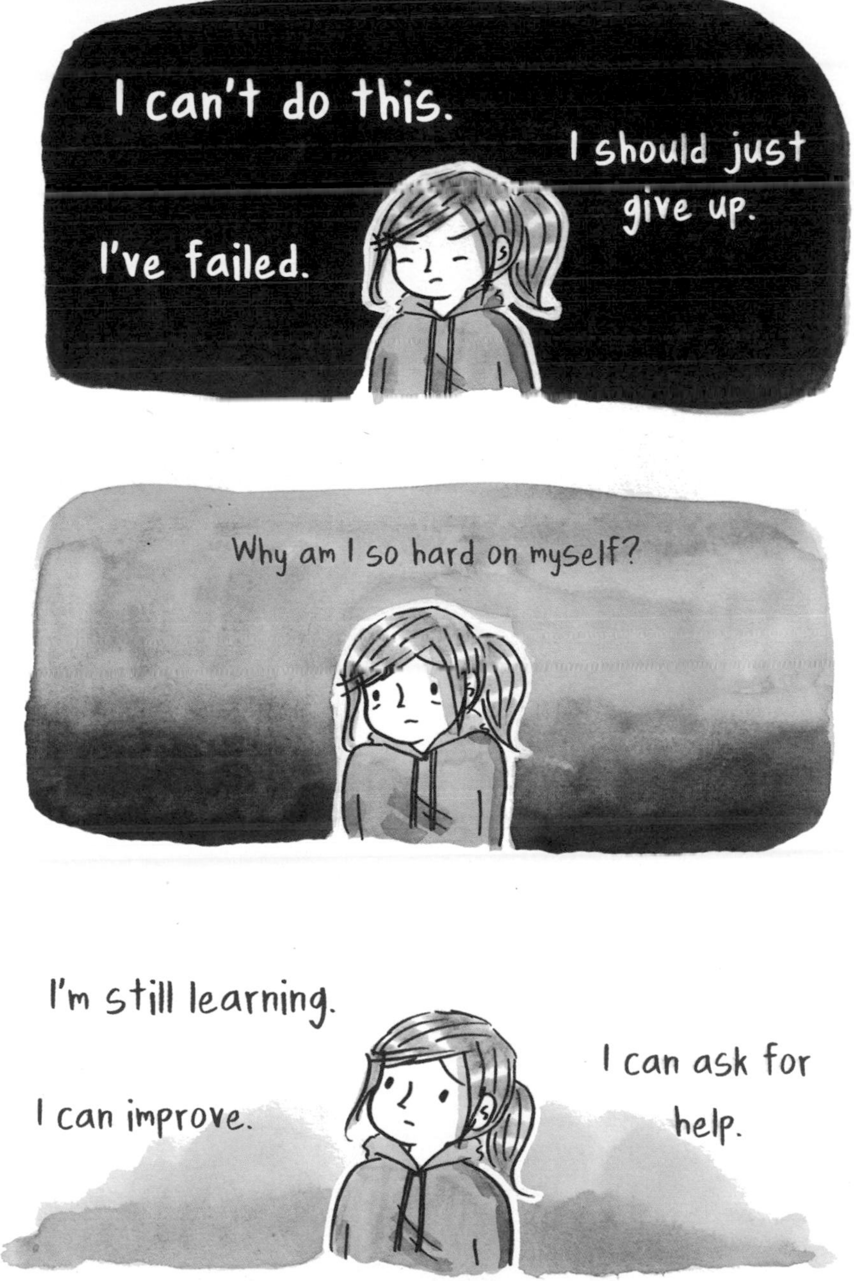
I can't do this.
I should just give up.
I've failed.
Why am I so hard on myself?
I'm still learning.
I can ask for help.
I can improve.

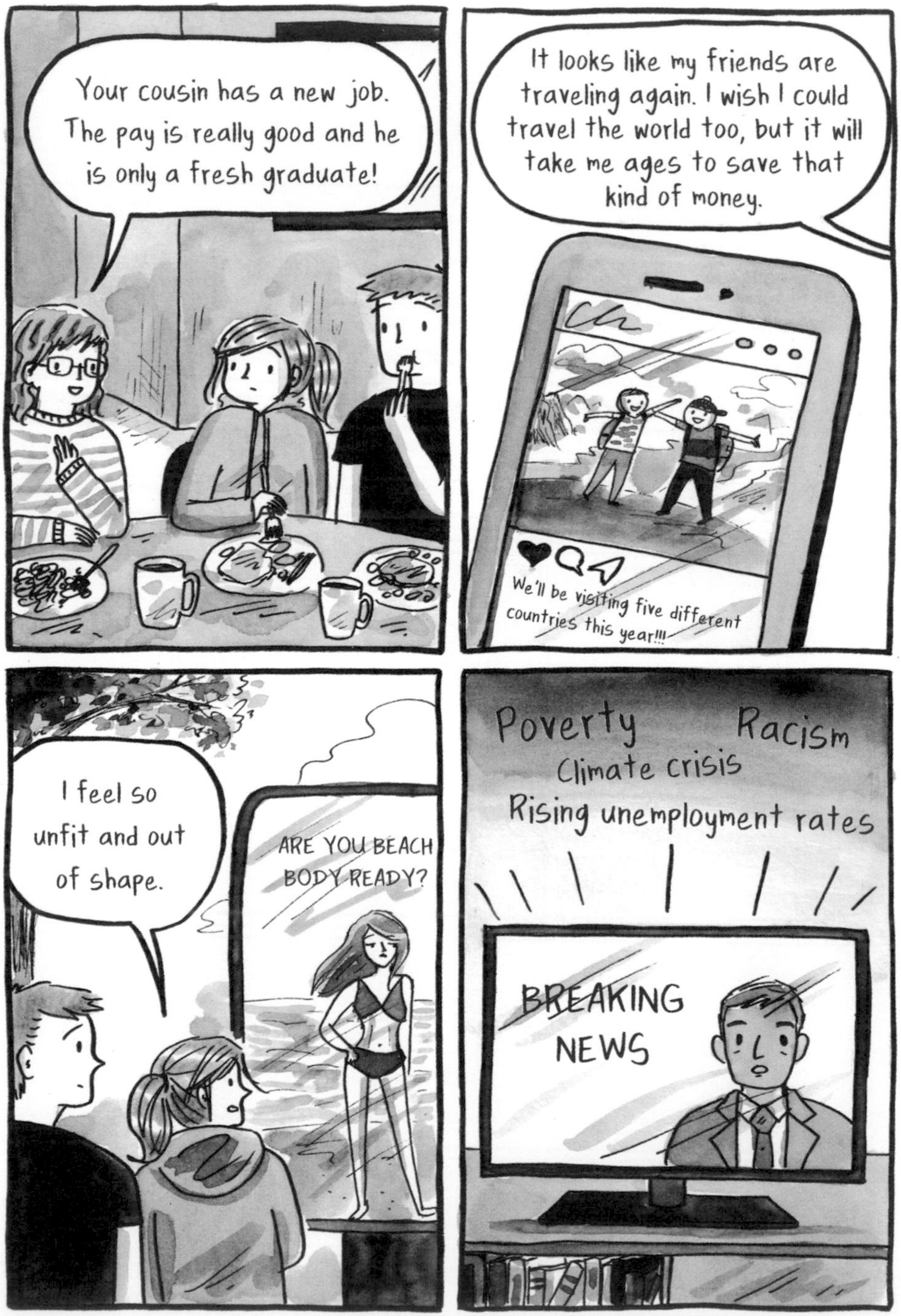
Your cousin has a new job. The pay is really good and he is only a fresh graduate!
It looks like my friends are traveling again. I wish I could travel the world too, but it will take me ages to save that kind of money.
We'll be visiting five different countries this year!!!
I feel so unfit and out of shape.
ARE YOU BEACH BODY READY?
Poverty
Racism
Climate crisis
Rising unemployment rates
BREAKING NEWS

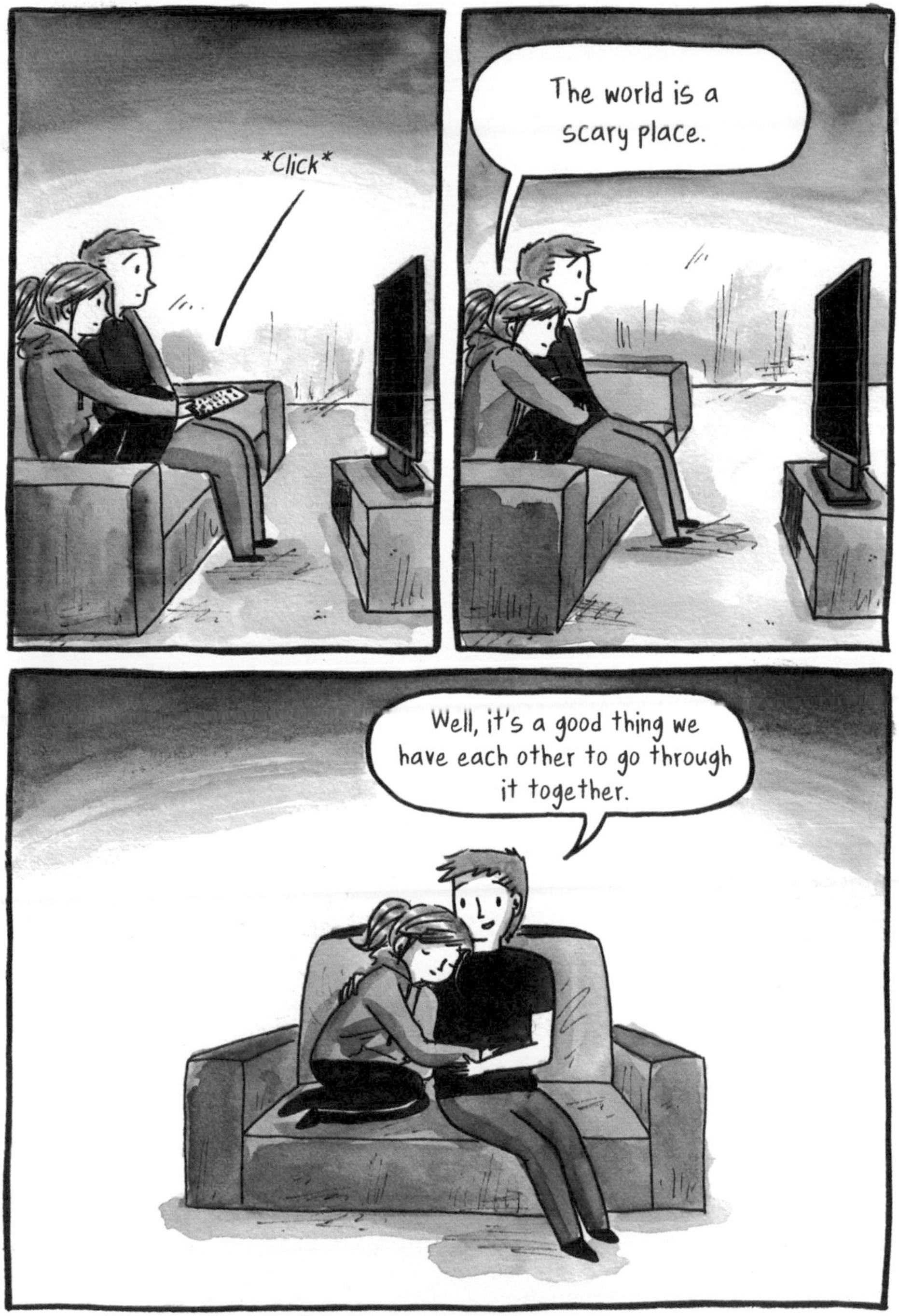
Click
The world is a scary place.
Well, it's a good thing we have each other to go through it together.

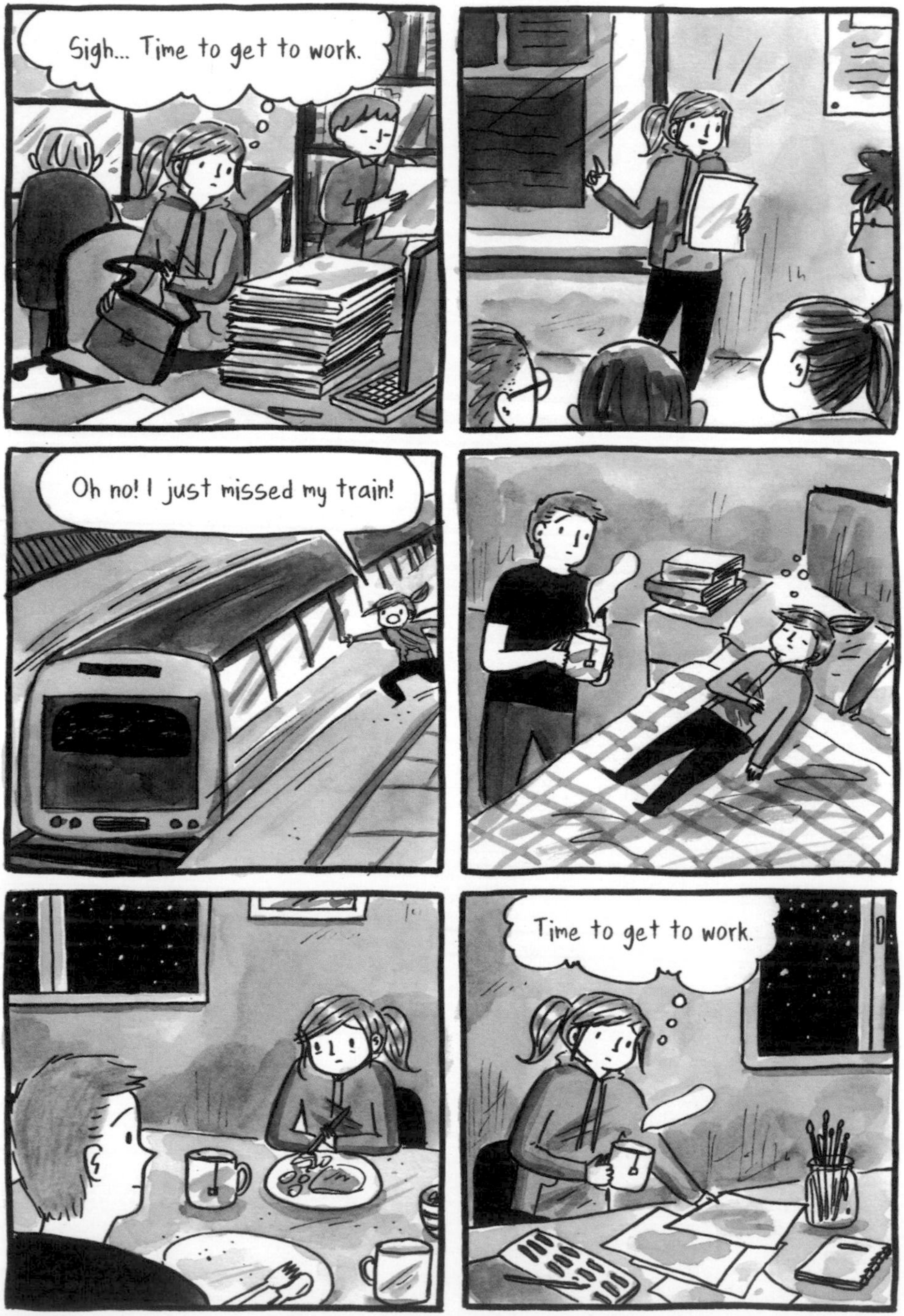
Sigh... Time to get to work.
Oh no! I just missed my train!
Time to get to work.

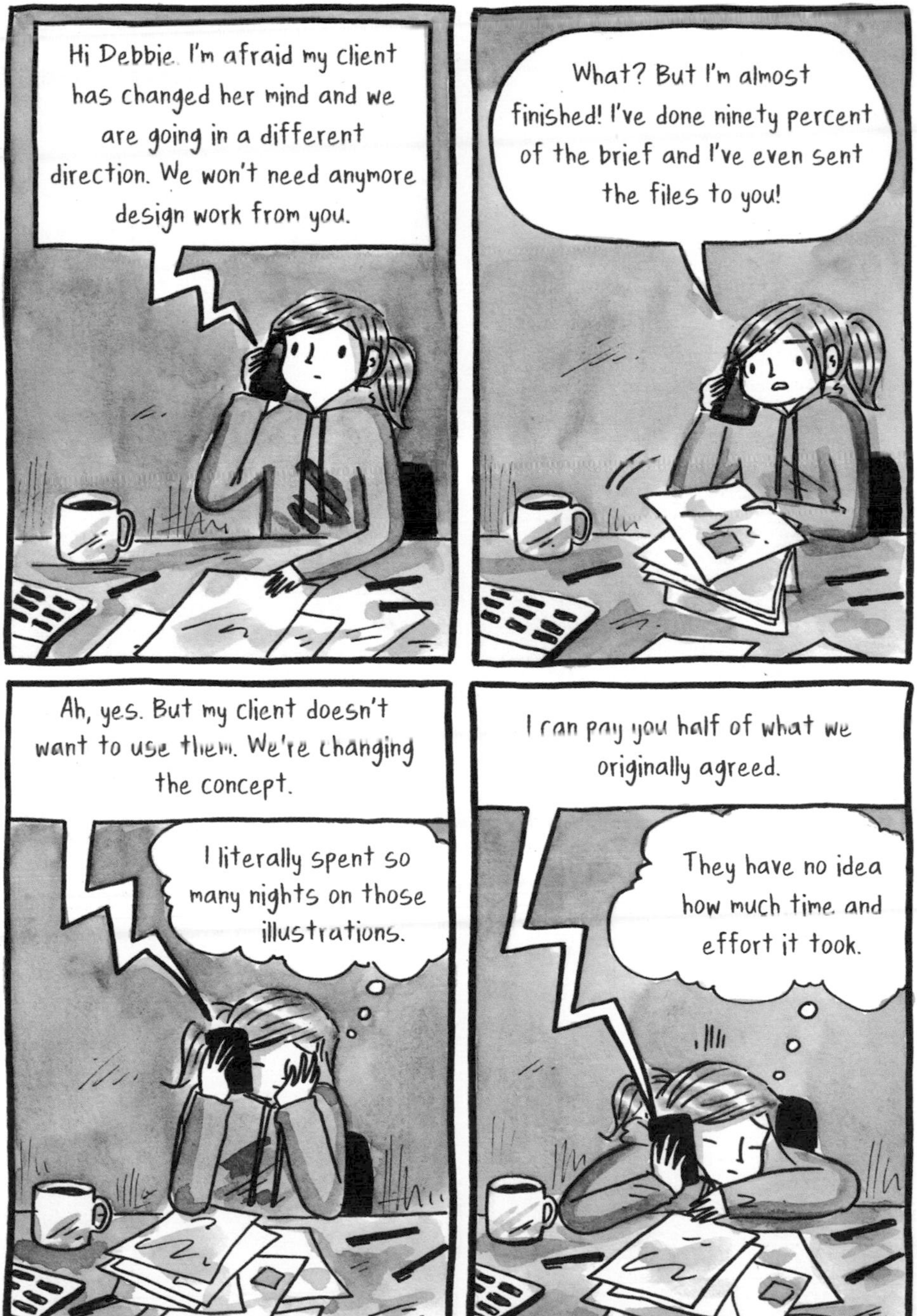
Hi Debbie. I'm afraid my client has changed her mind and we are going in a different direction. We won't need anymore design work from you.
What? But I'm almost finished! I've done ninety percent of the brief and I've even sent the files to you!
Ah, yes. But my client doesn't want to use them. We're changing the concept.
I literally spent so many nights on those illustrations.
I can pay you half of what we originally agreed.
They have no idea how much time and effort it took.

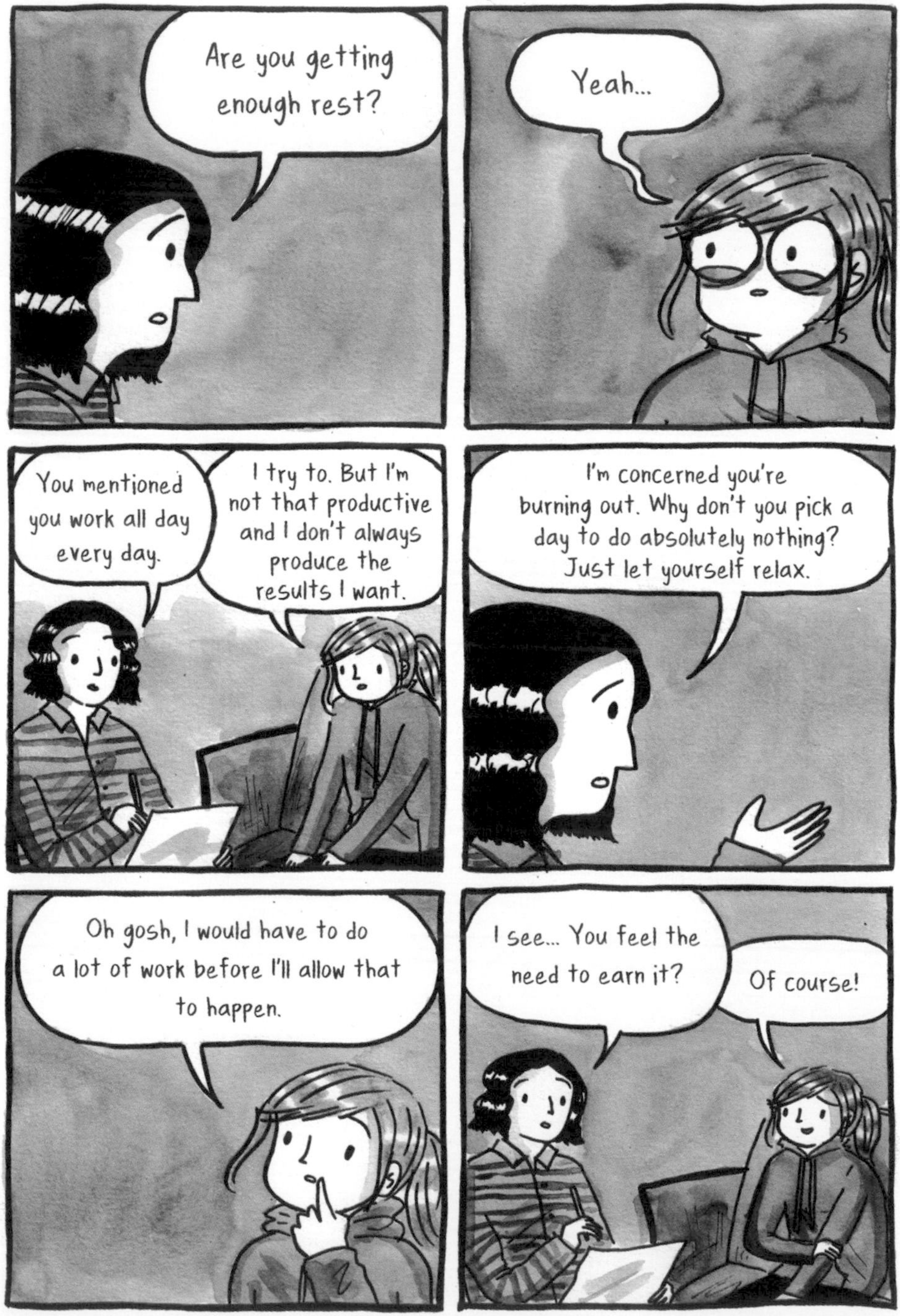
Are you getting enough rest?
Yeah...
You mentioned you work all day every day.
I try to. But I'm not that productive and I don't always produce the results I want.
I'm concerned you're burning out. Why don't you pick a day to do absolutely nothing? Just let yourself relax.
Oh gosh, I would have to do a lot of work before I'll allow that to happen.
I see... You feel the need to earn it?
Of course!

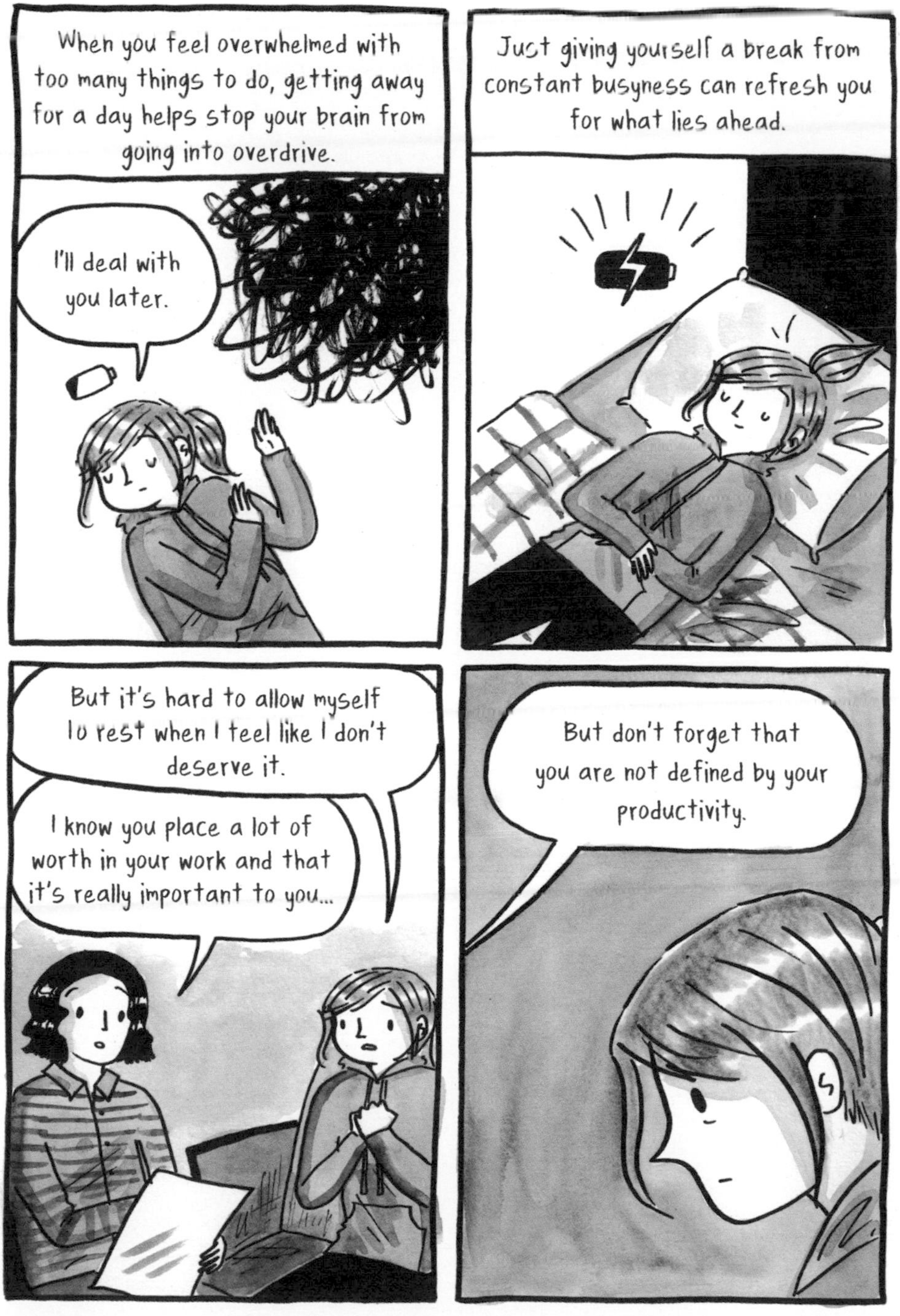
When you feel overwhelmed with too many things to do, getting away for a day helps stop your brain from going into overdrive.
I'll deal with you later.
Just giving yourself a break from constant busyness can refresh you for what lies ahead.
But it's hard to allow myself to rest when I feel like I don't deserve it.
I know you place a lot of worth in your work and that it's really important to you...
But don't forget that you are not defined by your productivity.

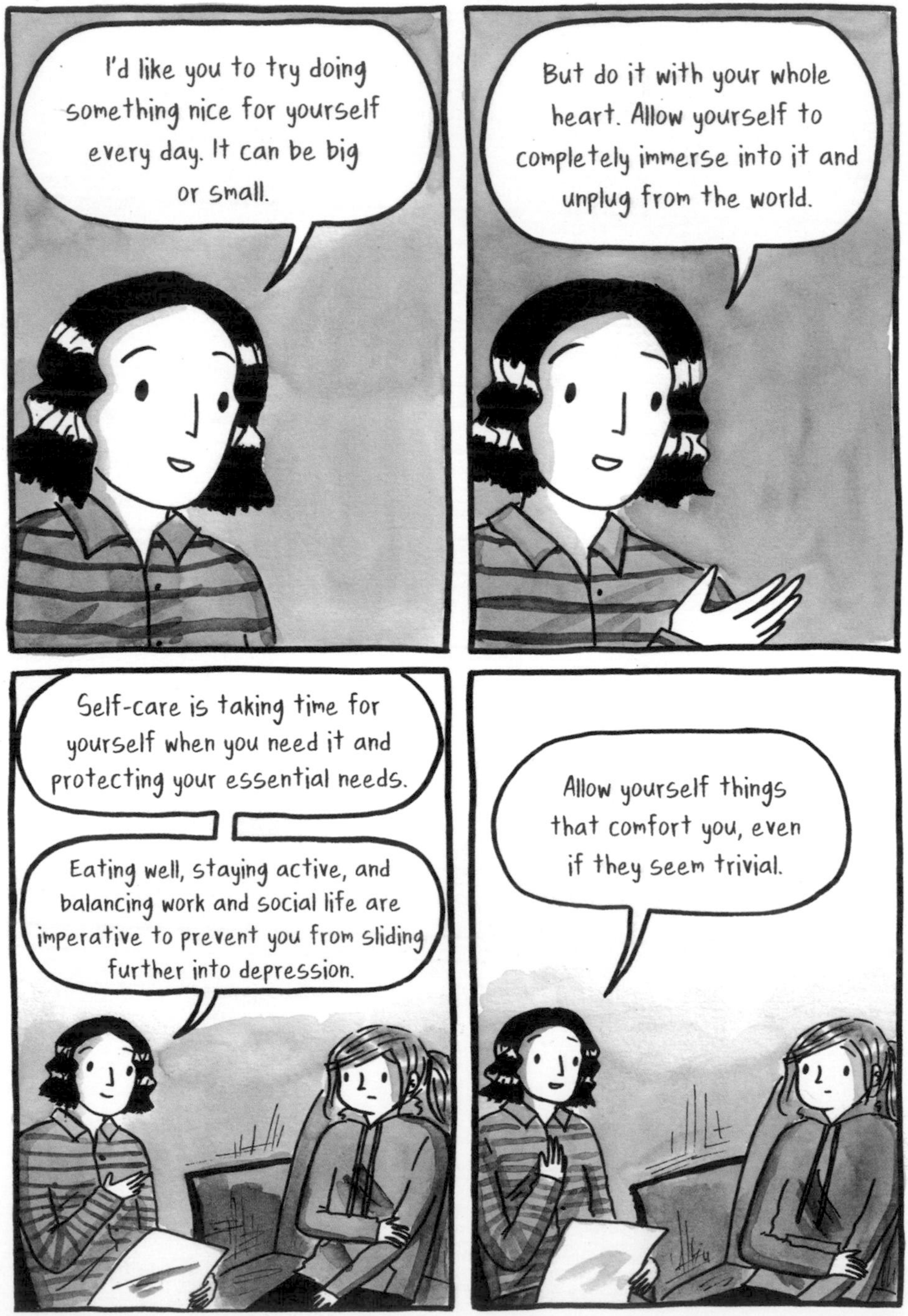
I'd like you to try doing something nice for yourself every day. It can be big or small.
But do it with your whole heart. Allow yourself to completely immerse into it and unplug from the world.
Self-care is taking time for yourself when you need it and protecting your essential needs.
Eating well, staying active, and balancing work and social life are imperative to prevent you from sliding further into depression.
Allow yourself things that comfort you, even if they seem trivial.

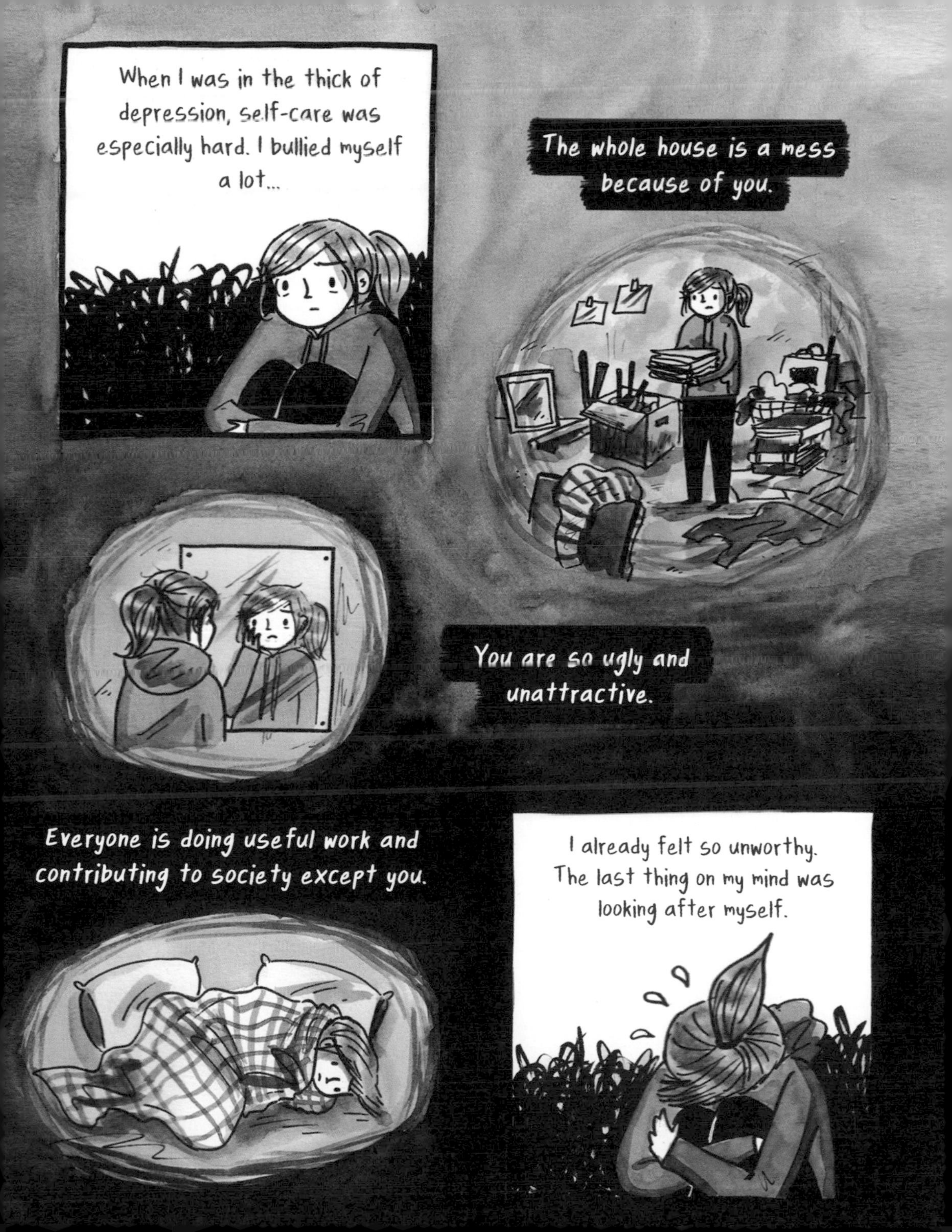
When I was in the thick of depression, self-care was especially hard. I bullied myself a lot...
The whole house is a mess because of you.
You are so ugly and unattractive.
Everyone is doing useful work and contributing to society except you.
I already felt so unworthy. The last thing on my mind was looking after myself.

Modern life encourages us to keep busy and value our worth based on our productivity. There is constant fear and pressure to achieve and there is always not enough time to get anything done.

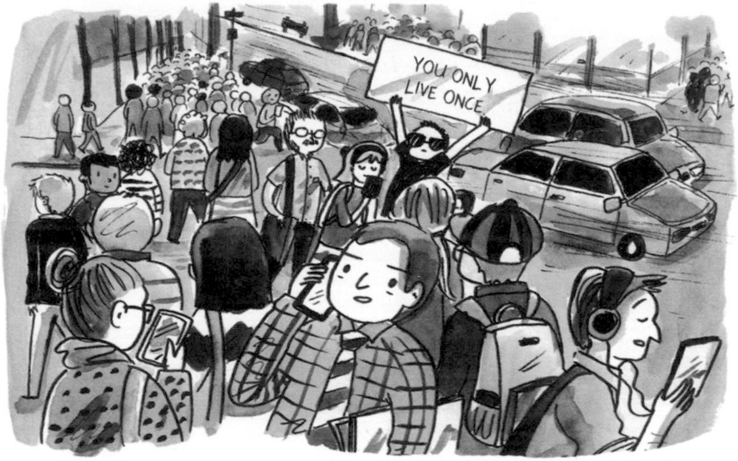
YOU ONLY LIVE ONCE

We all move so fast and consume so much. We often forget how much we are taking on board every day and how much we miss when we don't stop to look around.

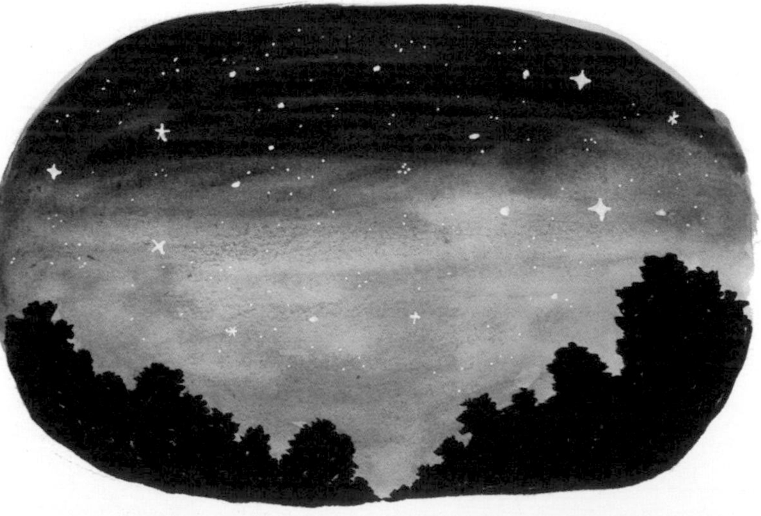

We overload ourselves.

We forget we have our limits.

My mind had a habit of telling me to keep pushing, keep rushing, keep checking off boxes on my to-do list.

I was burning out and my body was screaming for me to stop.

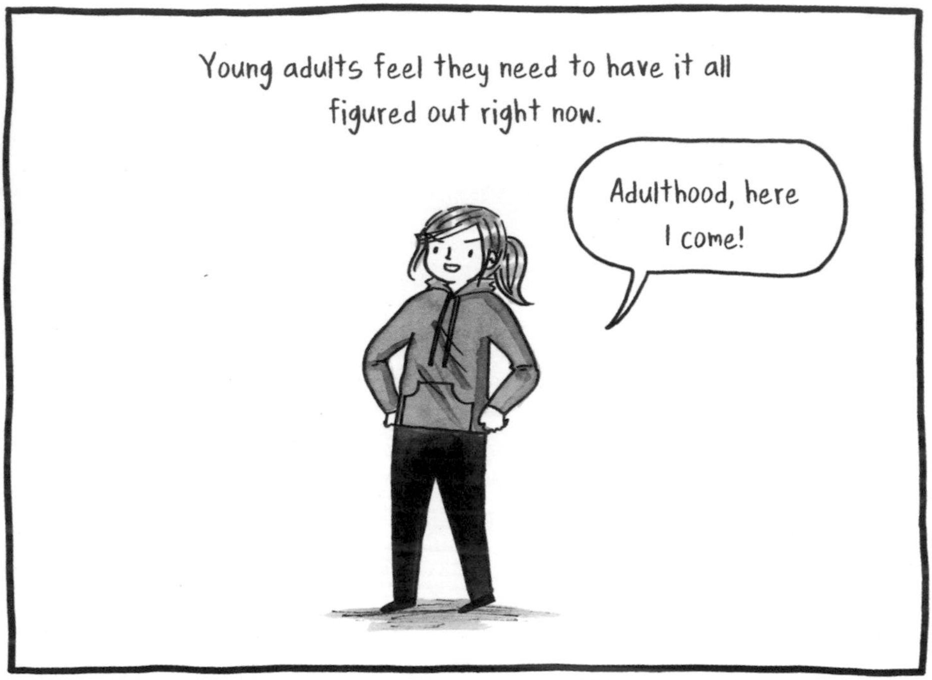
Young adults feel they need to have it all figured out right now.
Adulthood, here I come!

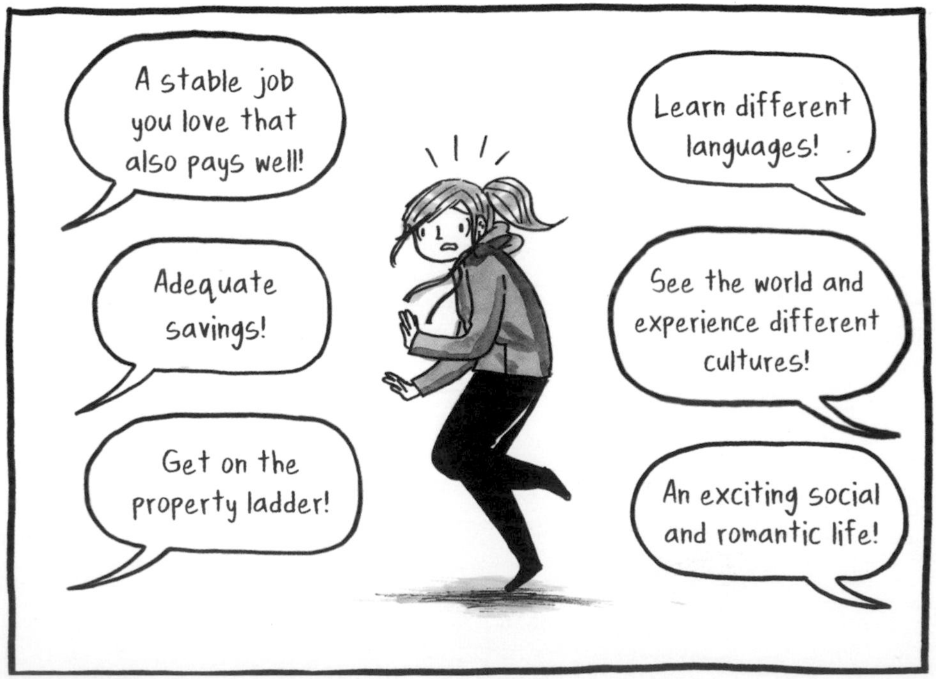
A stable job you love that also pays well!
Learn different languages!
Adequate savings!
See the world and experience different cultures!
Get on the property ladder!
An exciting social and romantic life!

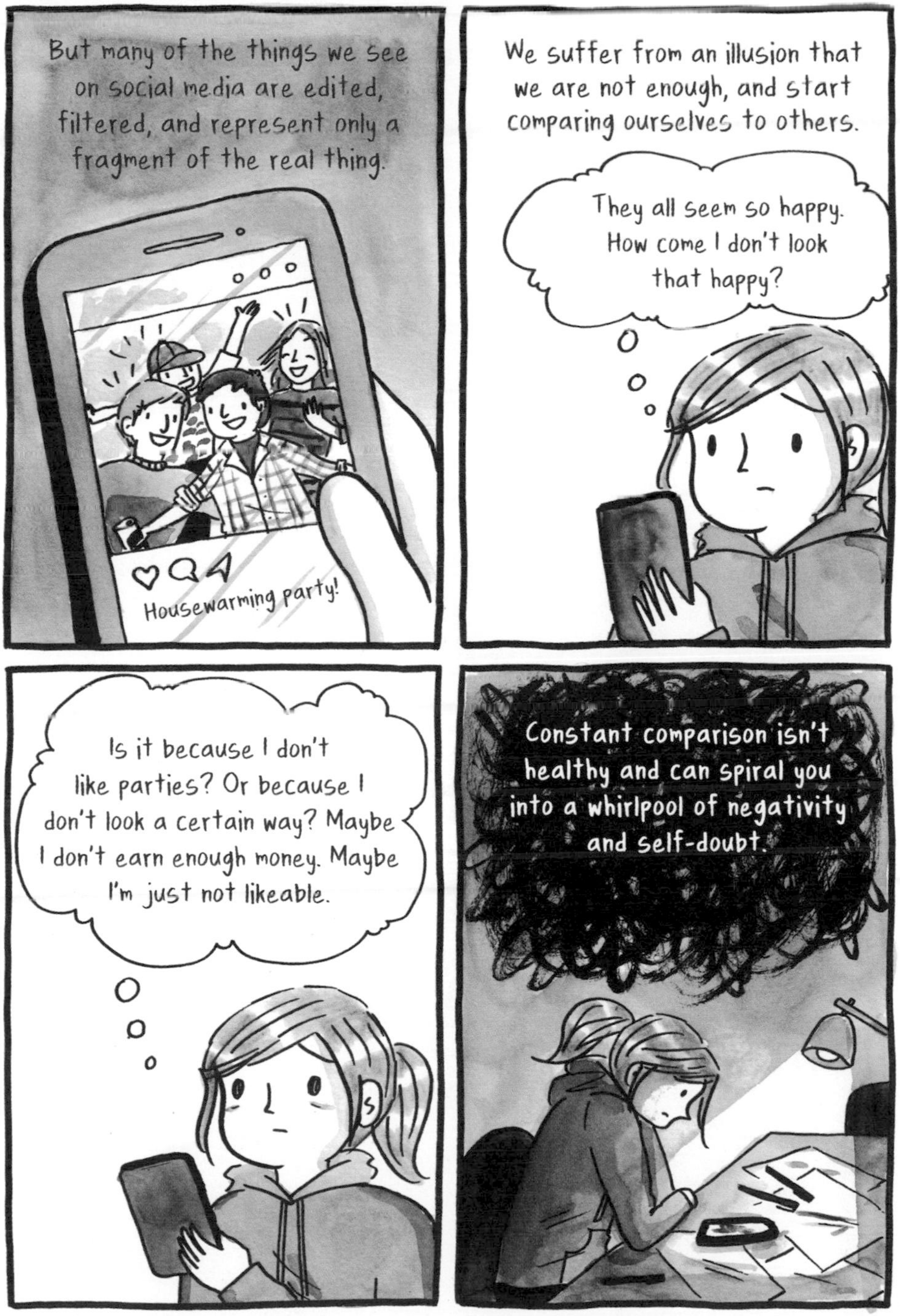
But many of the things we see on social media are edited, filtered, and represent only a fragment of the real thing.
Housewarming party!
We suffer from an illusion that we are not enough, and start comparing ourselves to others.
They all seem so happy. How come I don't look that happy?
Is it because I don't like parties? Or because I don't look a certain way? Maybe I don't earn enough money. Maybe I'm just not likeable.
Constant comparison isn't healthy and can spiral you into a whirlpool of negativity and self-doubt.

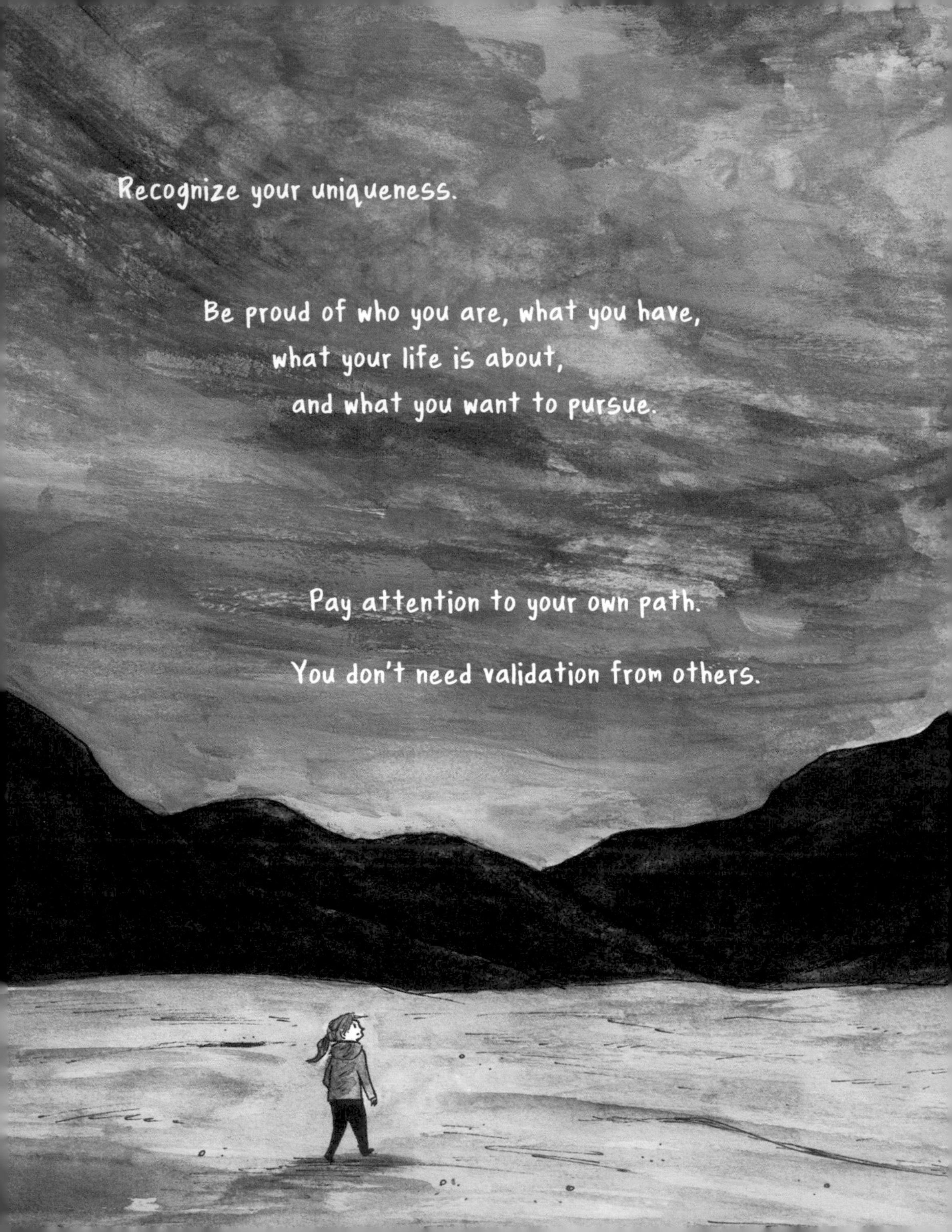
Recognize your uniqueness.
Be proud of who you are, what you have, what your life is about, and what you want to pursue.
Pay attention to your own path.
You don't need validation from others.

Instead of caring about what others think and
changing who you are to fit in...

Maybe it's time to focus on
learning to accept yourself completely.

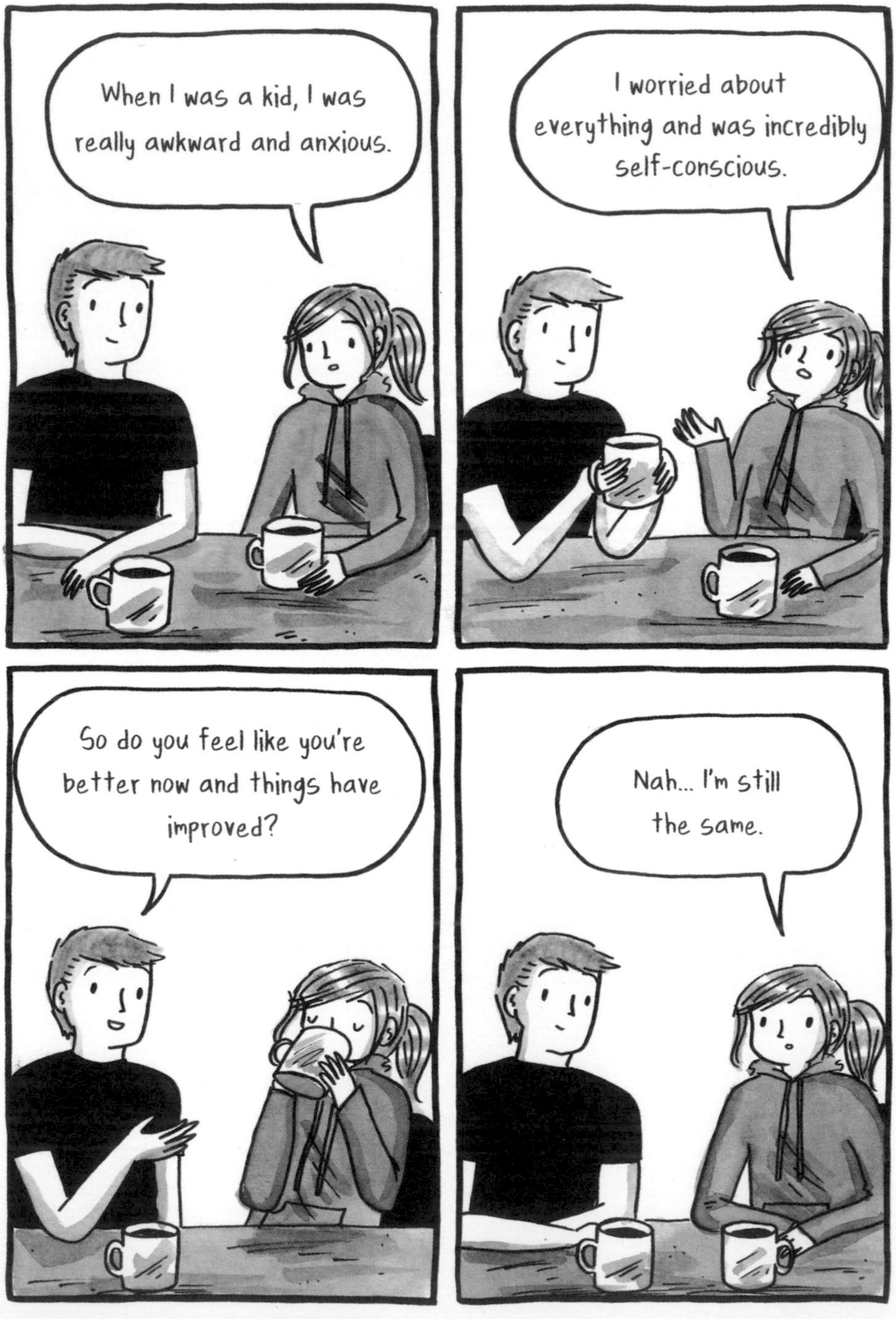
When I was a kid, I was really awkward and anxious.
I worried about everything and was incredibly self-conscious.
So do you feel like you're better now and things have improved?
Nah... I'm still the same.

Embrace your

awkwardness!

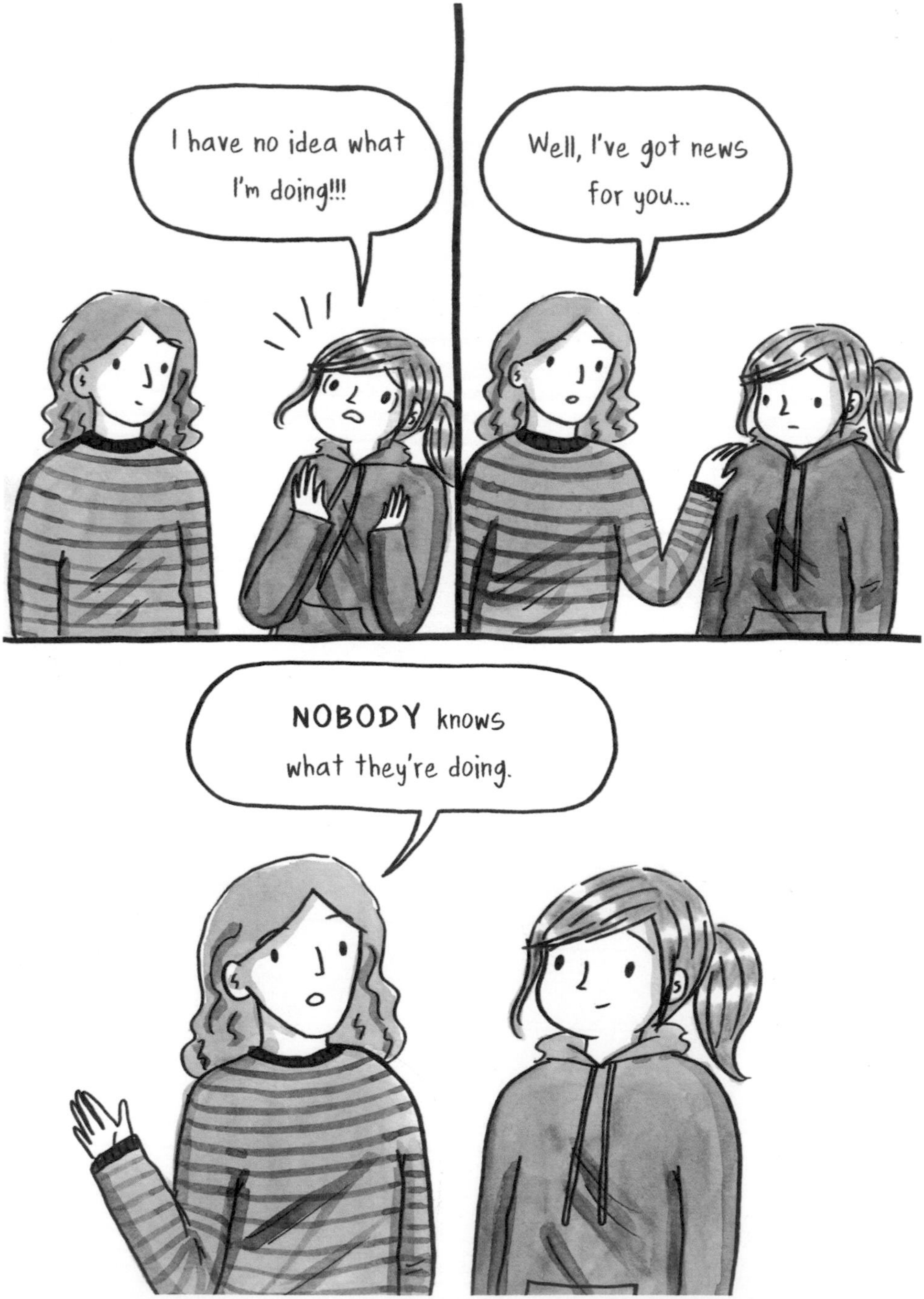
I have no idea what I'm doing!!!
Well, I've got news for you...
NOBODY knows what they're doing.

We expect that by the time we become adults, we will have a secure life plan right in front of us.

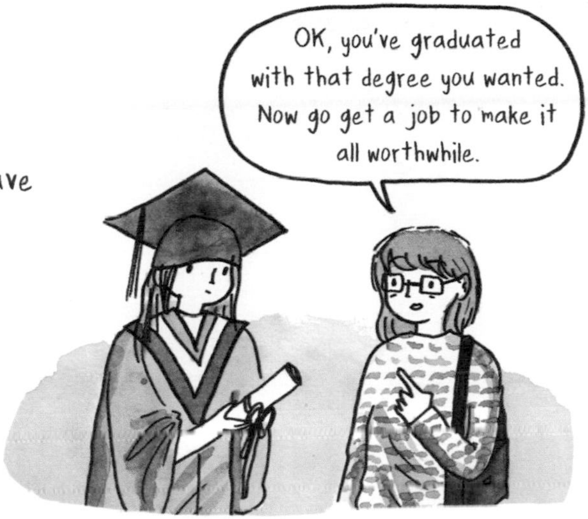
OK, you've graduated with that degree you wanted. Now go get a job to make it all worthwhile.

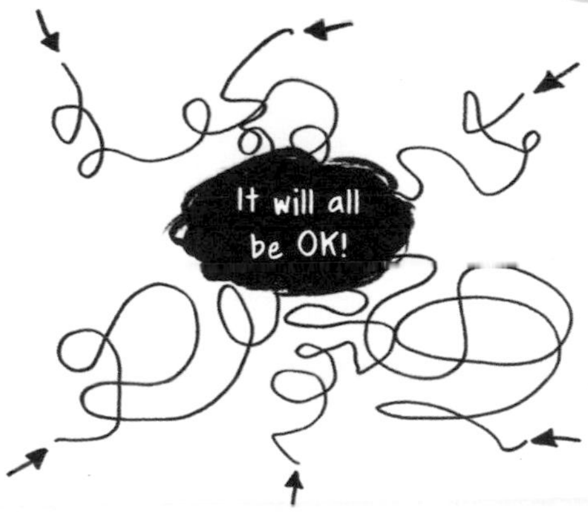
It will all be OK!

The thing is, there is no right way to do life.

We are all winging it.

And we are all doing the best we can.

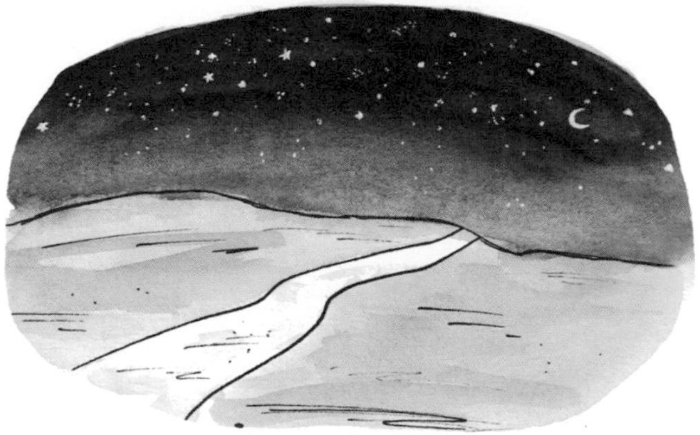

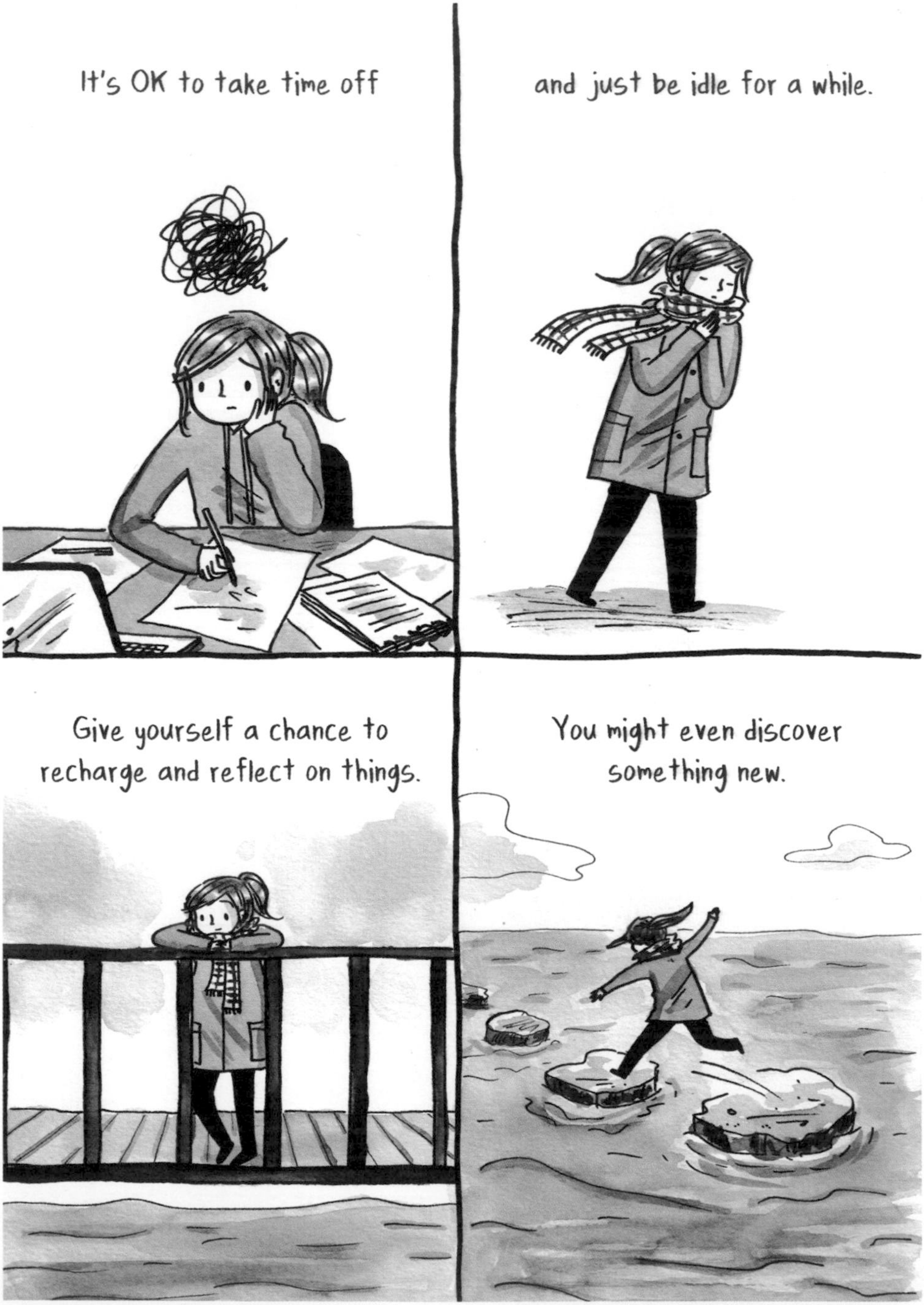
It's OK to take time off
and just be idle for a while.
Give yourself a chance to recharge and reflect on things.
You might even discover something new.

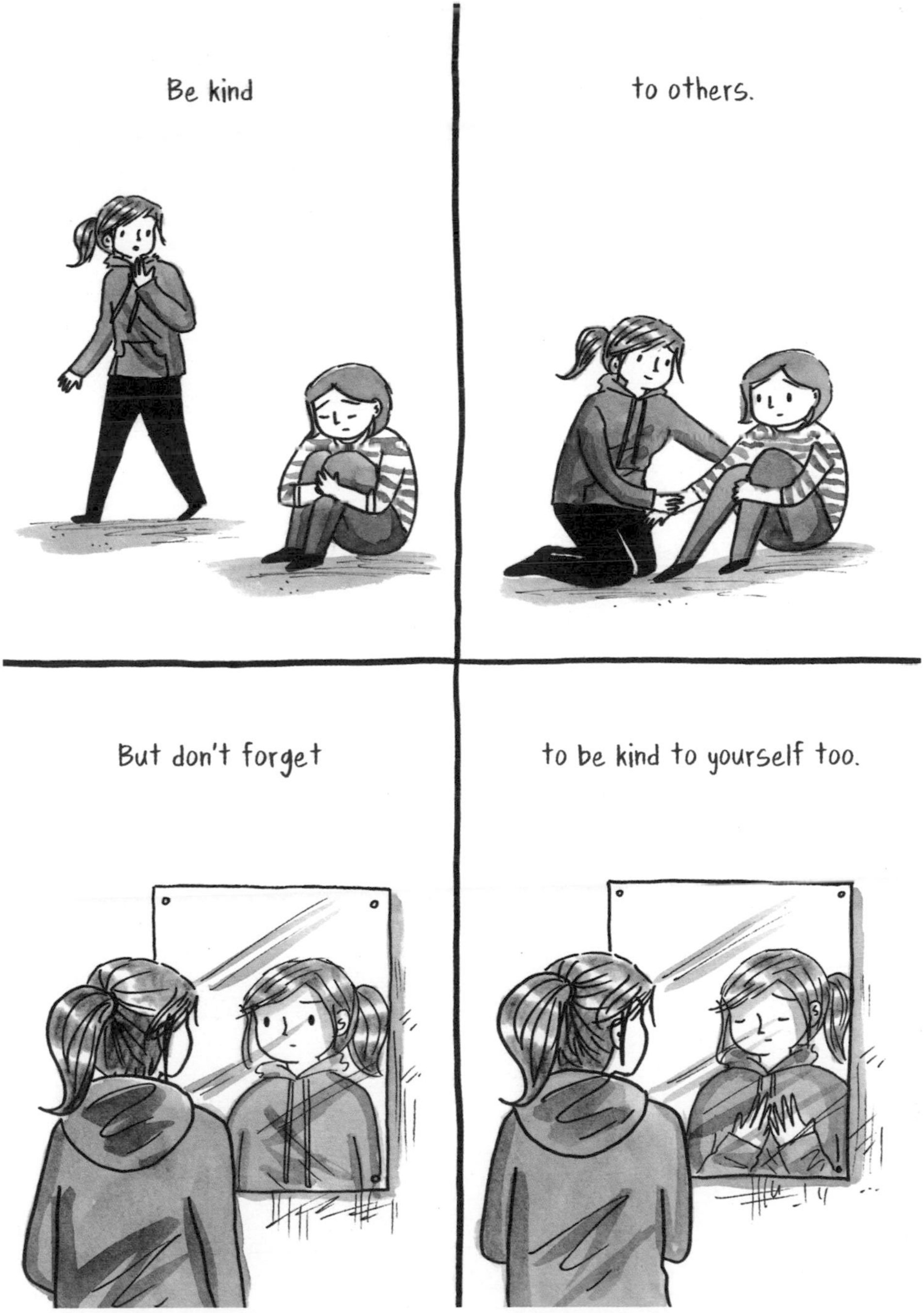
Be kind
to others.
But don't forget
to be kind to yourself too.

Today I woke up early without hitting the snooze button

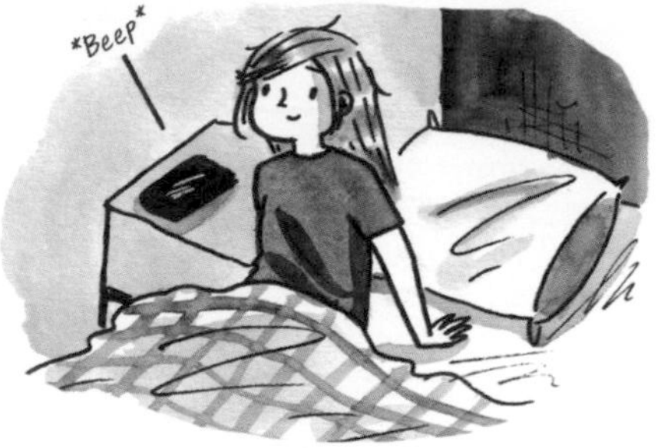
Beep

I got my chores done

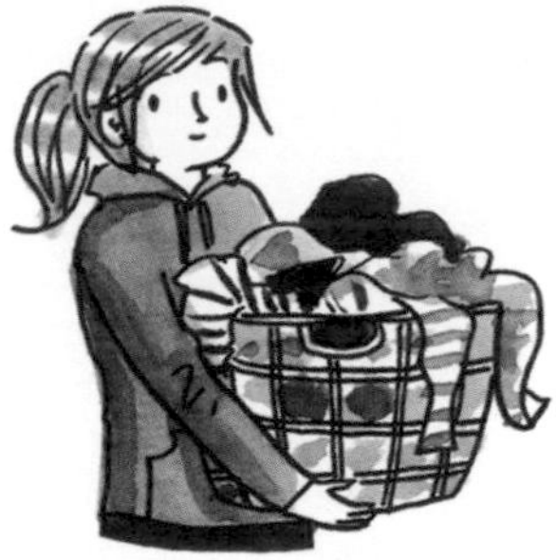

made some important phone calls

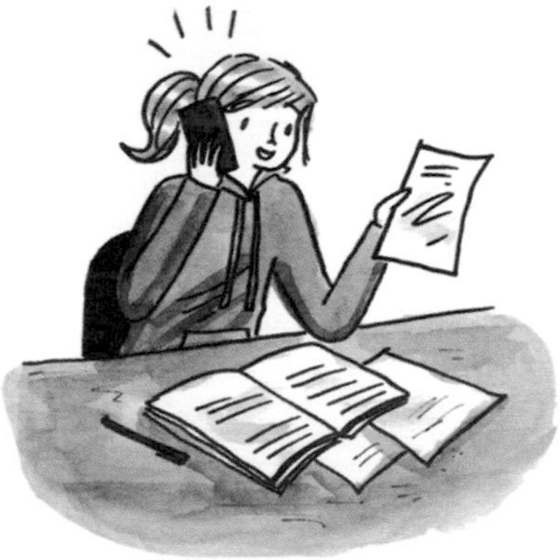

and took a break when I needed it.

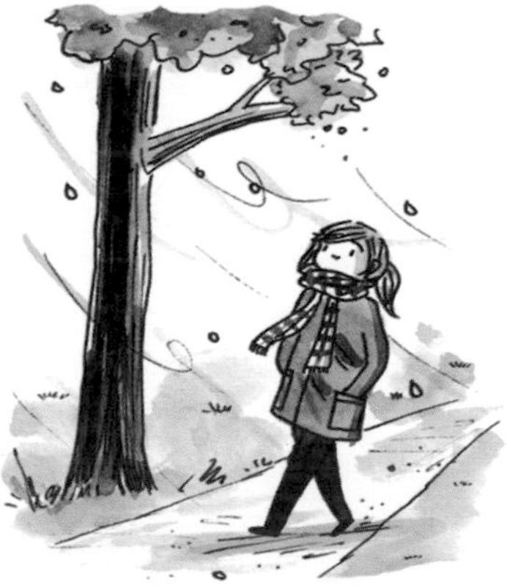

It's the little victories that keep me going.

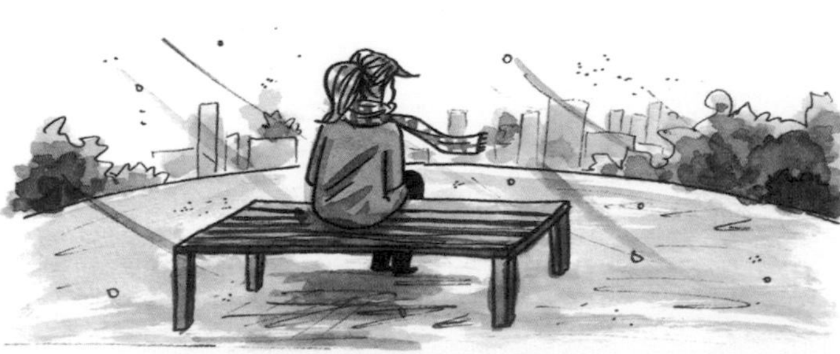

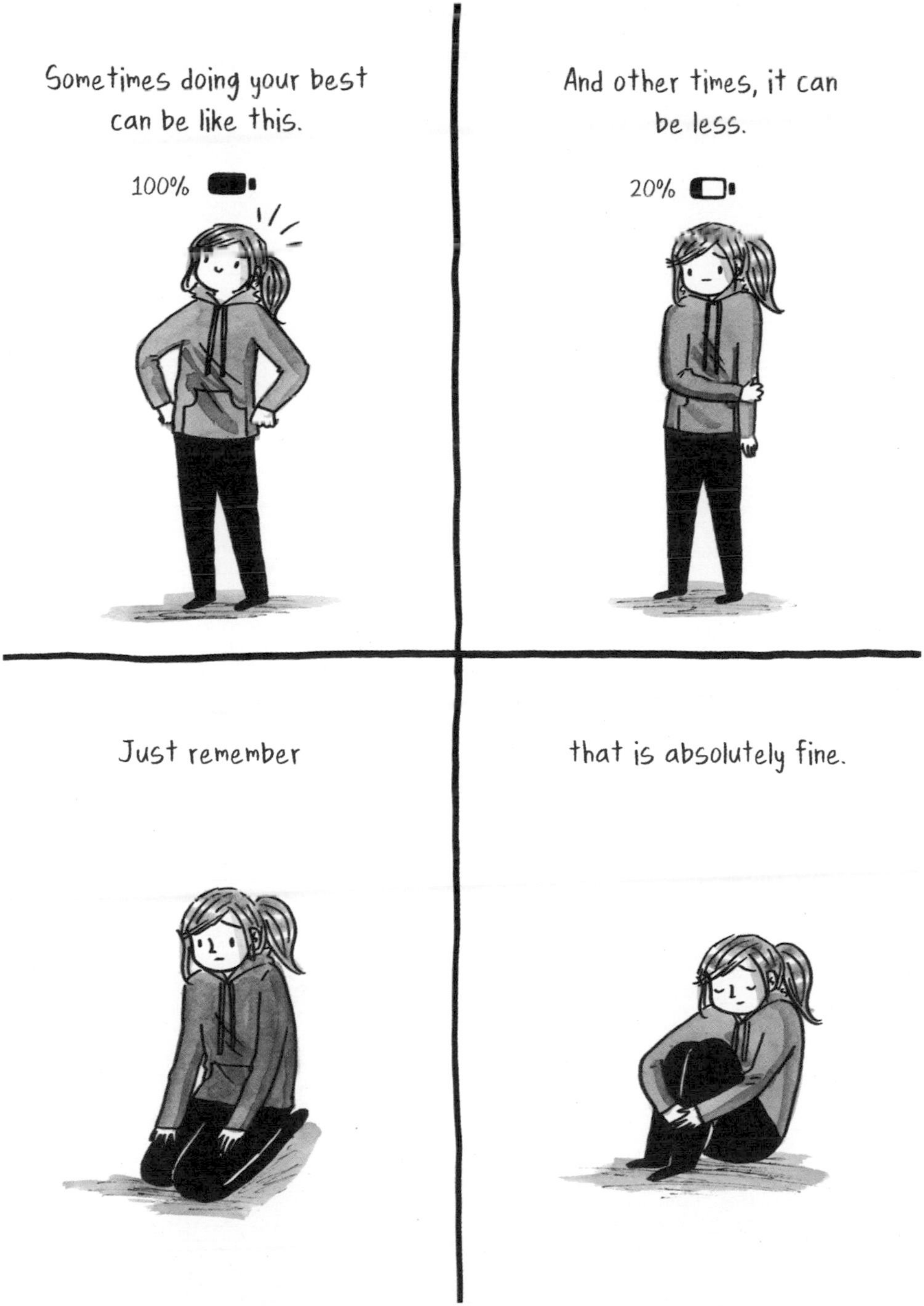
Sometimes doing your best can be like this.
100%
And other times, it can be less.
20%
Just remember
that is absolutely fine.

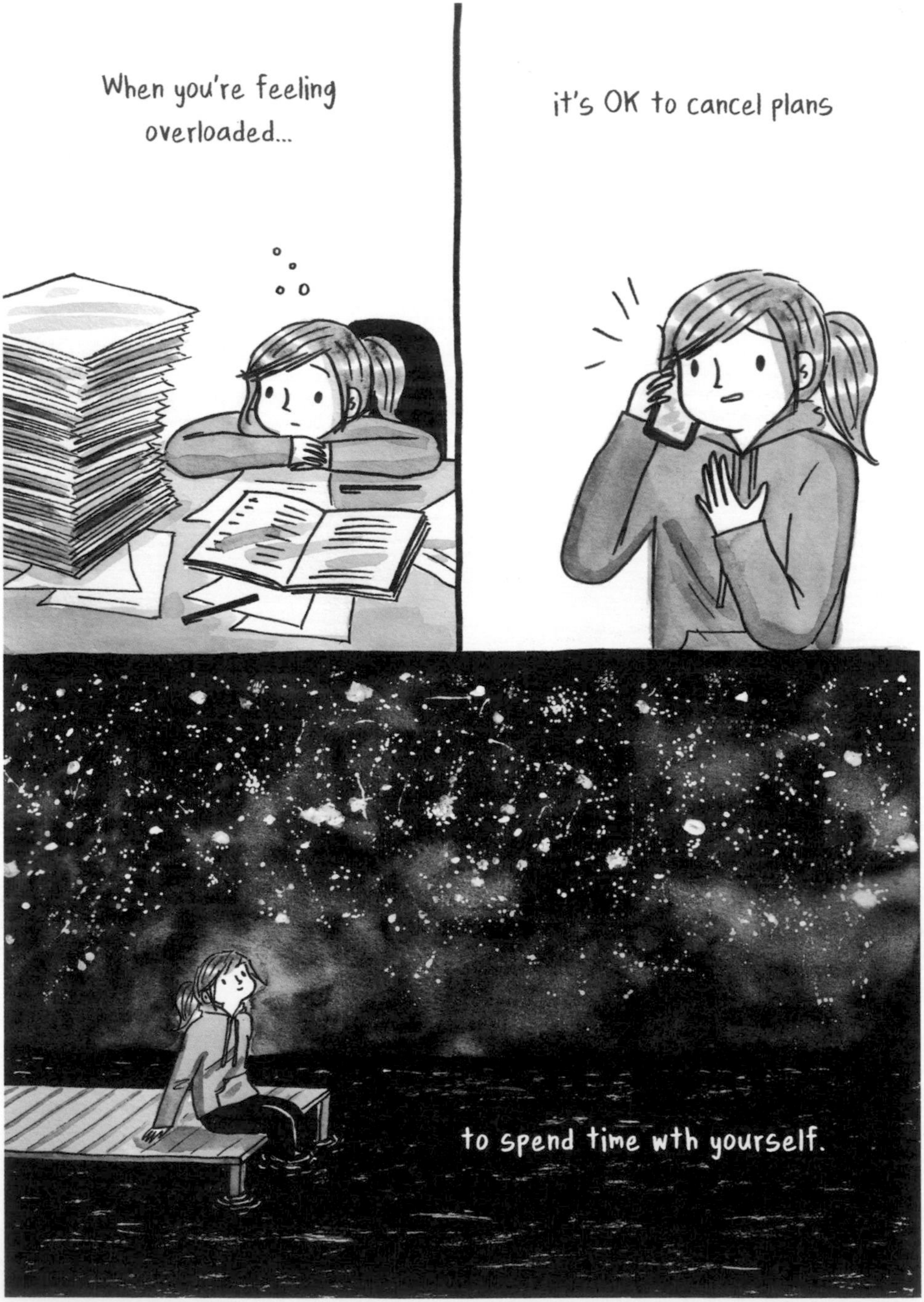
When you're feeling overloaded...
it's OK to cancel plans
to spend time wth yourself.

If I did something nice for myself, even a small thing, I realize that they all eventually add up.

And each time I did more stuff that made myself feel good...

It contributed to my overall happiness.

It's not always the big things that count. Joy comes in little and ordinary moments.

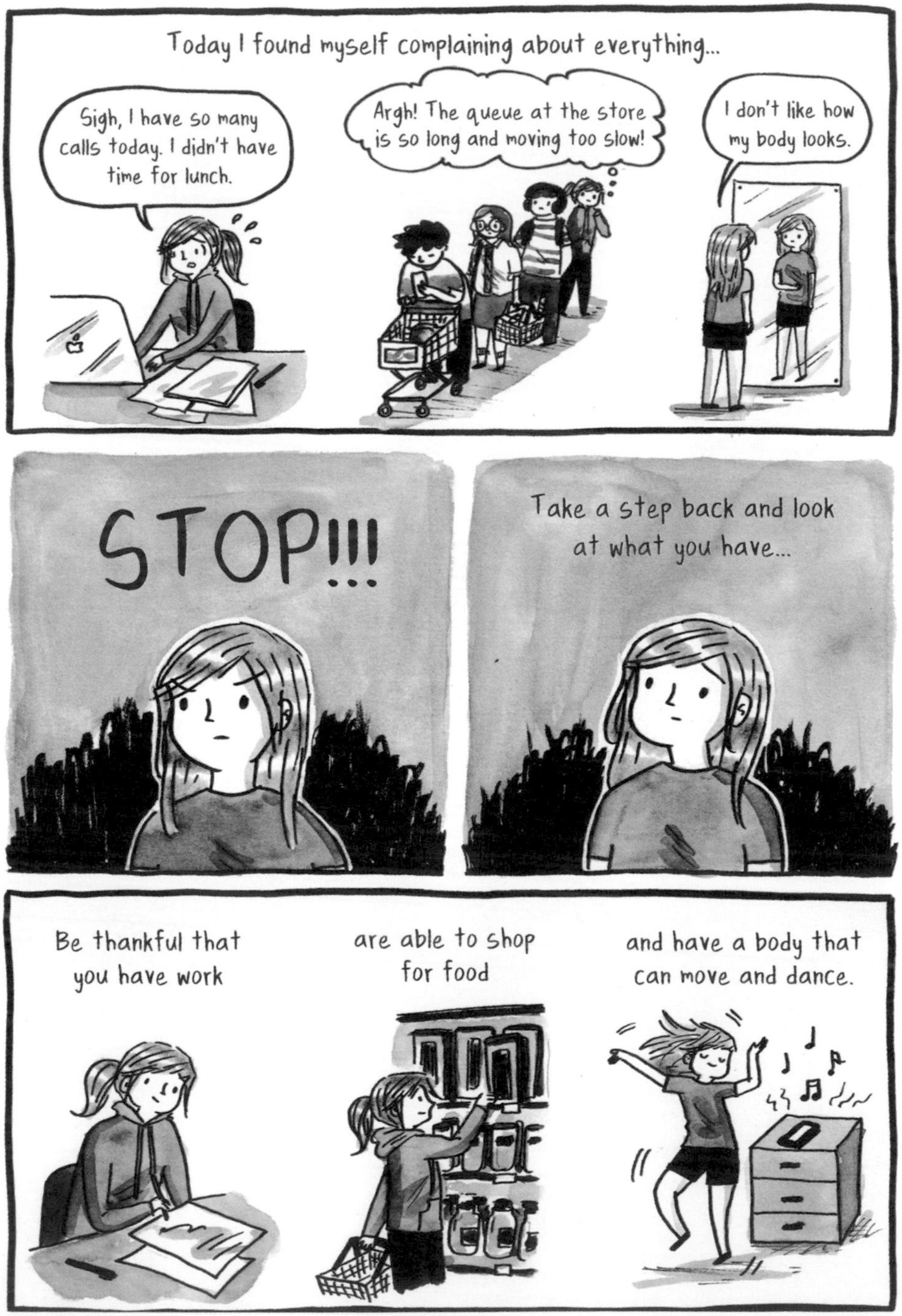
Today I found myself complaining about everything...
Sigh, I have so many calls today. I didn't have time for lunch.
Argh! The queue at the store is so long and moving too slow!
I don't like how my body looks.
STOP!!!
Take a step back and look at what you have...
Be thankful that you have work
are able to shop for food
and have a body that can move and dance.

Little things I'm grateful for today

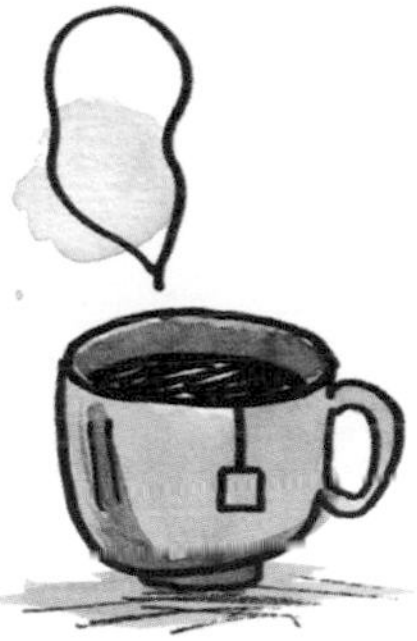

A hot drink

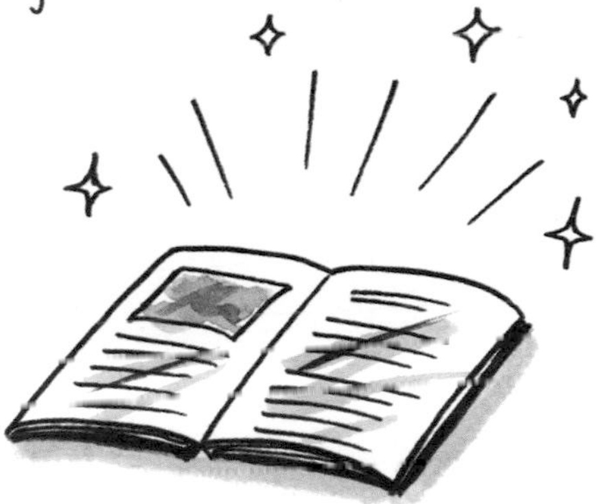

Inspiring stories

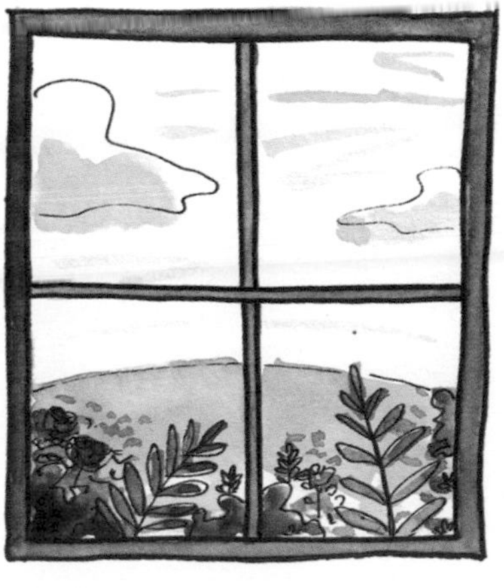

The view outside my window

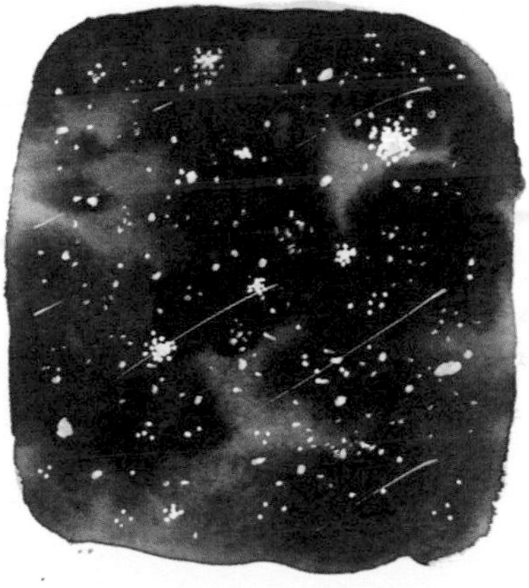

Quiet moments of introspection

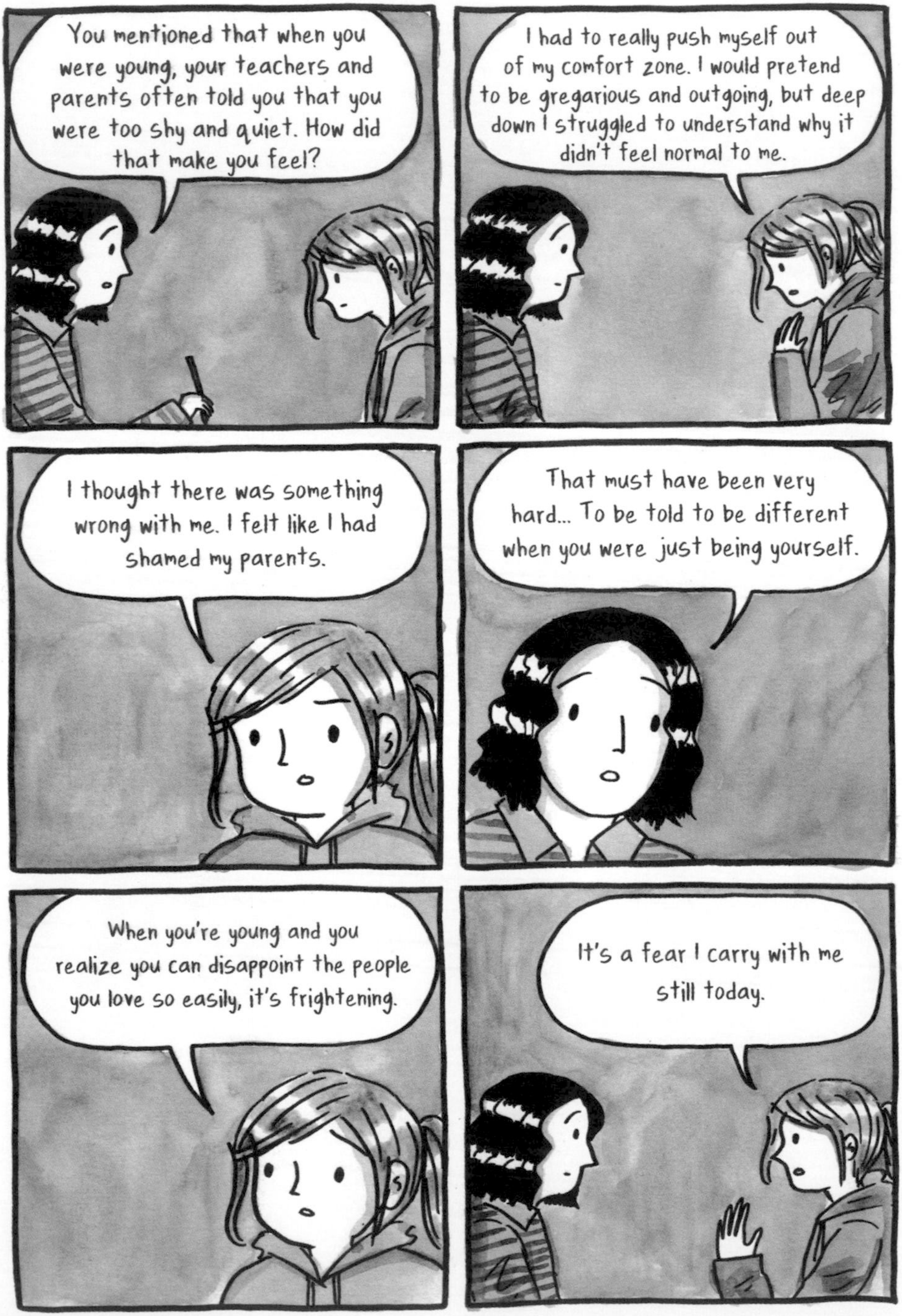
You mentioned that when you were young, your teachers and parents often told you that you were too shy and quiet. How did that make you feel?
I had to really push myself out of my comfort zone. I would pretend to be gregarious and outgoing, but deep down I struggled to understand why it didn't feel normal to me.
I thought there was something wrong with me. I felt like I had shamed my parents.
That must have been very hard... To be told to be different when you were just being yourself.
When you're young and you realize you can disappoint the people you love so easily, it's frightening.
It's a fear I carry with me still today.

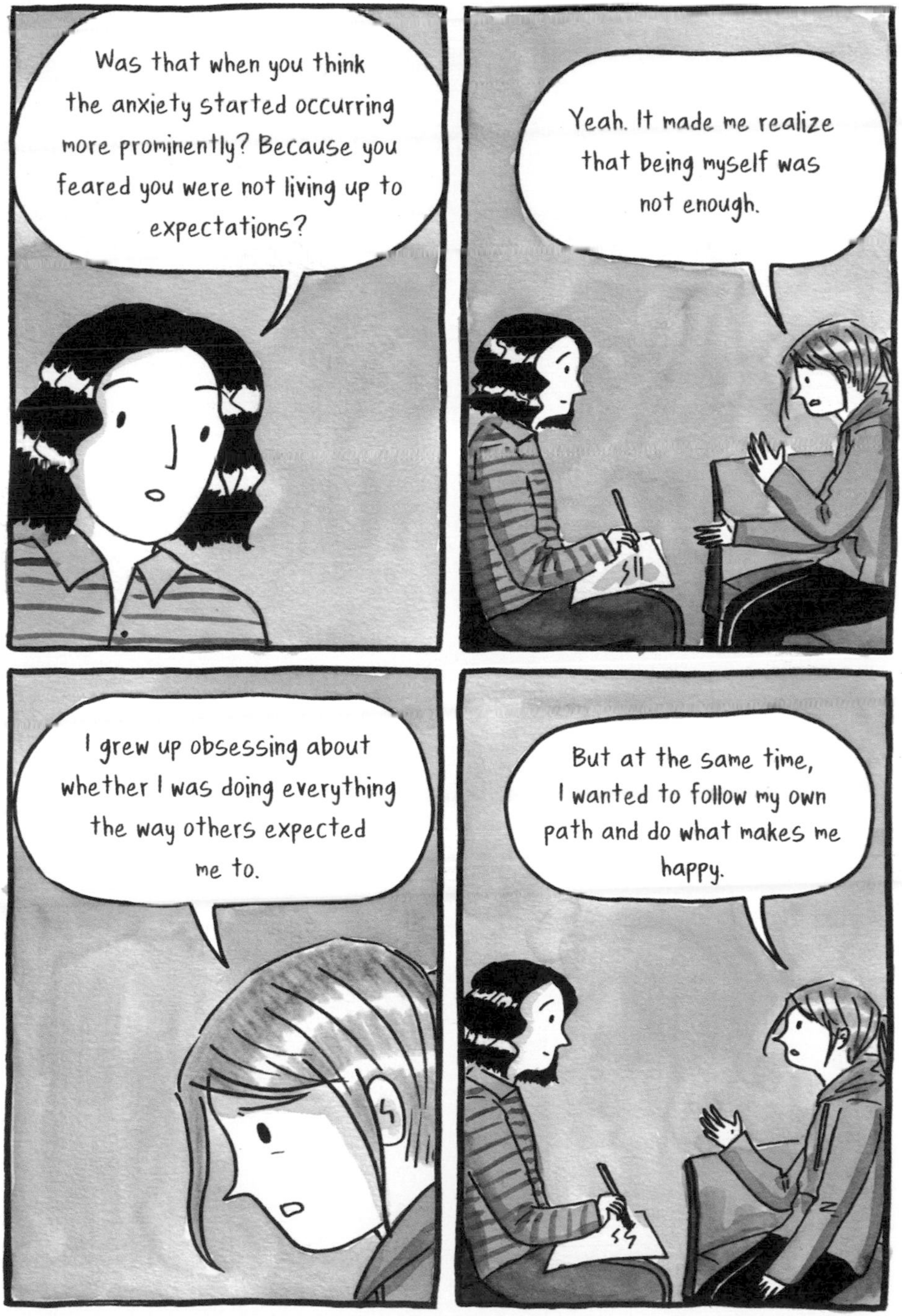
Was that when you think the anxiety started occurring more prominently? Because you feared you were not living up to expectations?
Yeah. It made me realize that being myself was not enough.
I grew up obsessing about whether I was doing everything the way others expected me to.
But at the same time, I wanted to follow my own path and do what makes me happy.

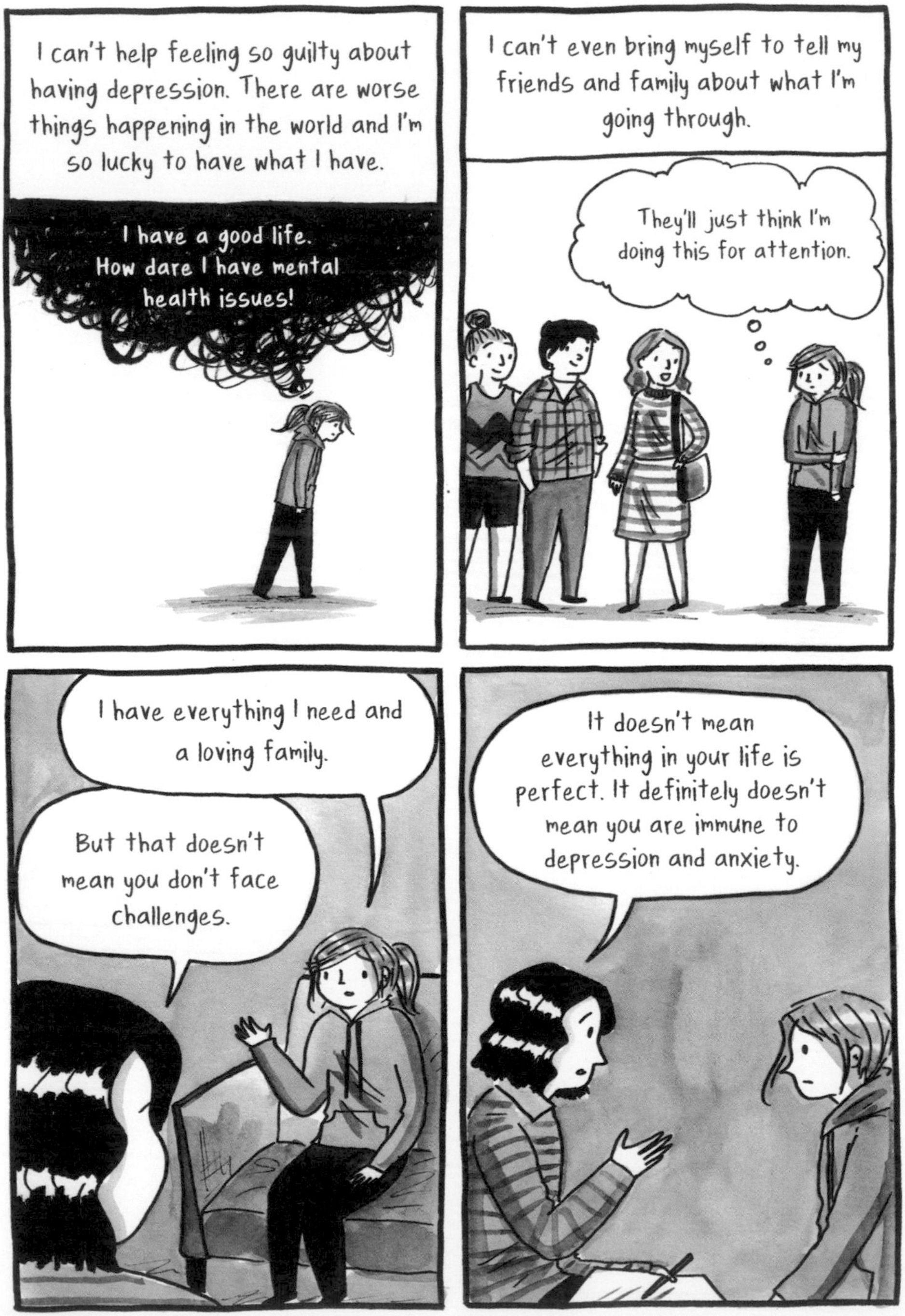

I can't help feeling so guilty about having depression. There are worse things happening in the world and I'm so lucky to have what I have.
I have a good life. How dare I have mental health issues!
I can't even bring myself to tell my friends and family about what I'm going through.
They'll just think I'm doing this for attention.
I have everything I need and a loving family.
But that doesn't mean you don't face challenges.
It doesn't mean everything in your life is perfect. It definitely doesn't mean you are immune to depression and anxiety.

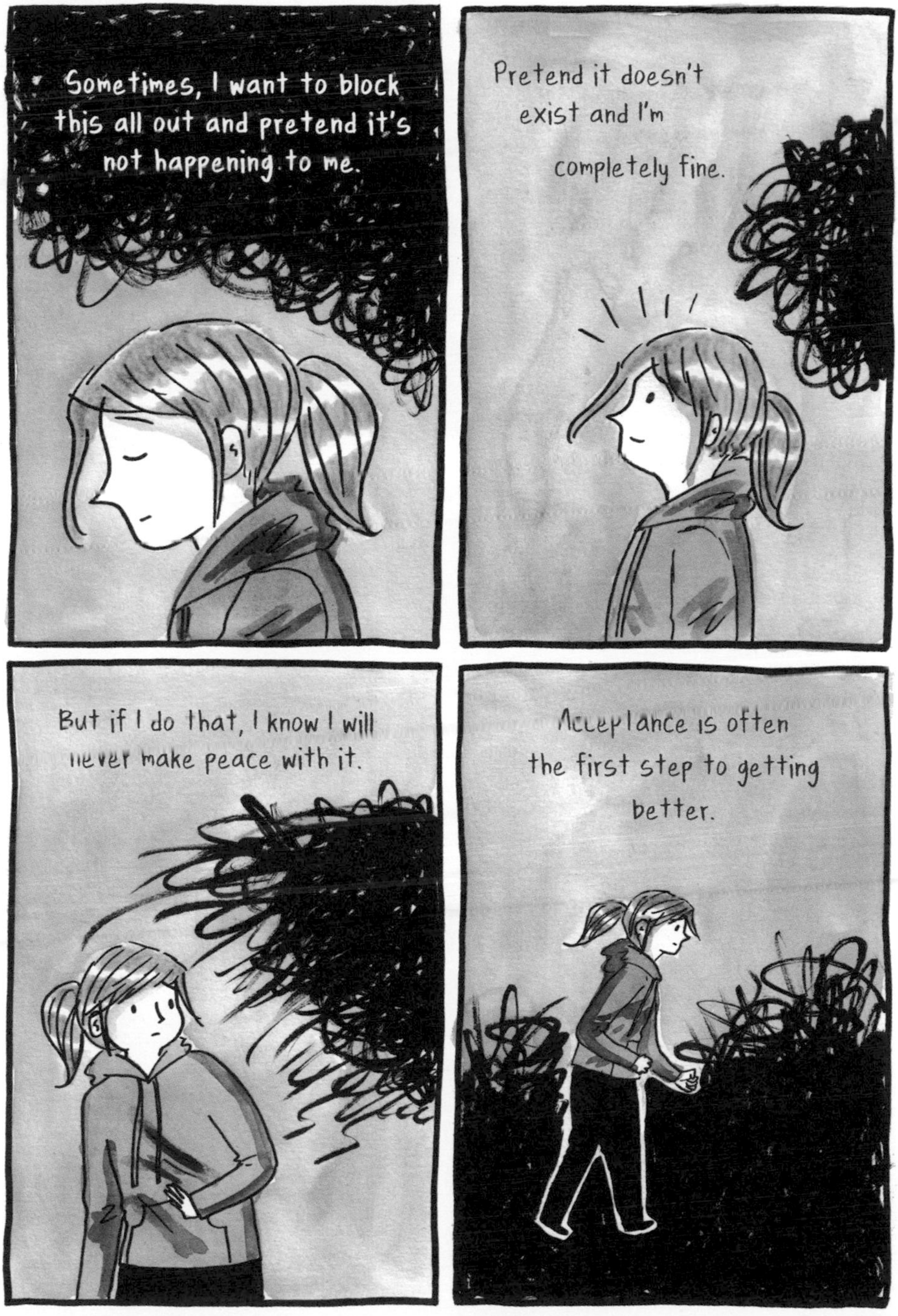
Sometimes, I want to block this all out and pretend it's not happening to me.
Pretend it doesn't exist and I'm
completely fine.
But if I do that, I know I will never make peace with it.
Acceptance is often the first step to getting better.

Everyone's struggles are real and valid. I can't get through my pain by simply muting and denying it.

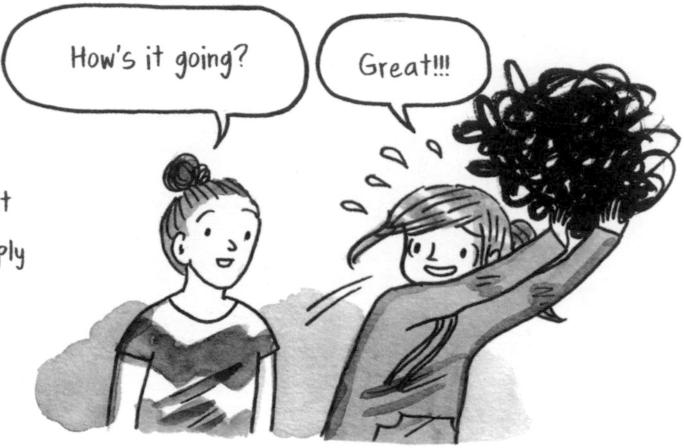
How's it going?
Great!!!

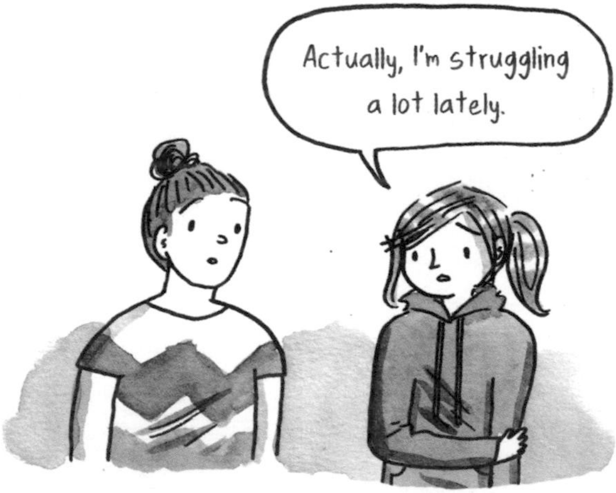
Actually, I'm struggling a lot lately.

There is no shame when challenges in life become too overwhelming.

There is no shame in struggling with my mental health.

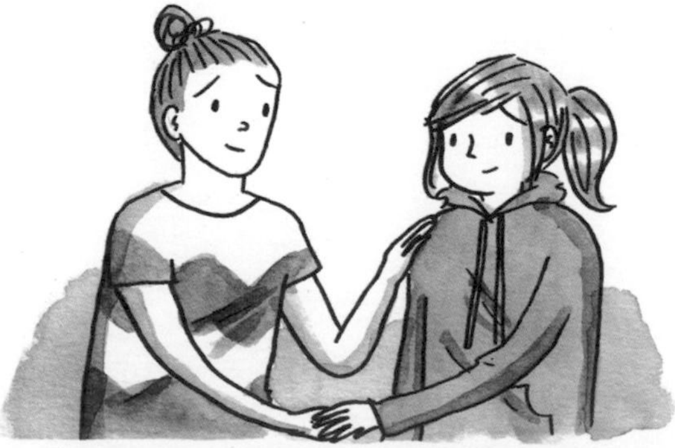

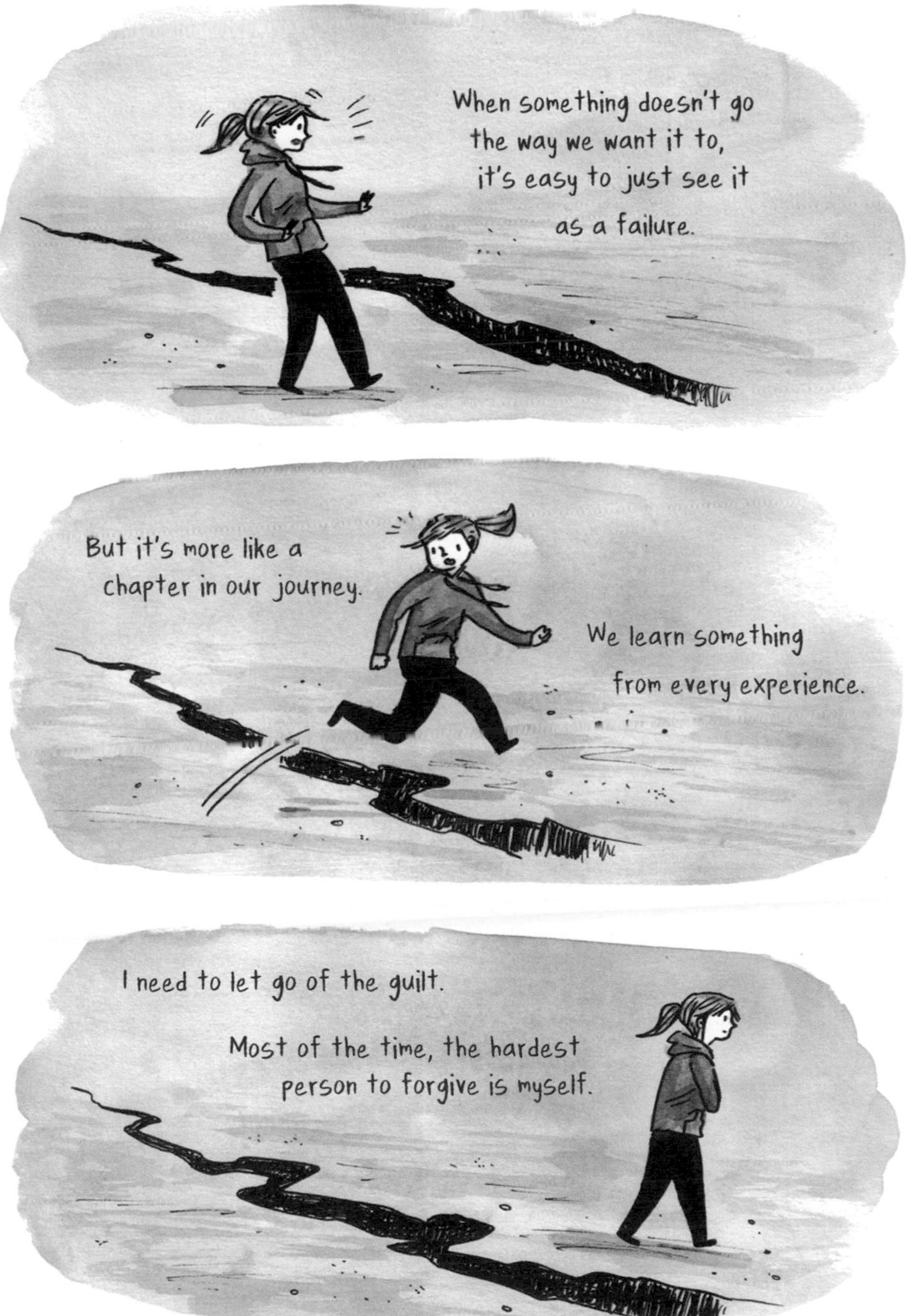
When something doesn't go the way we want it to, it's easy to just see it as a failure.
But it's more like a chapter in our journey.
We learn something from every experience.
I need to let go of the guilt.
Most of the time, the hardest person to forgive is myself.

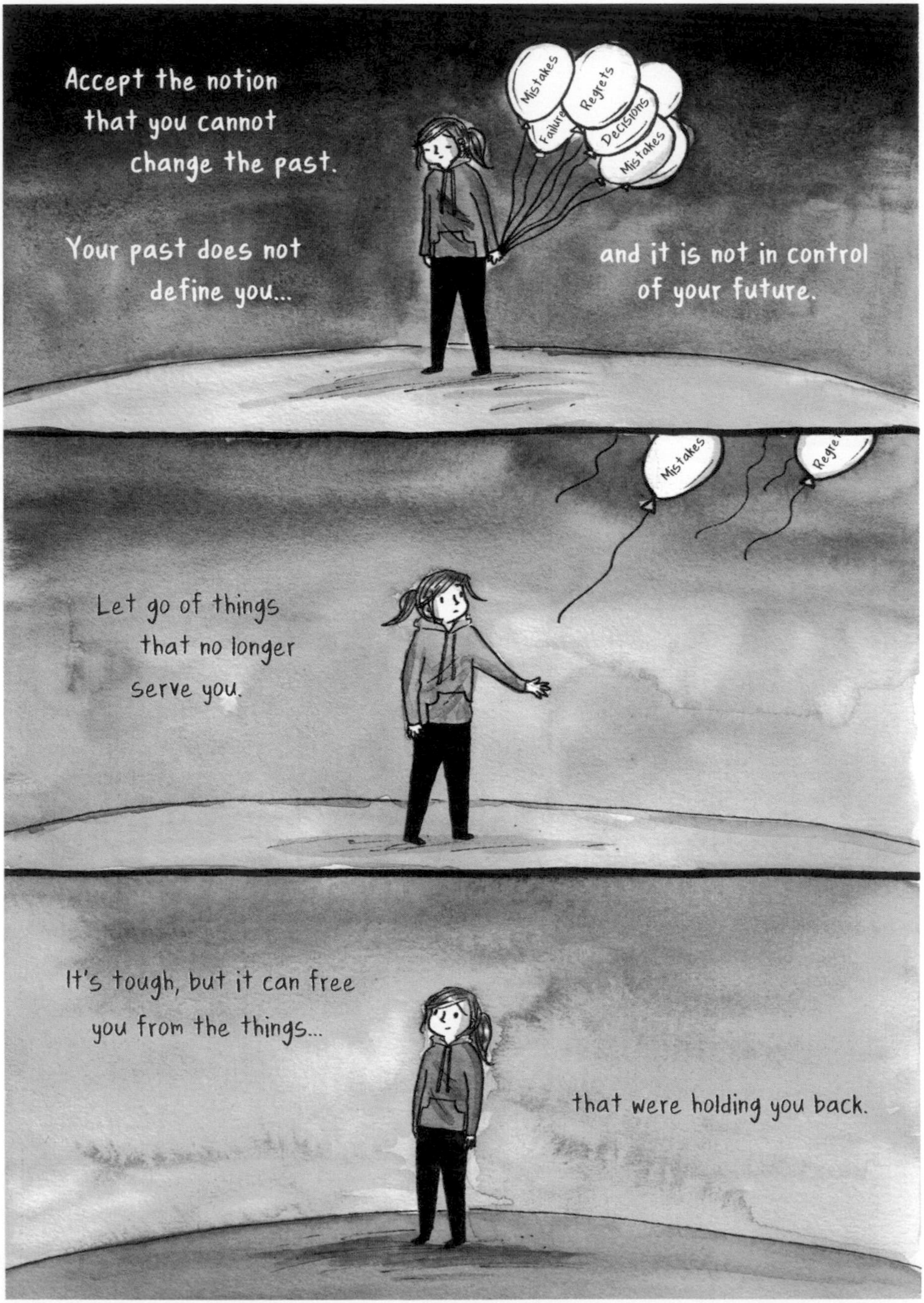
Accept the notion that you cannot change the past.
Mistakes
Failure
Regrets
Decisions
Mistakes
Your past does not define you...
and it is not in control of your future.
Mistakes
Let go of things that no longer serve you.
It's tough, but it can free you from the things...
that were holding you back.

Forgive yourself for your regrets
and bad decisions.

Making mistakes does not mean
you are a bad person.

You are allowed to mess up.

And you are allowed to
start again.

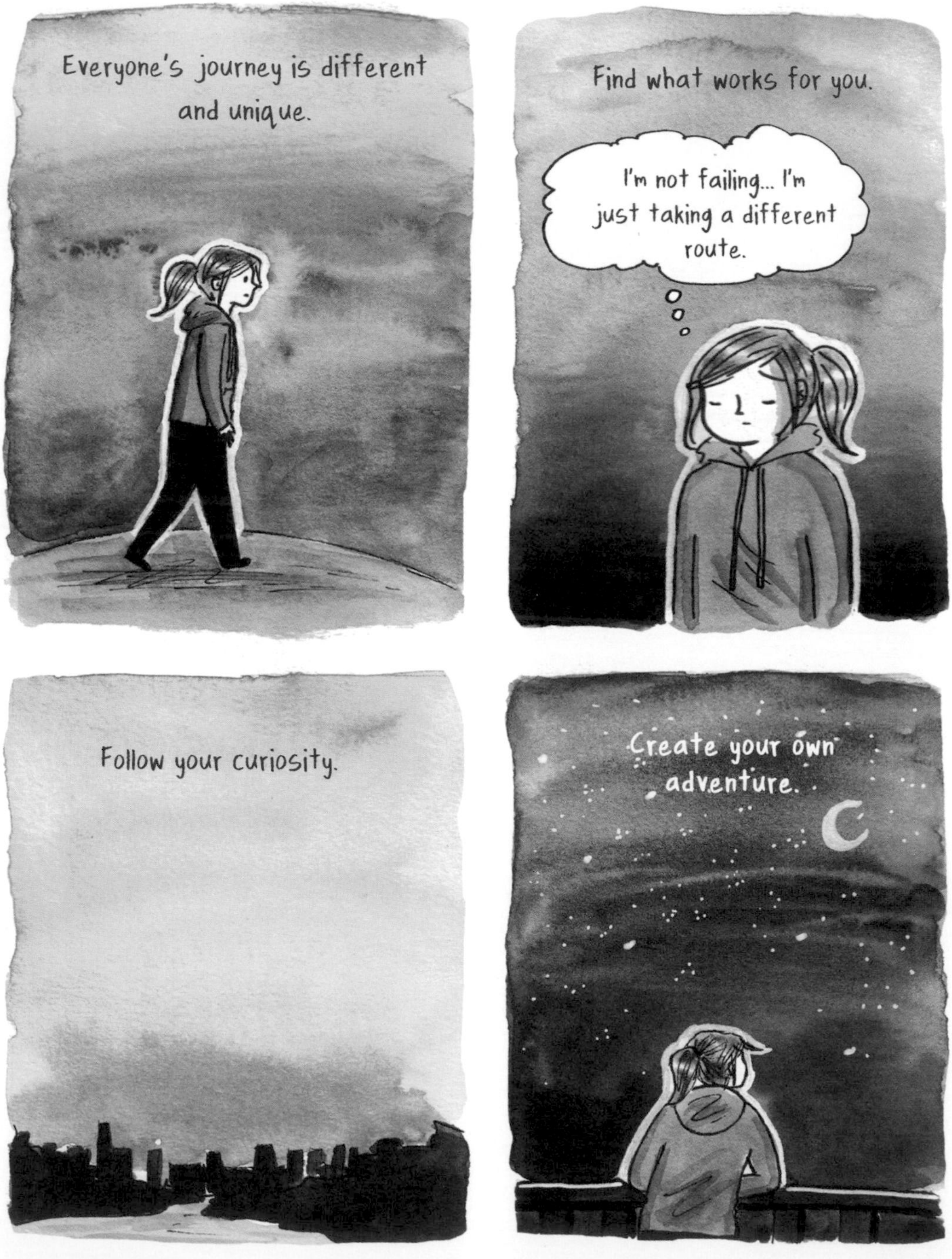
Everyone's journey is different and unique.
Find what works for you.
I'm not failing... I'm just taking a different route.
Follow your curiosity.
Create your own adventure.

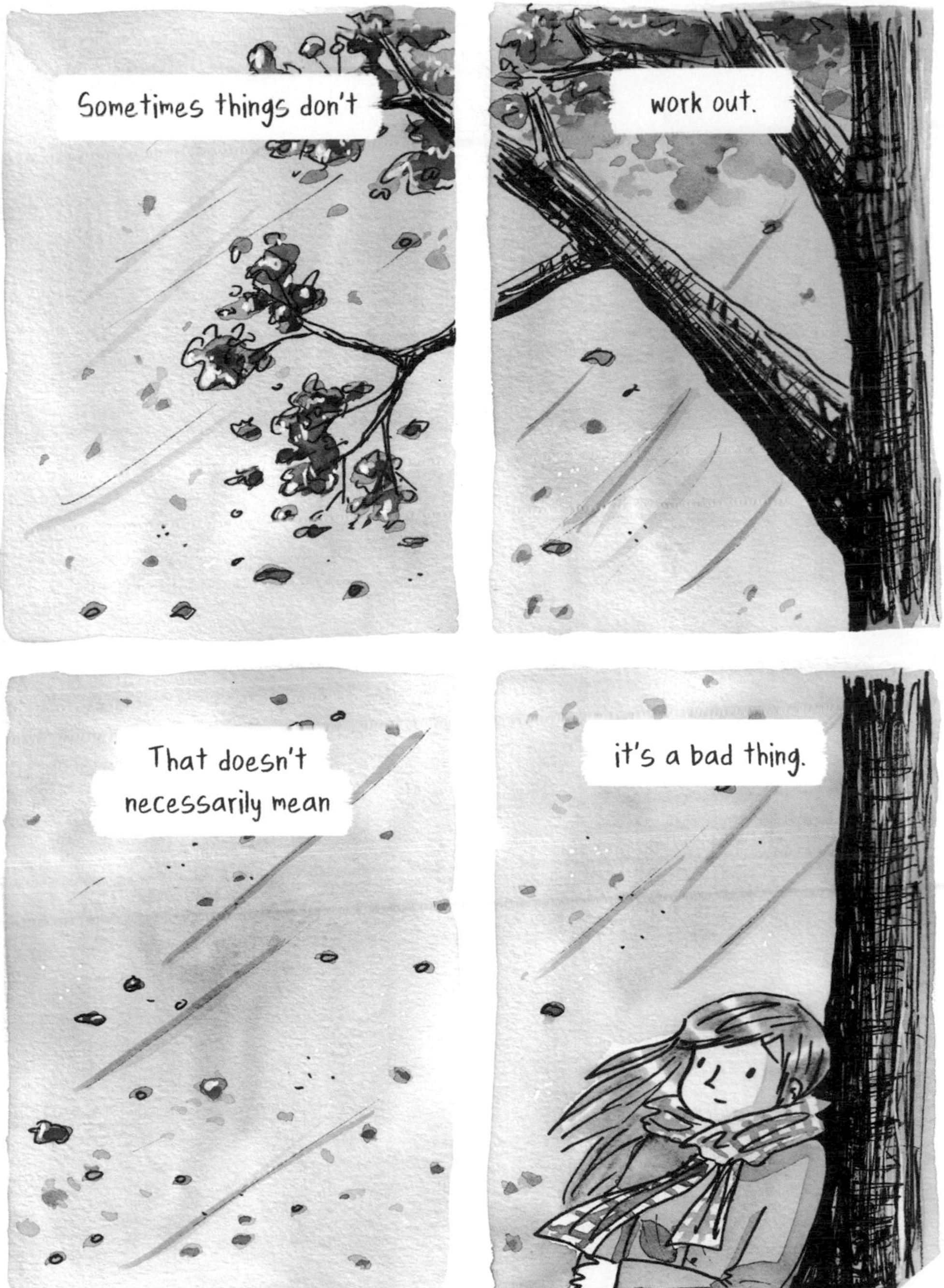
Sometimes things don't
work out.
That doesn't necessarily mean
it's a bad thing.

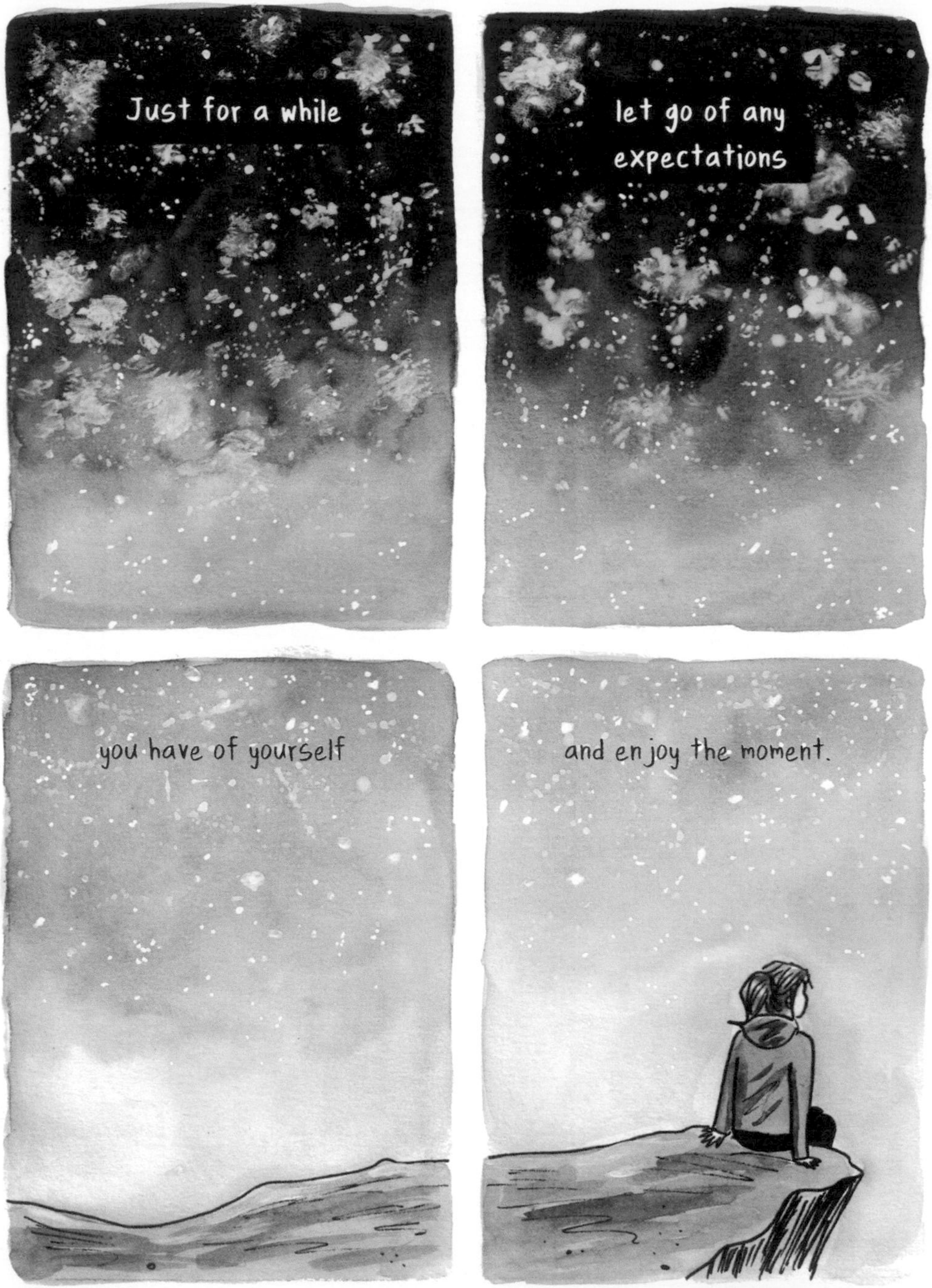
Just for a while
let go of any expectations
you have of yourself
and enjoy the moment.

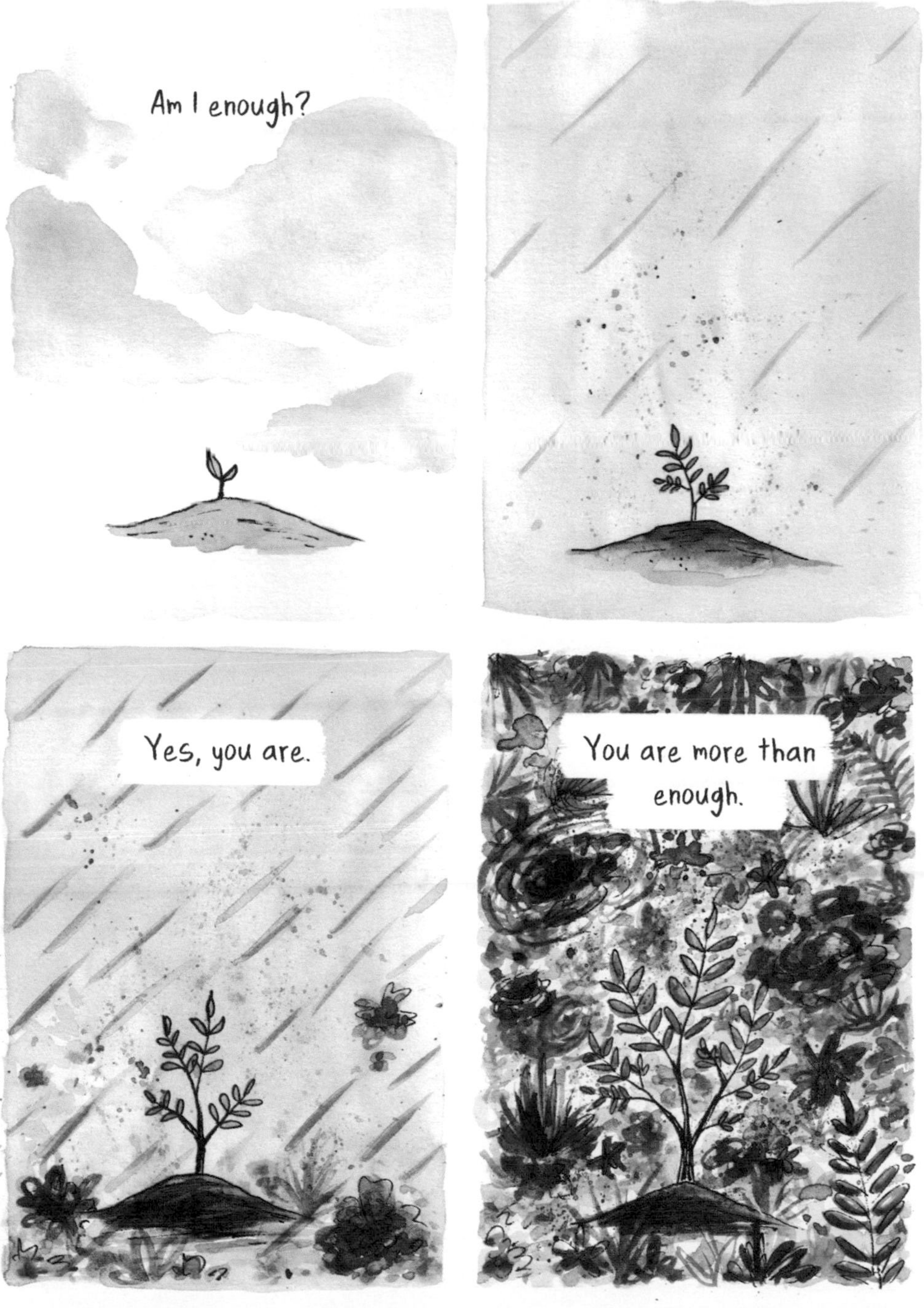
Am I enough?
Yes, you are.
You are more than enough.

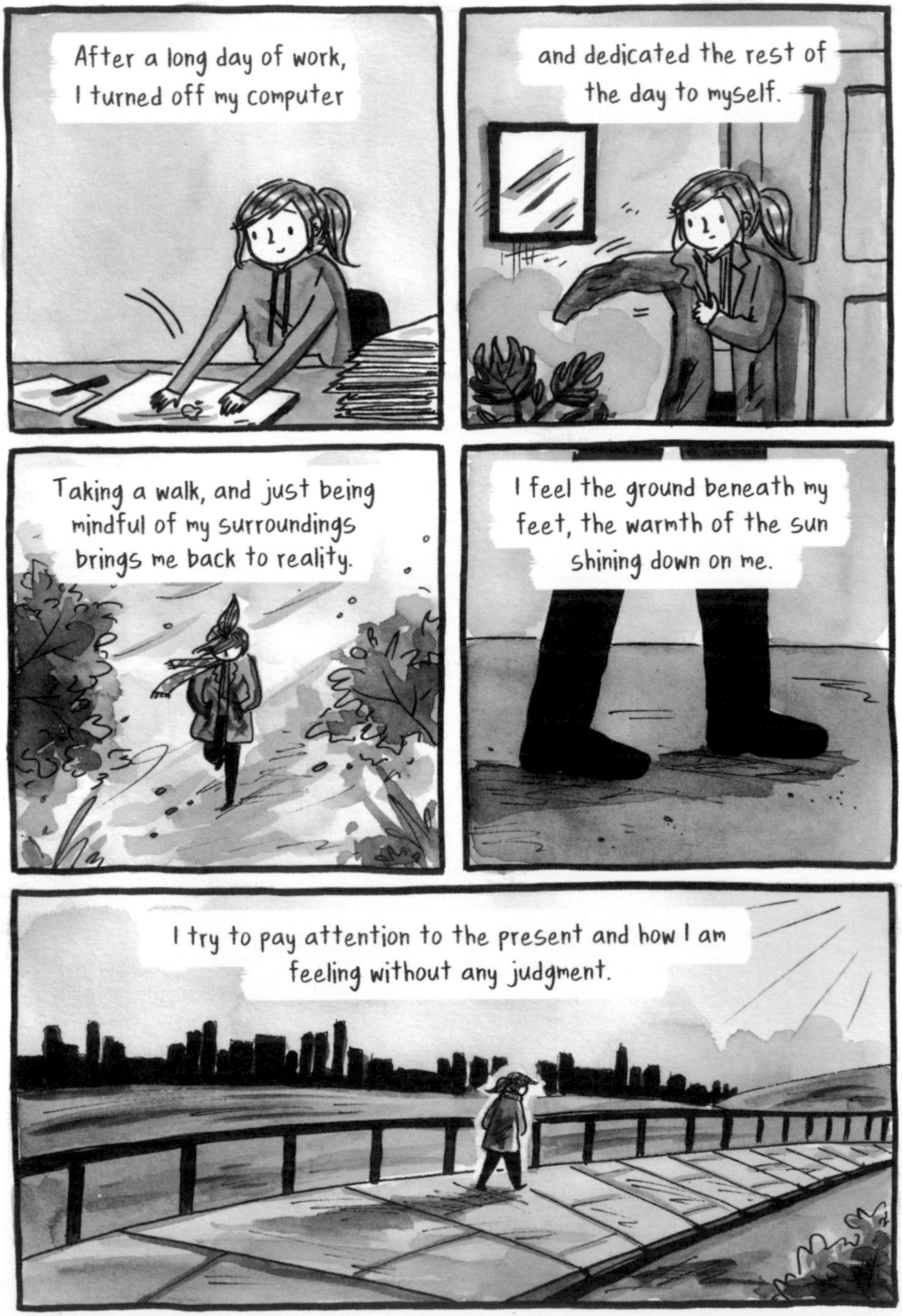
After a long day of work, I turned off my computer
and dedicated the rest of the day to myself.
Taking a walk, and just being mindful of my surroundings brings me back to reality.
I feel the ground beneath my feet, the warmth of the sun shining down on me.
I try to pay attention to the present and how I am feeling without any judgment.

Mindfulness helps to quiet your mind and pull you away from the anxious and critical thoughts.

Allow yourself to enter a space that feels safe.

Breathe.

Enough with the self-sabotage and self-bullying.

Take a few moments to come out of the dark clouds.

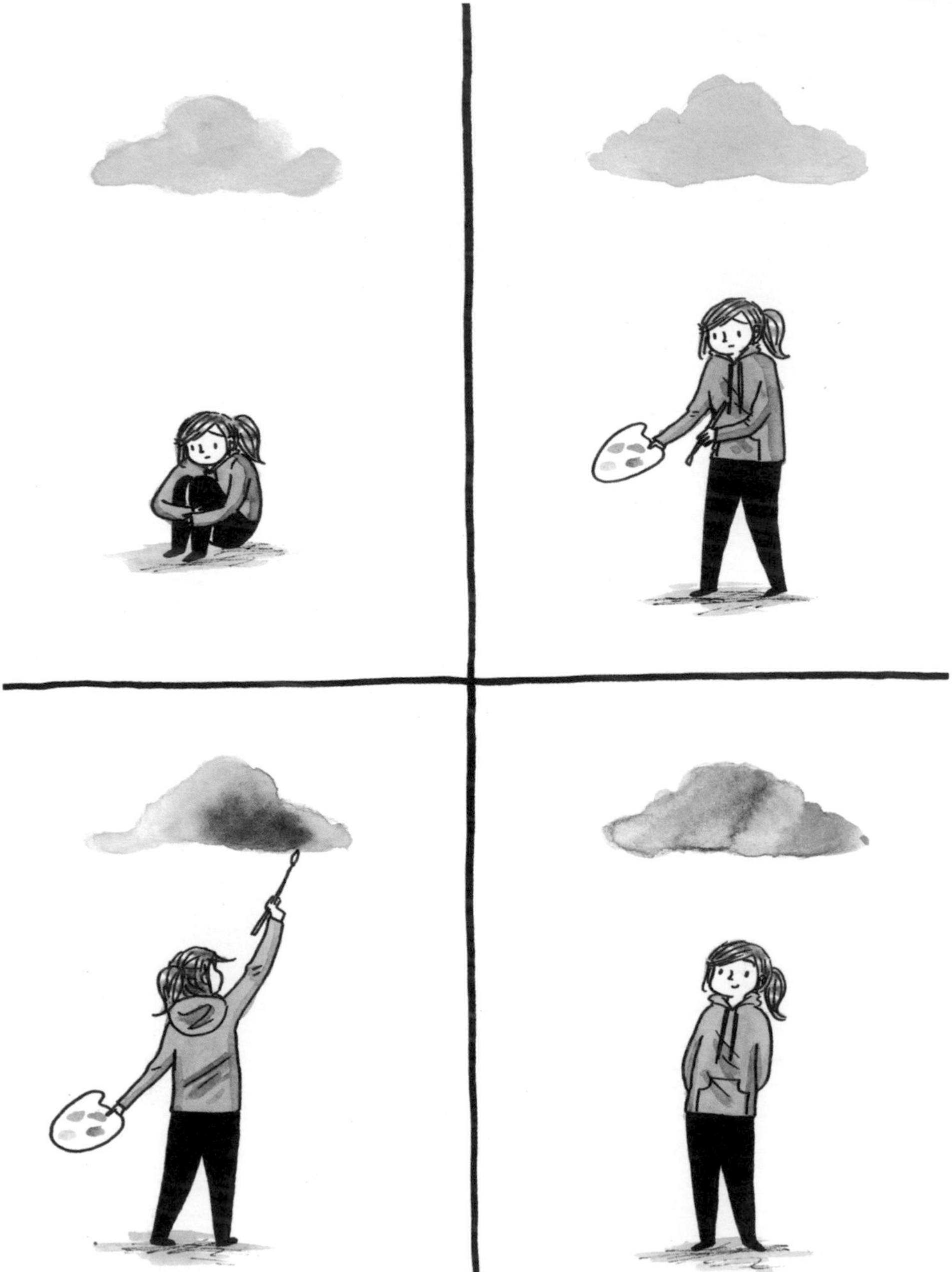

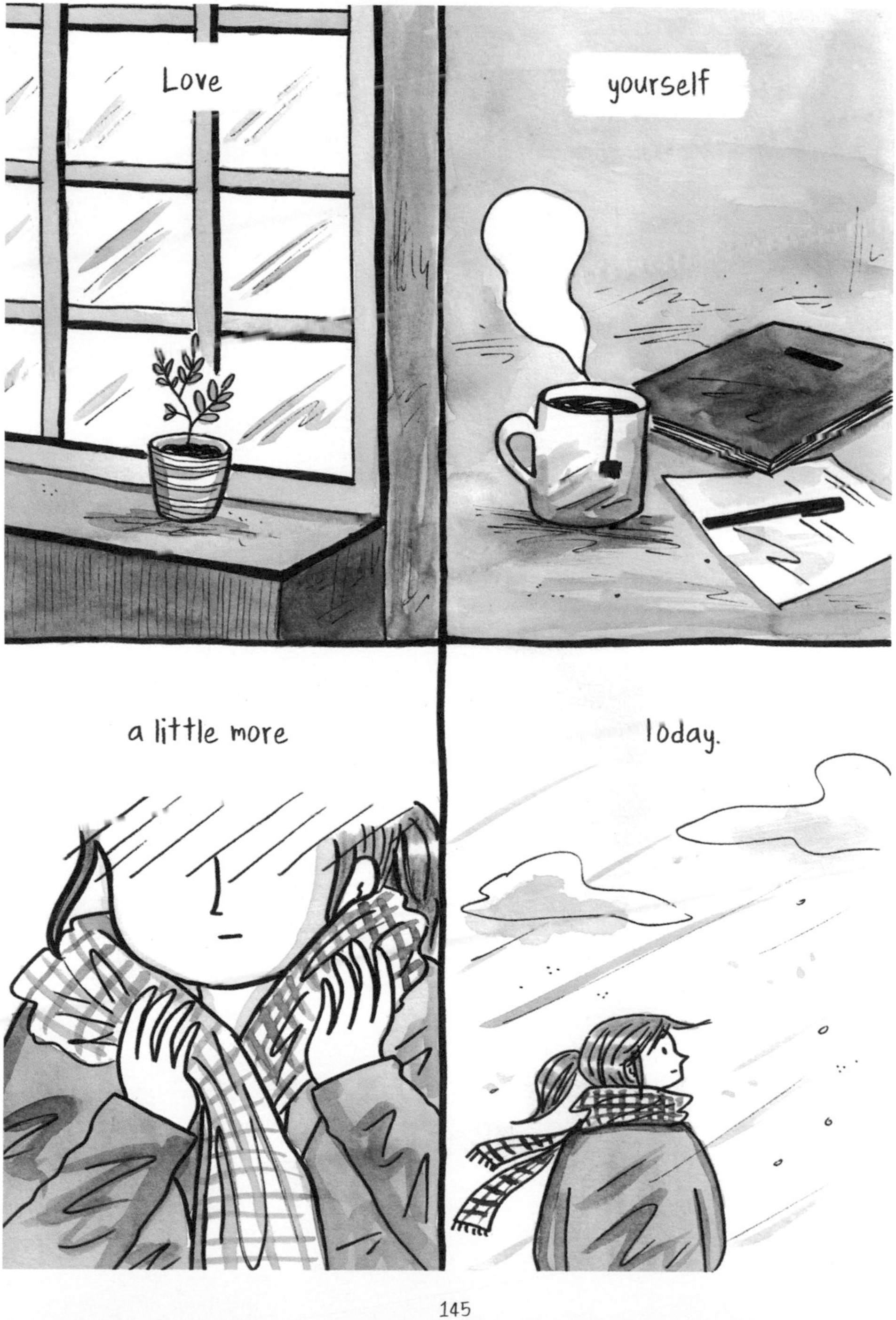
Love
yourself
a little more
today.

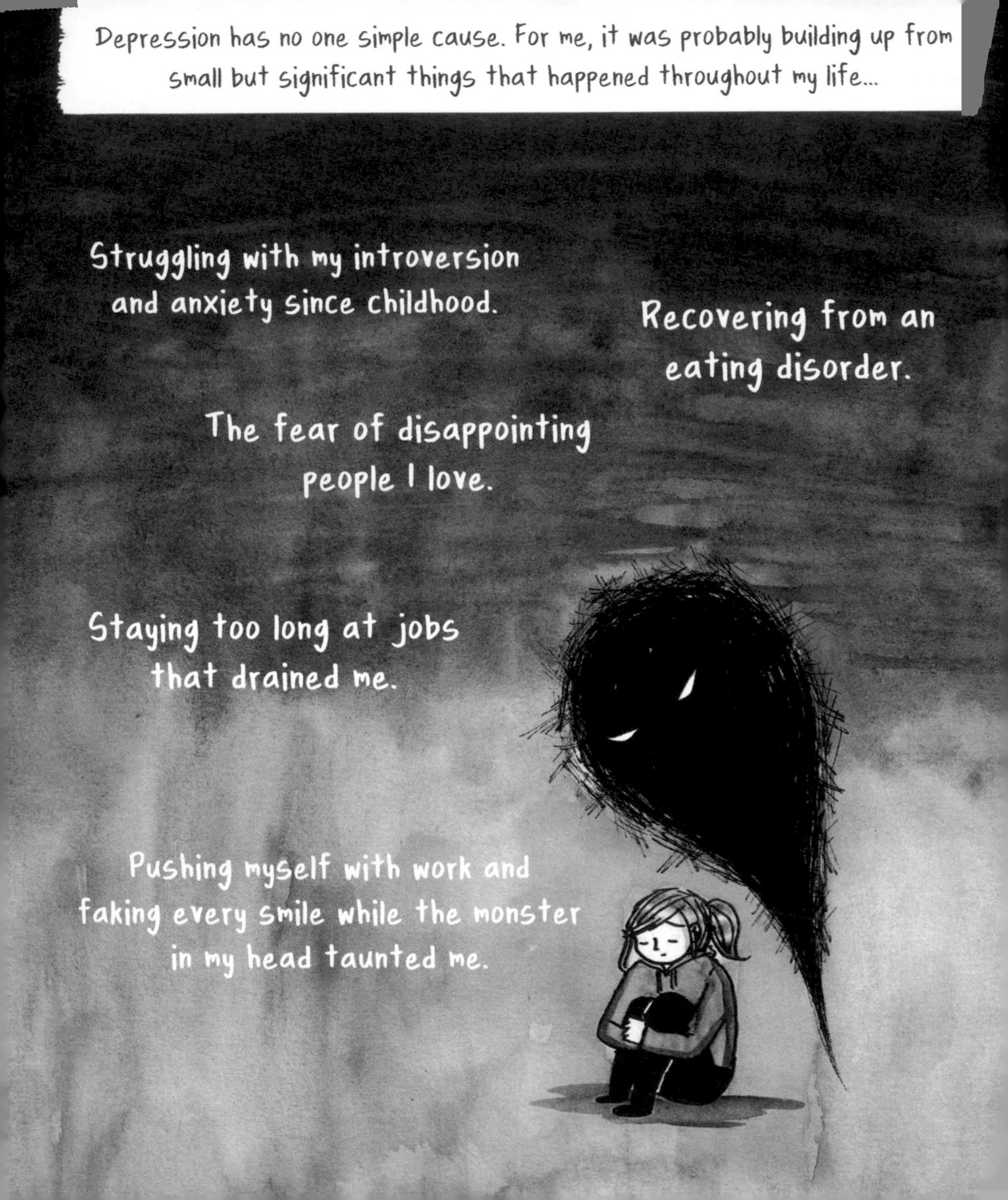
Depression has no one simple cause. For me, it was probably building up from small but significant things that happened throughout my life...
Struggling with my introversion and anxiety since childhood.
Recovering from an eating disorder.
The fear of disappointing people I love.
Staying too long at jobs that drained me.
Pushing myself with work and faking every smile while the monster in my head taunted me.

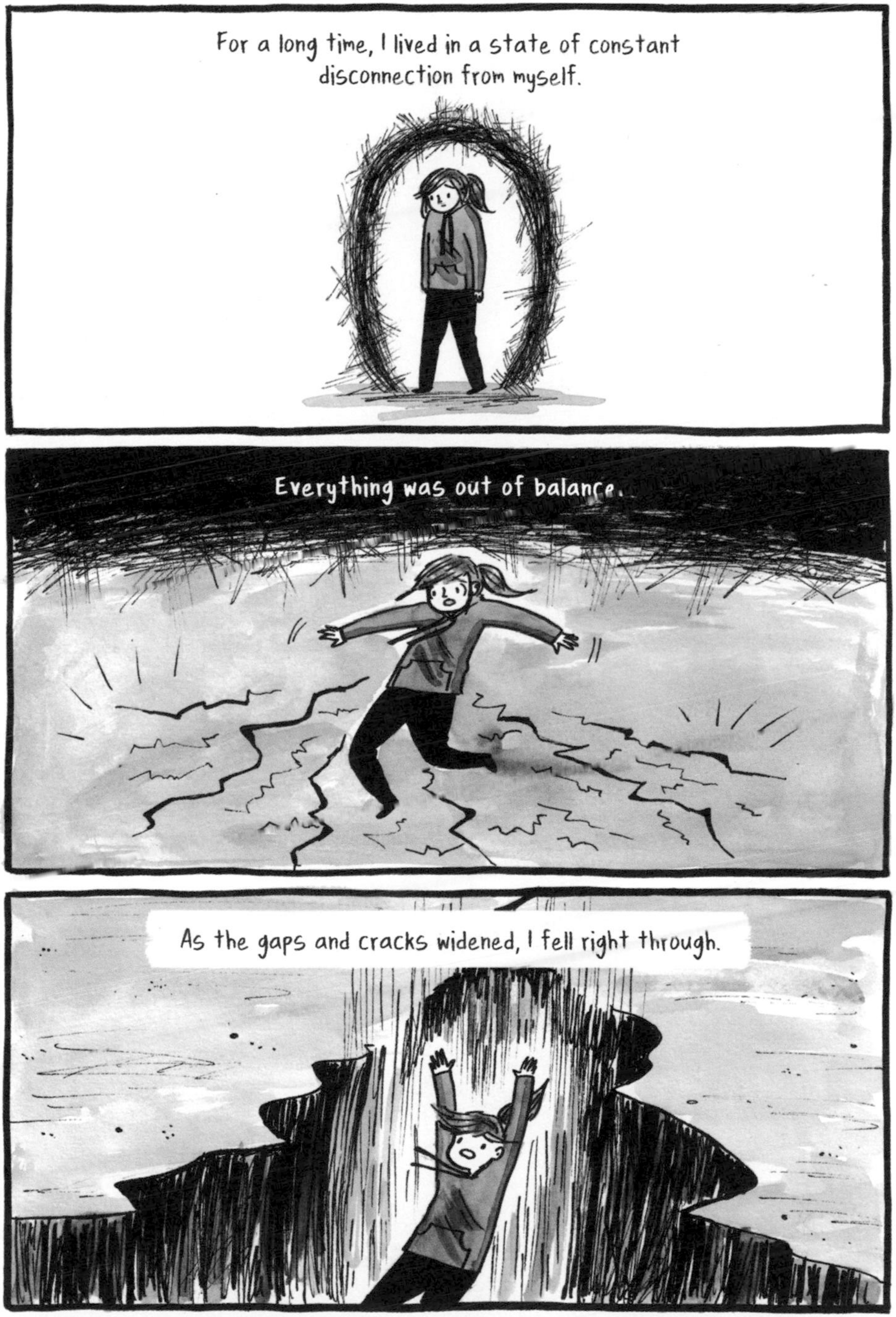
For a long time, I lived in a state of constant disconnection from myself.
Everything was out of balance.
As the gaps and cracks widened, I fell right through.

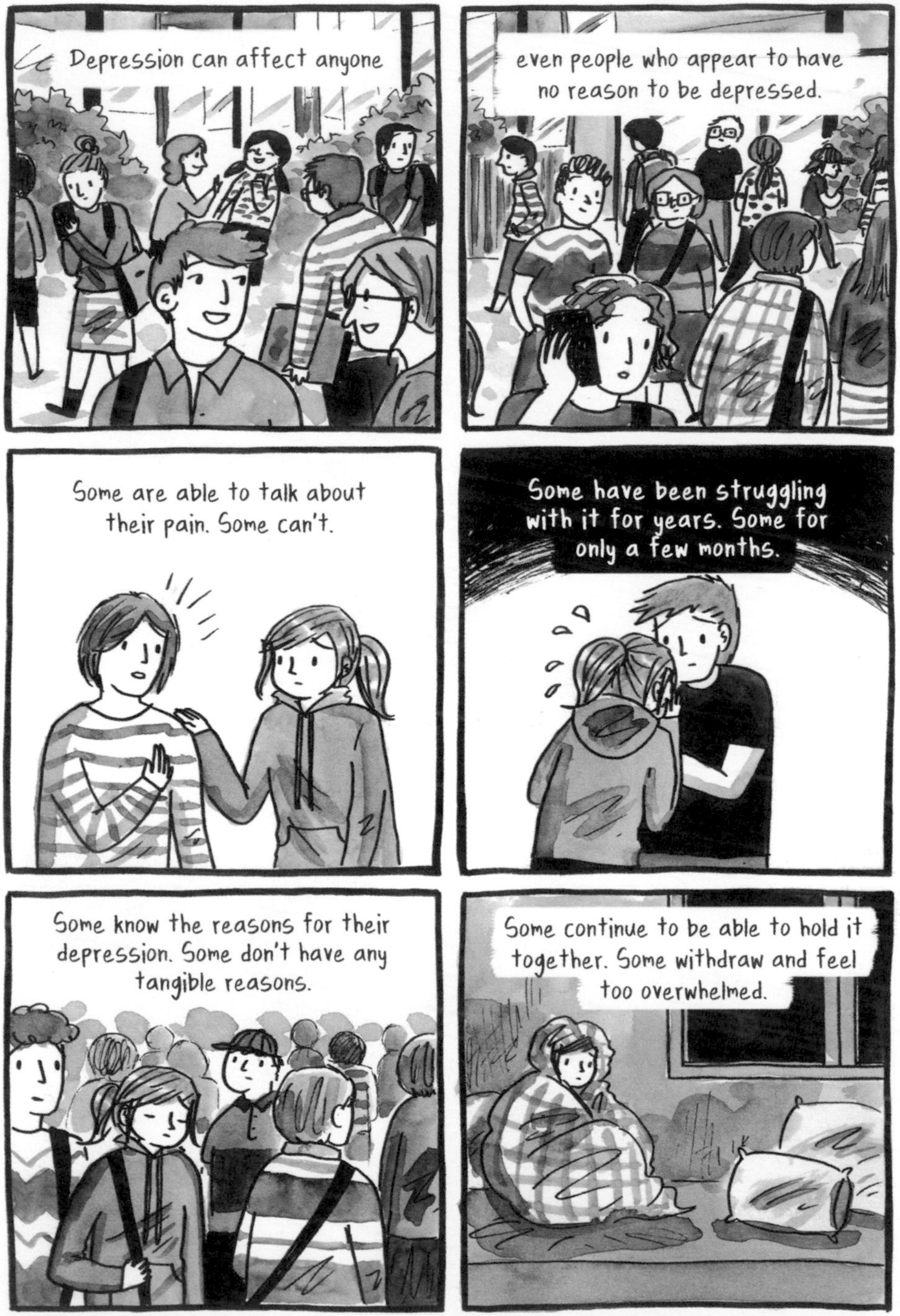
Depression can affect anyone
even people who appear to have no reason to be depressed.
Some are able to talk about their pain. Some can't.
Some have been struggling with it for years. Some for only a few months.
Some know the reasons for their depression. Some don't have any tangible reasons.
Some continue to be able to hold it together. Some withdraw and feel too overwhelmed.

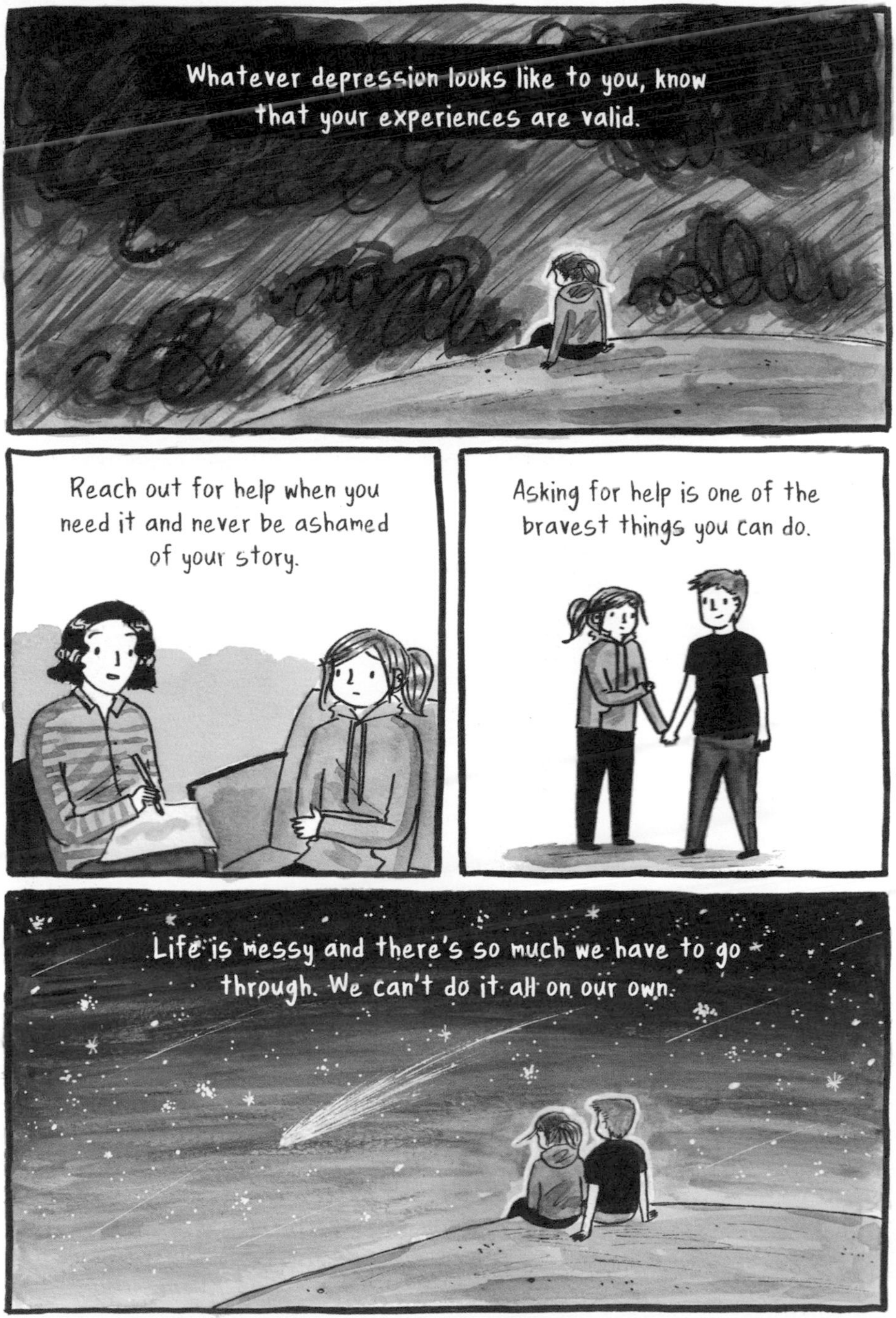
Whatever depression looks like to you, know that your experiences are valid.
Reach out for help when you need it and never be ashamed of your story.
Asking for help is one of the bravest things you can do.
Life is messy and there's so much we have to go through. We can't do it all on our own.

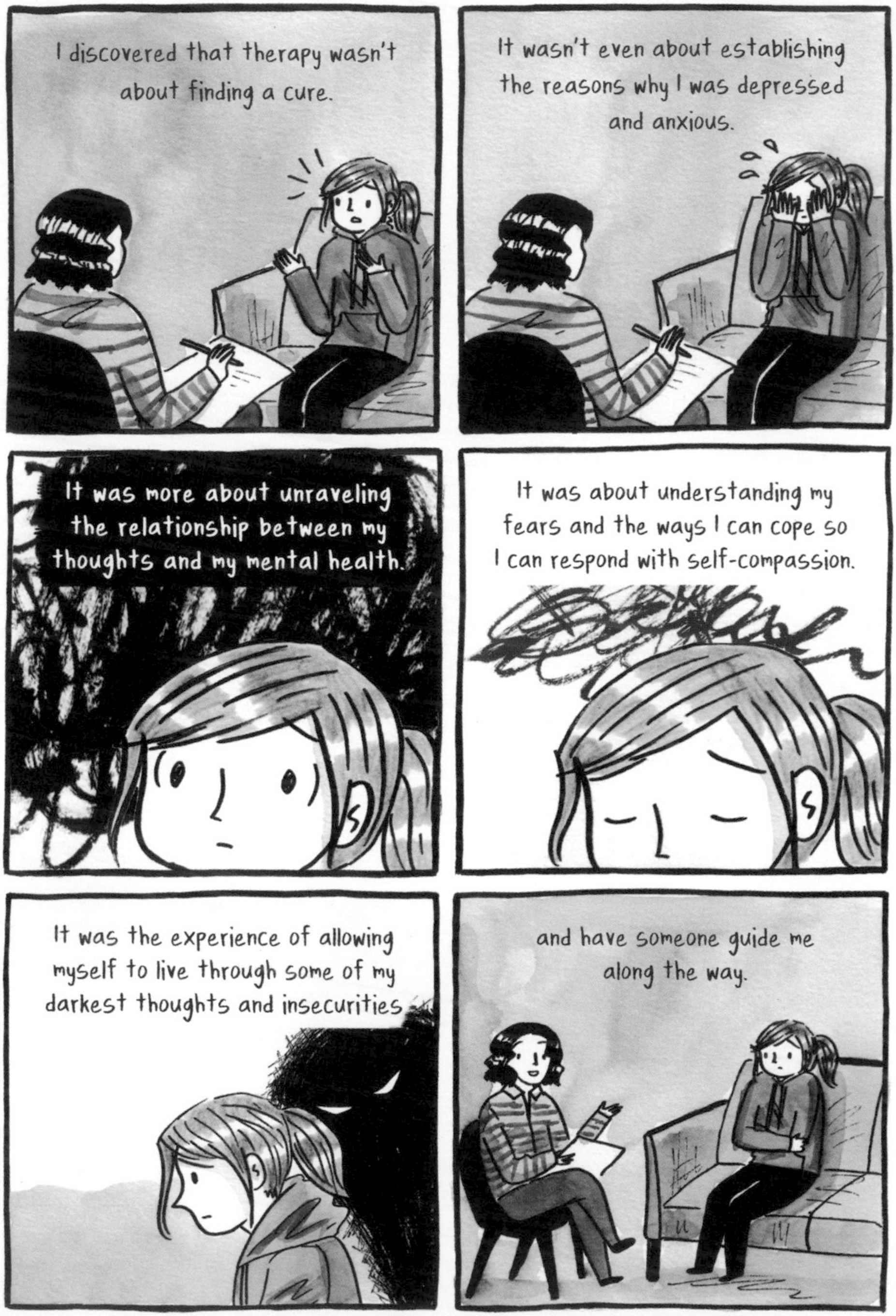

I discovered that therapy wasn't about finding a cure.
It wasn't even about establishing the reasons why I was depressed and anxious.
It was more about unraveling the relationship between my thoughts and my mental health.
It was about understanding my fears and the ways I can cope so I can respond with self-compassion.
It was the experience of allowing myself to live through some of my darkest thoughts and insecurities
and have someone guide me along the way.

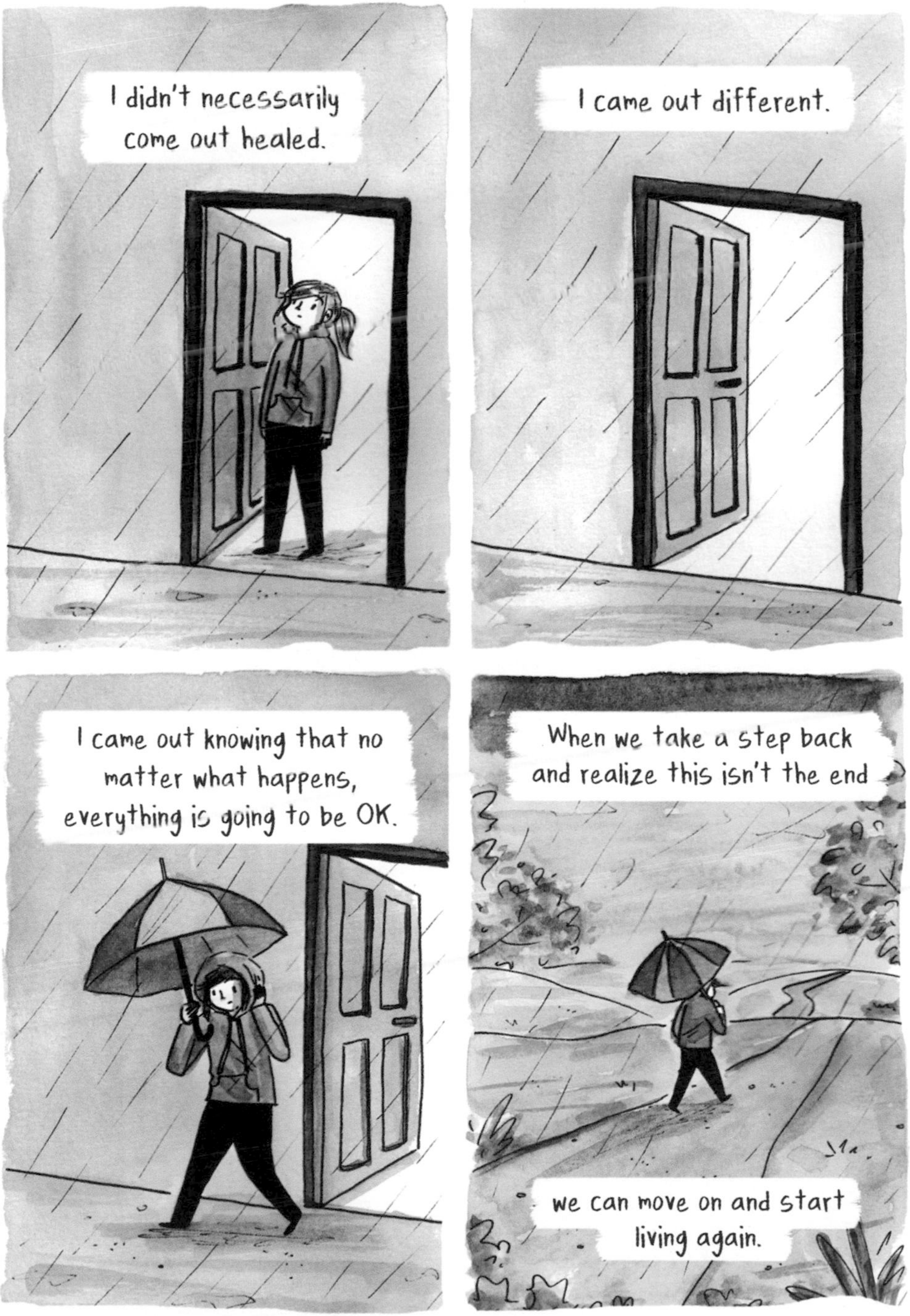
I didn't necessarily come out healed.
I came out different.
I came out knowing that no matter what happens, everything is going to be OK.
When we take a step back and realize this isn't the end
we can move on and start living again.

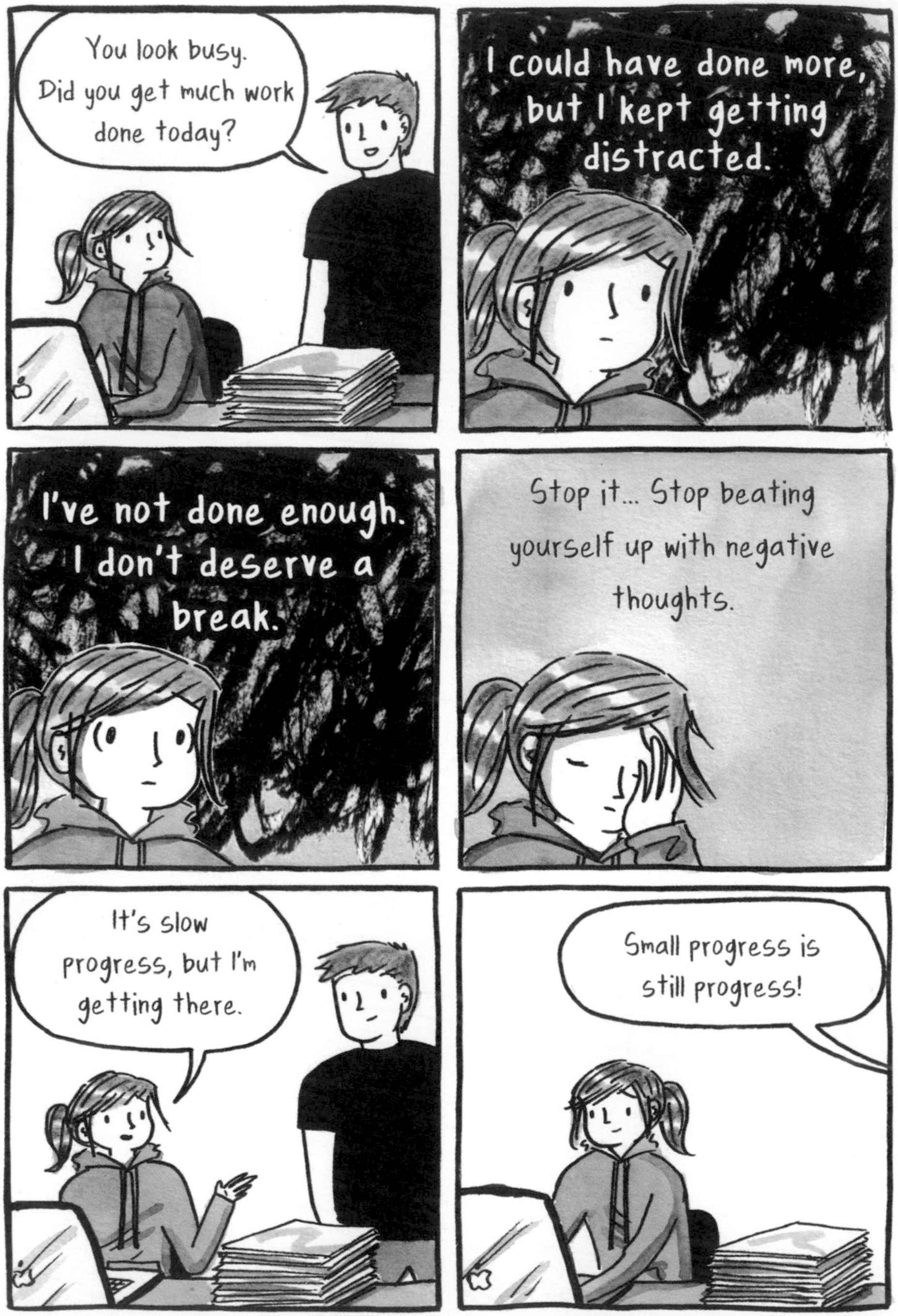
You look busy. Did you get much work done today?
I could have done more, but I kept getting distracted.
I've not done enough. I don't deserve a break.
Stop it... Stop beating yourself up with negative thoughts.
It's slow progress, but I'm getting there.
Small progress is still progress!

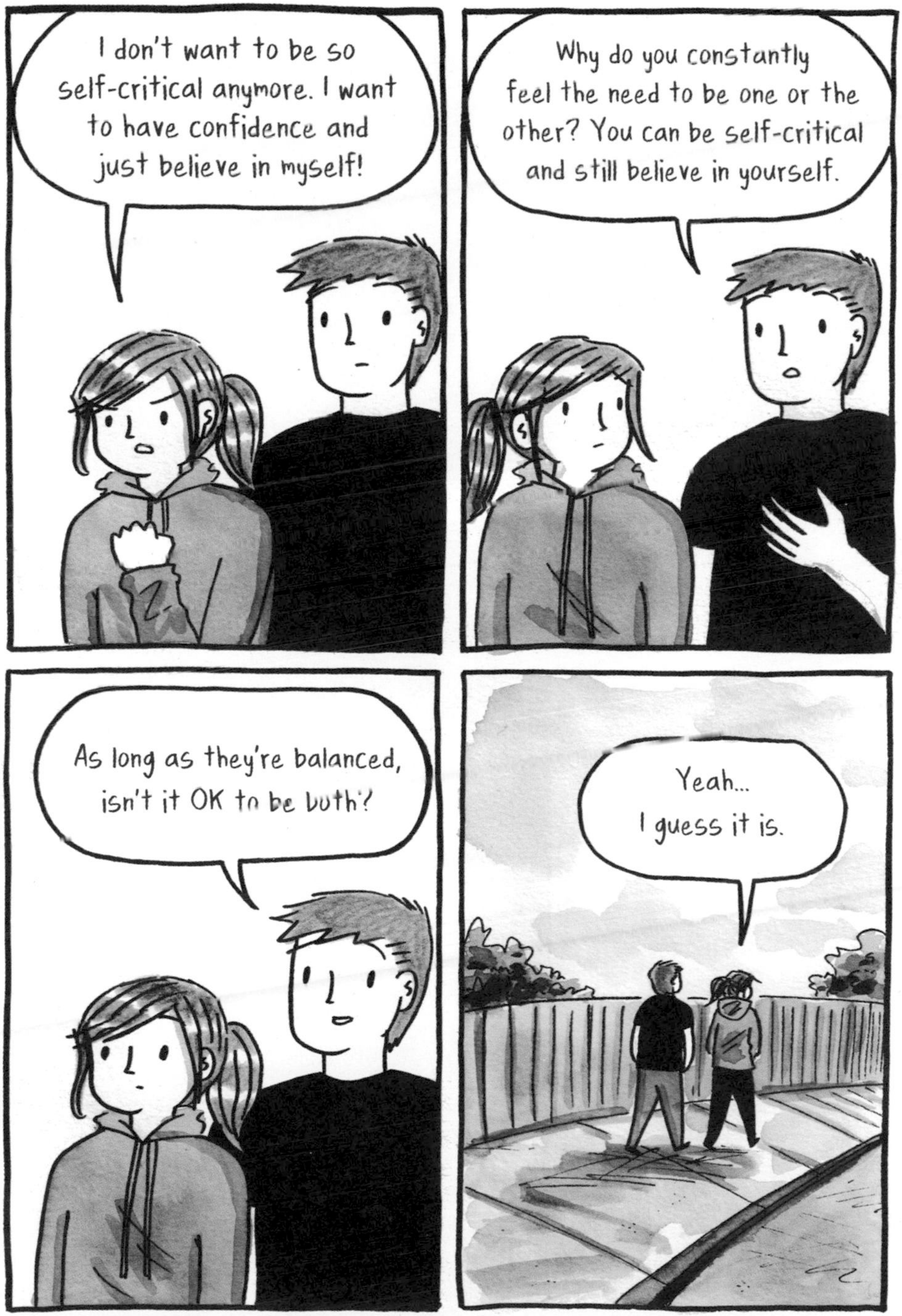
I don't want to be so self-critical anymore. I want to have confidence and just believe in myself!
Why do you constantly feel the need to be one or the other? You can be self-critical and still believe in yourself.
As long as they're balanced, isn't it OK to be both?
Yeah... I guess it is.

Some days can be hard.

But keep putting
one foot in front of
the other.

You don't need to have
all the answers.

You don't have to be
able to see the
finish line.

Just showing up
and getting on with things
is being brave.

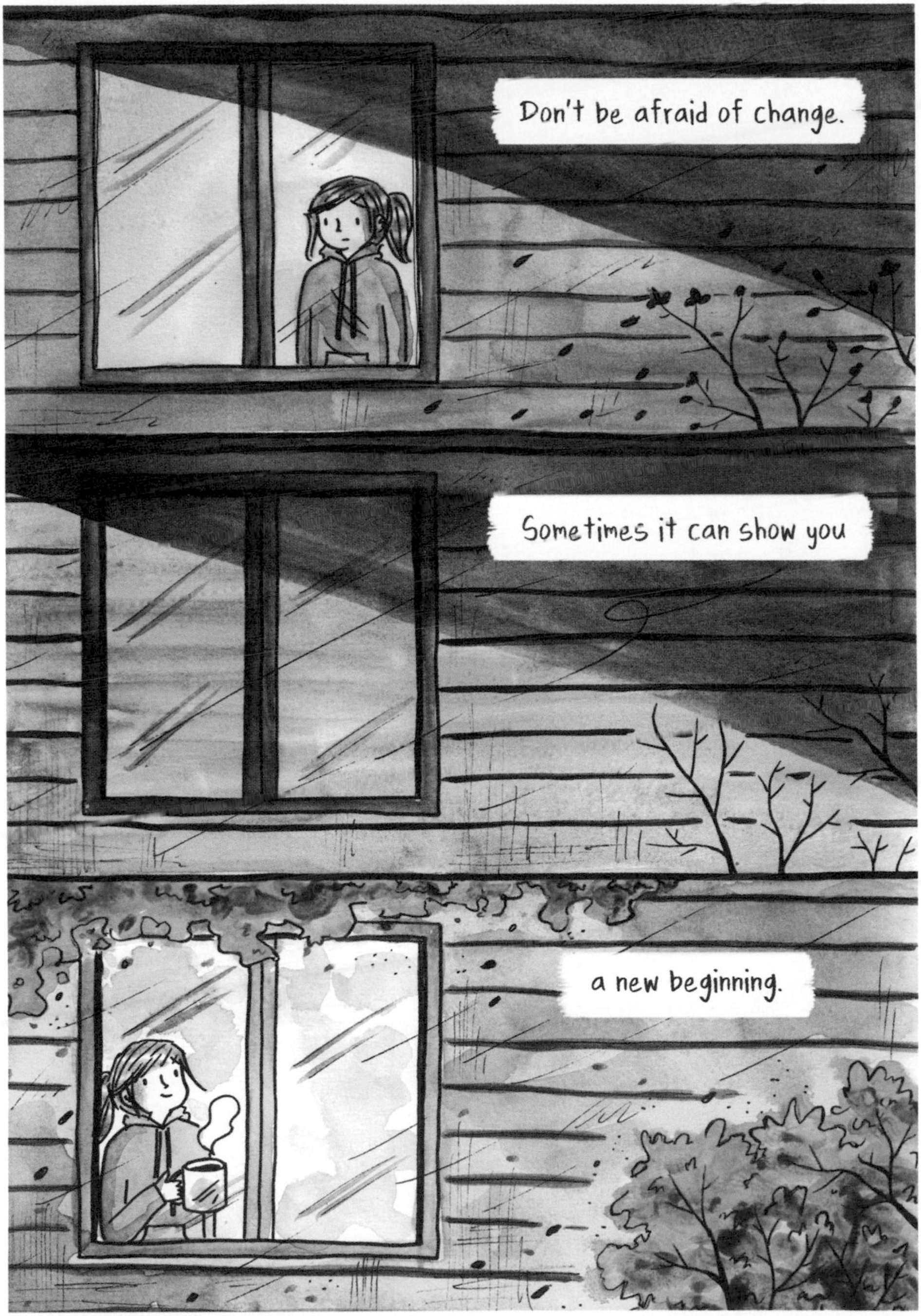
Don't be afraid of change.
Sometimes it can show you
a new beginning.

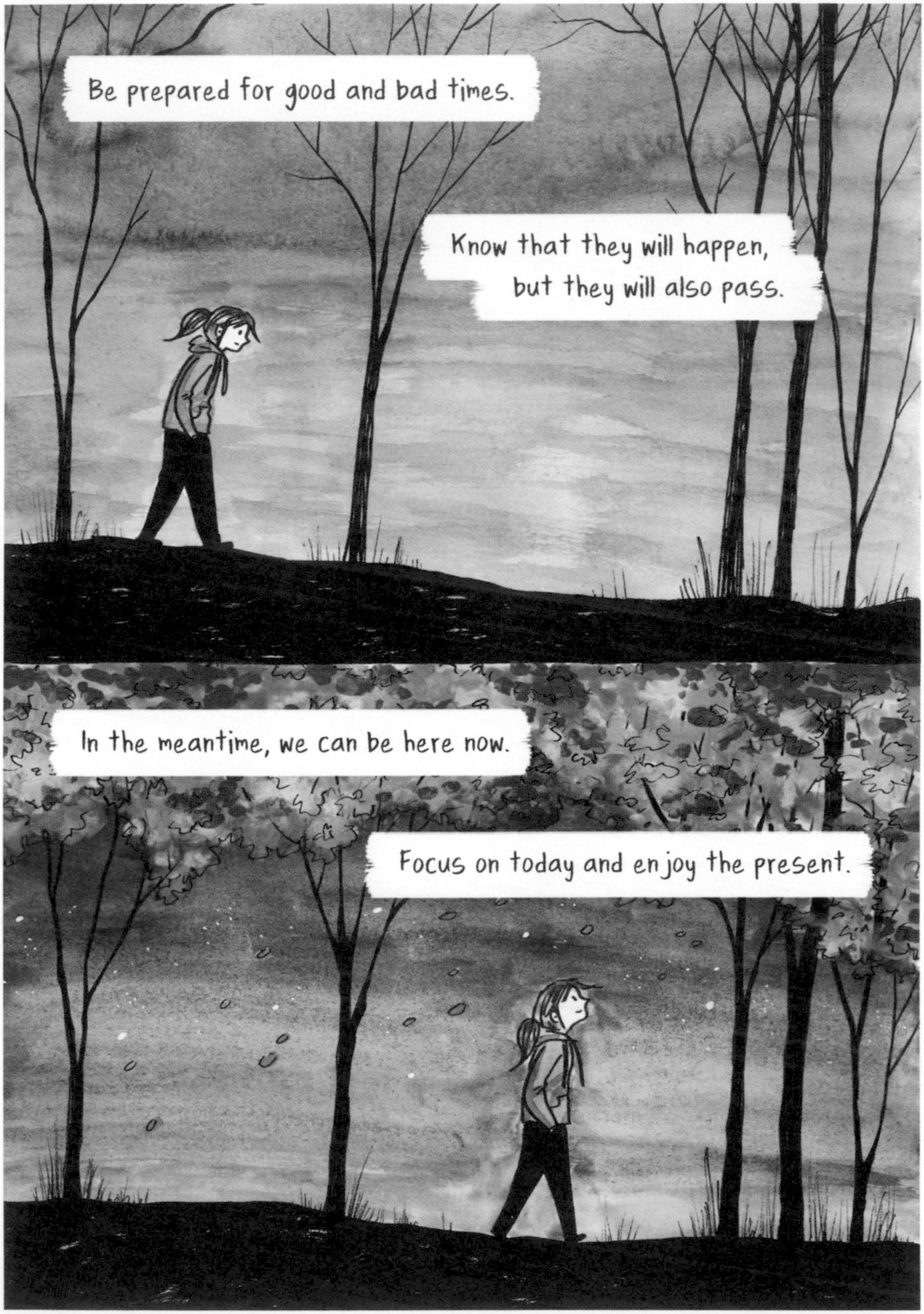
Be prepared for good and bad times.
Know that they will happen, but they will also pass.
In the meantime, we can be here now.
Focus on today and enjoy the present.

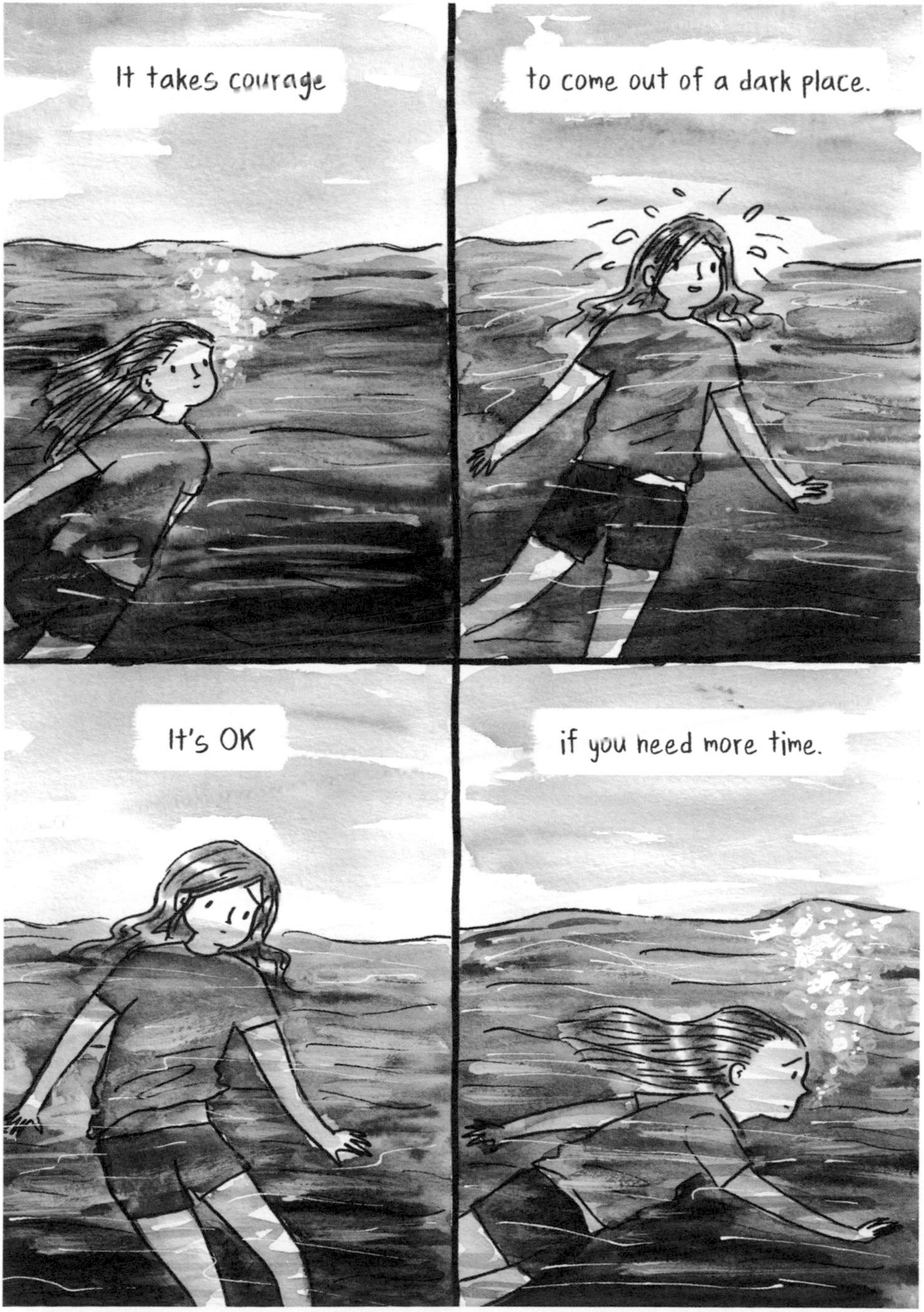
It takes courage
to come out of a dark place.
It's OK
if you need more time.

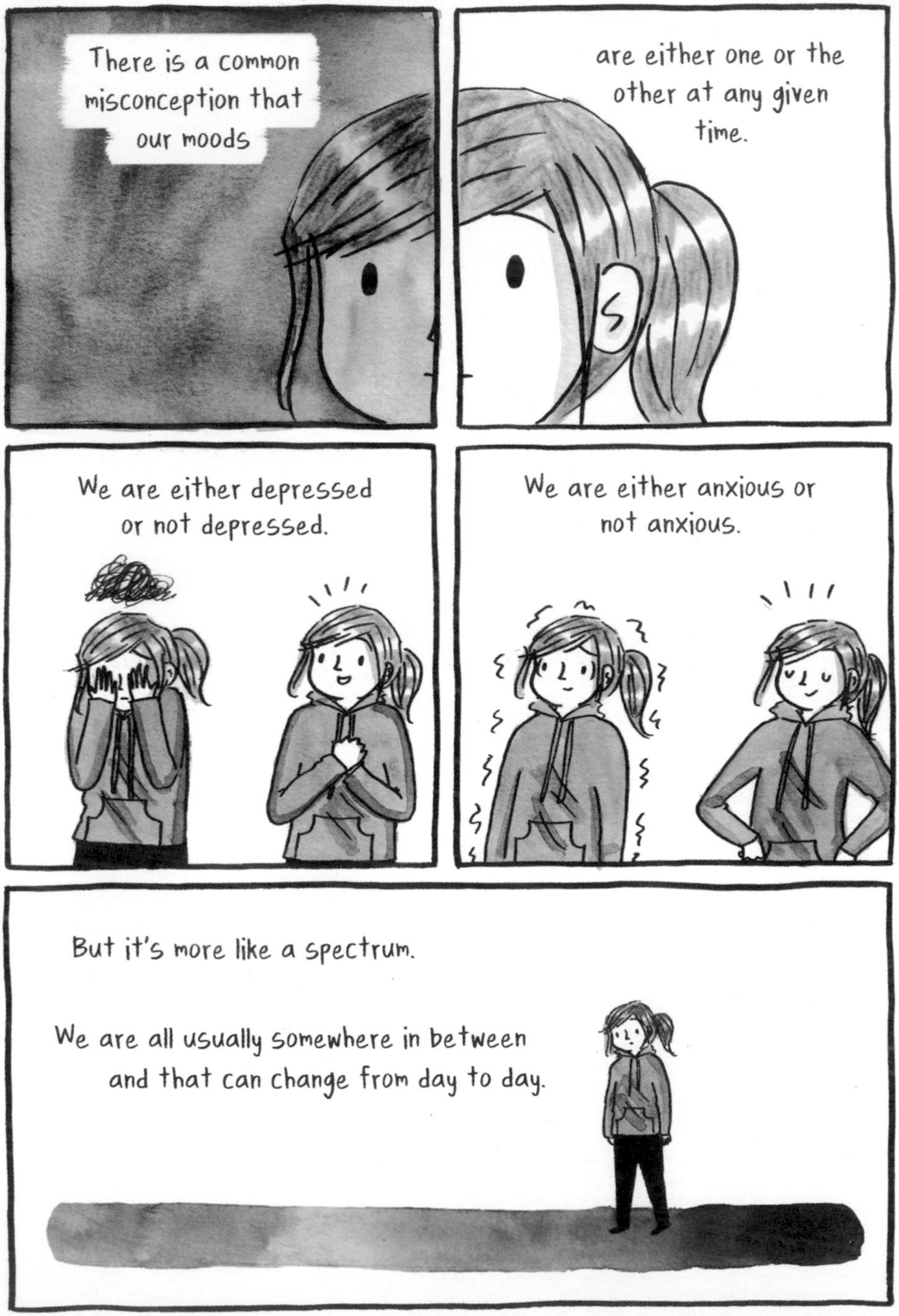
There is a common misconception that our moods
are either one or the other at any given time.
We are either depressed or not depressed.
We are either anxious or not anxious.
But it's more like a spectrum.
We are all usually somewhere in between and that can change from day to day.

Spread kindness always.

You never know who else is suffering.

At the end of the day, love wins.

When I start to feel anxious

I try to tell myself that it's perfectly fine
to feel this way.

I'll get through this.

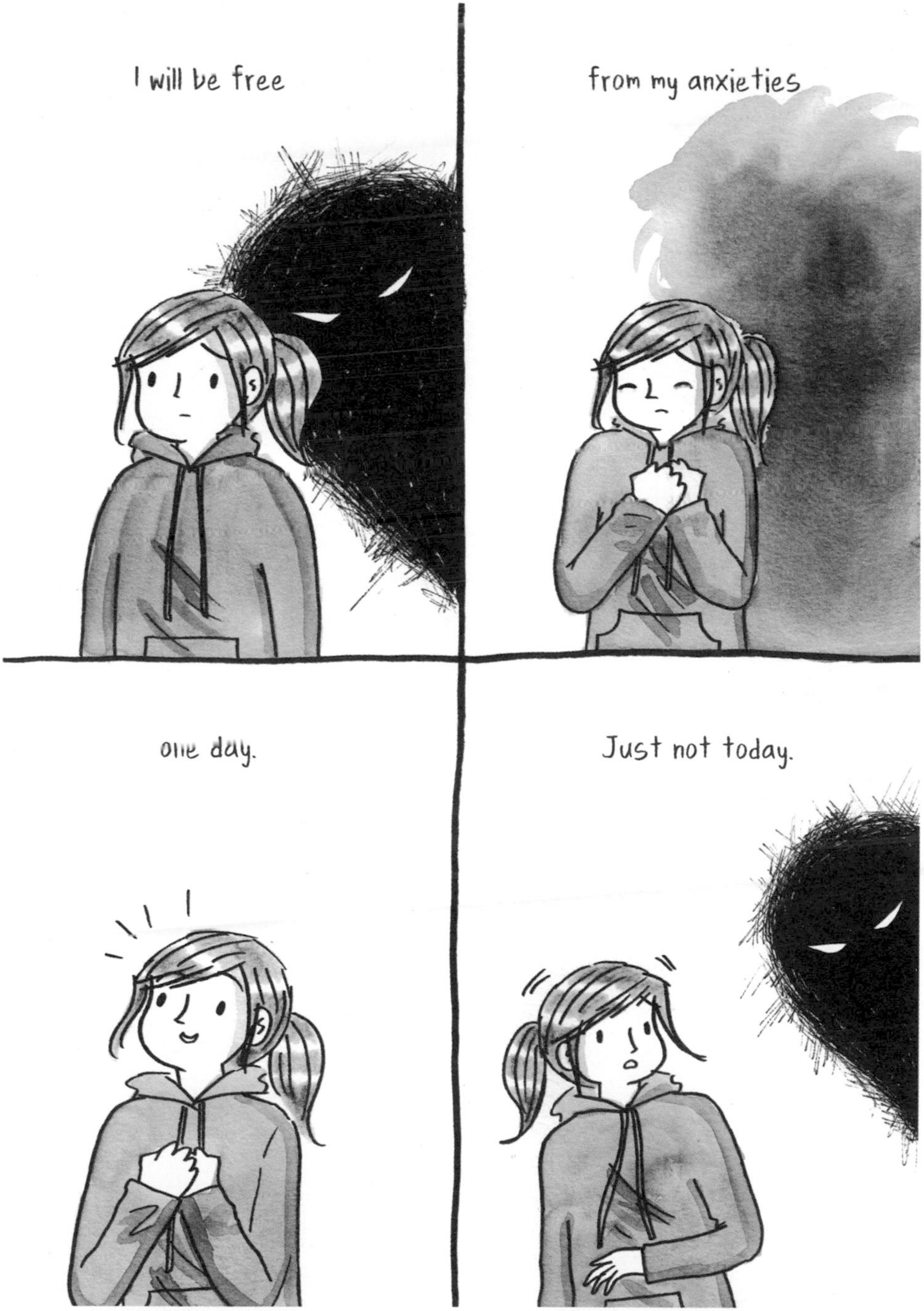
I will be free
from my anxieties
one day.
Just not today.

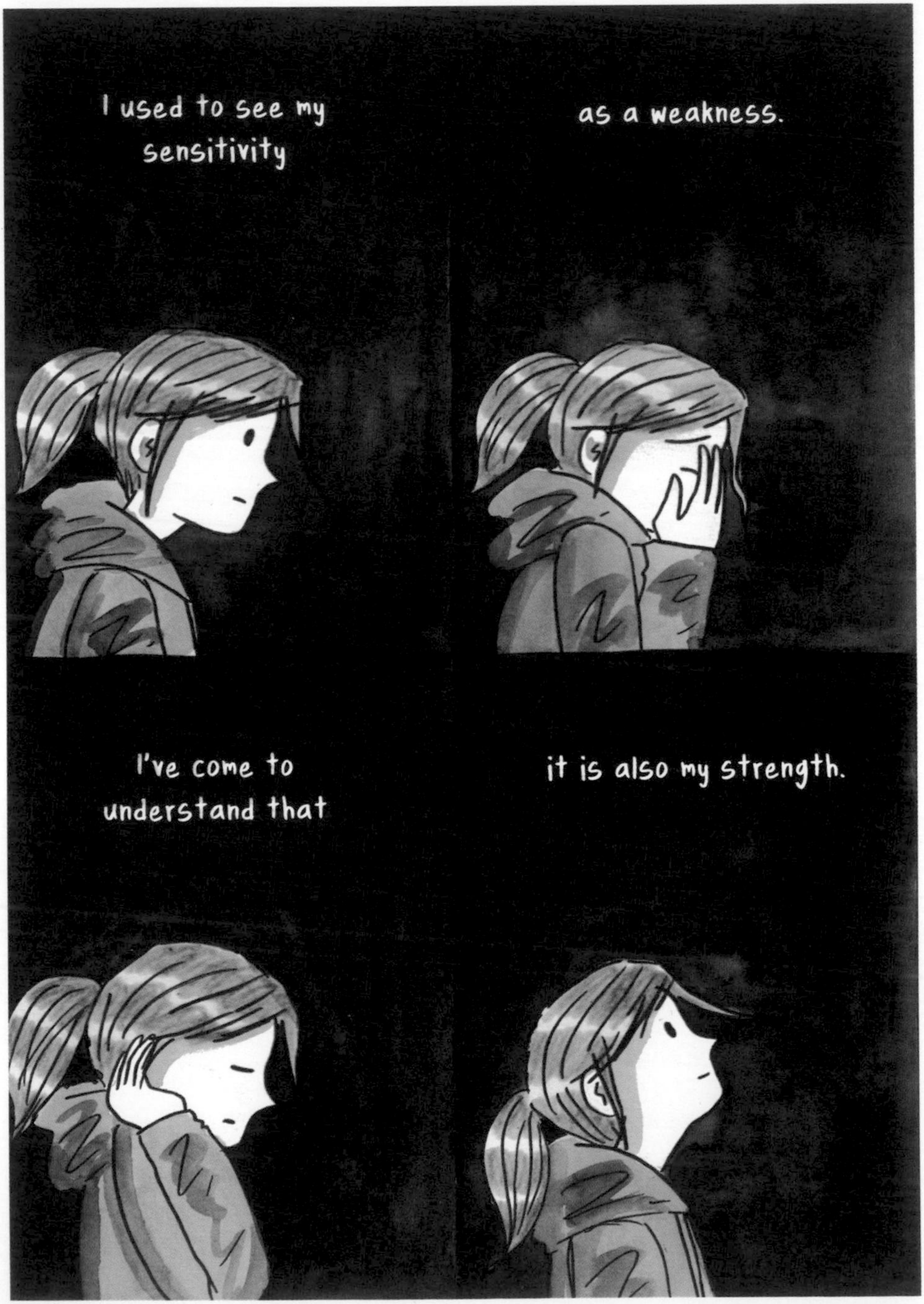
I used to see my sensitivity
as a weakness.
I've come to understand that
it is also my strength.

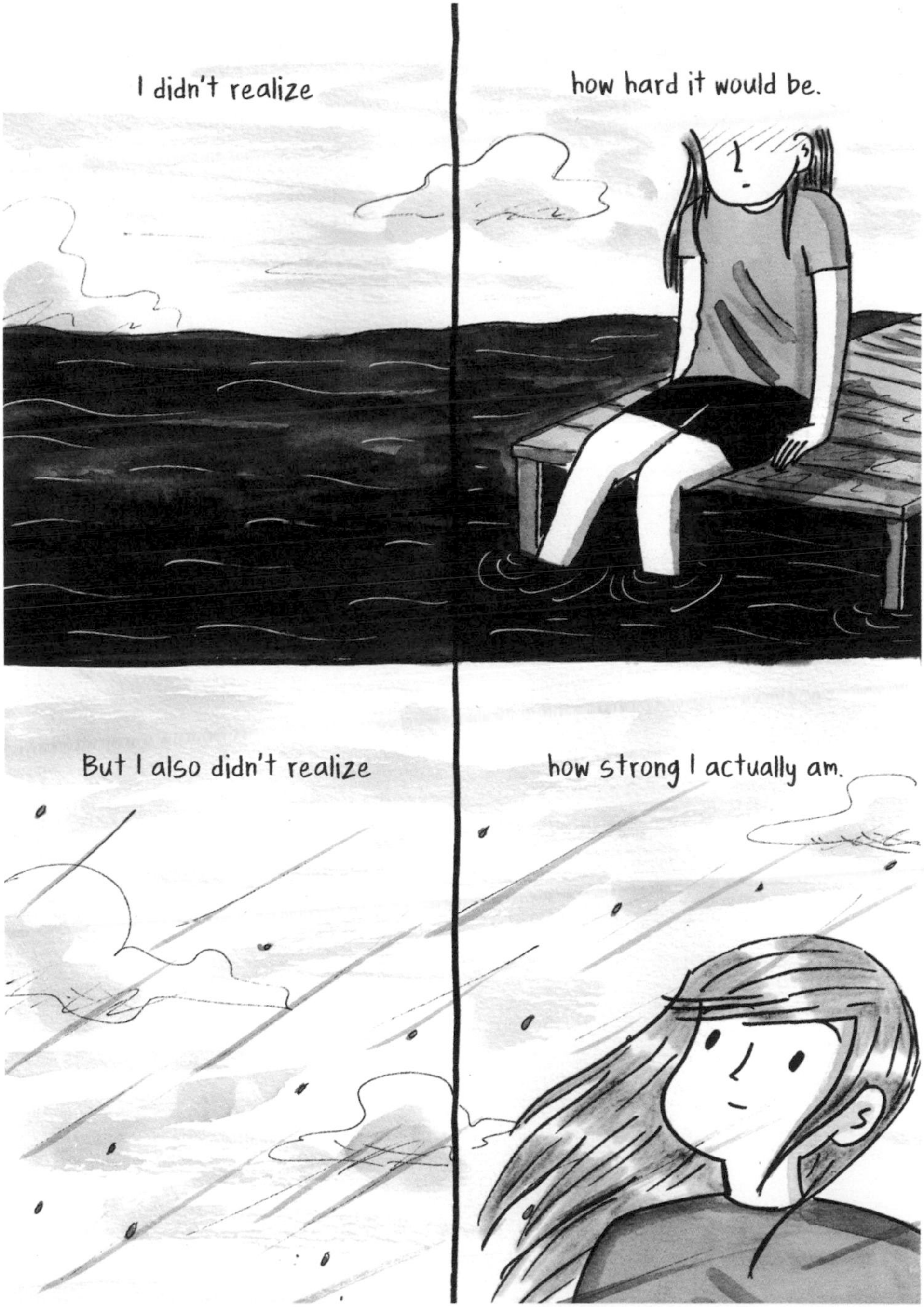
I didn't realize
how hard it would be.
But I also didn't realize
how strong I actually am.

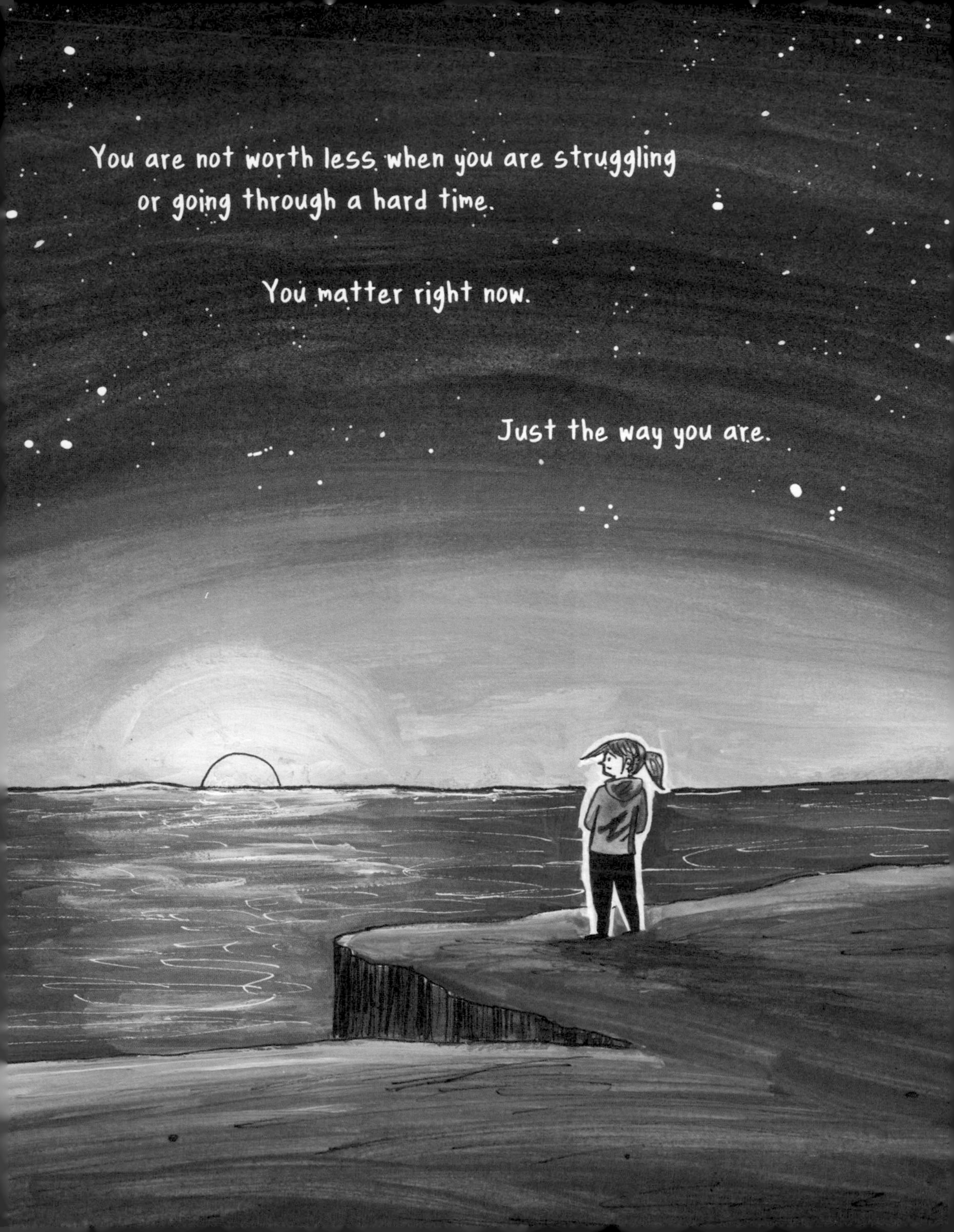
You are not worth less when you are struggling or going through a hard time.
You matter right now.
Just the way you are.

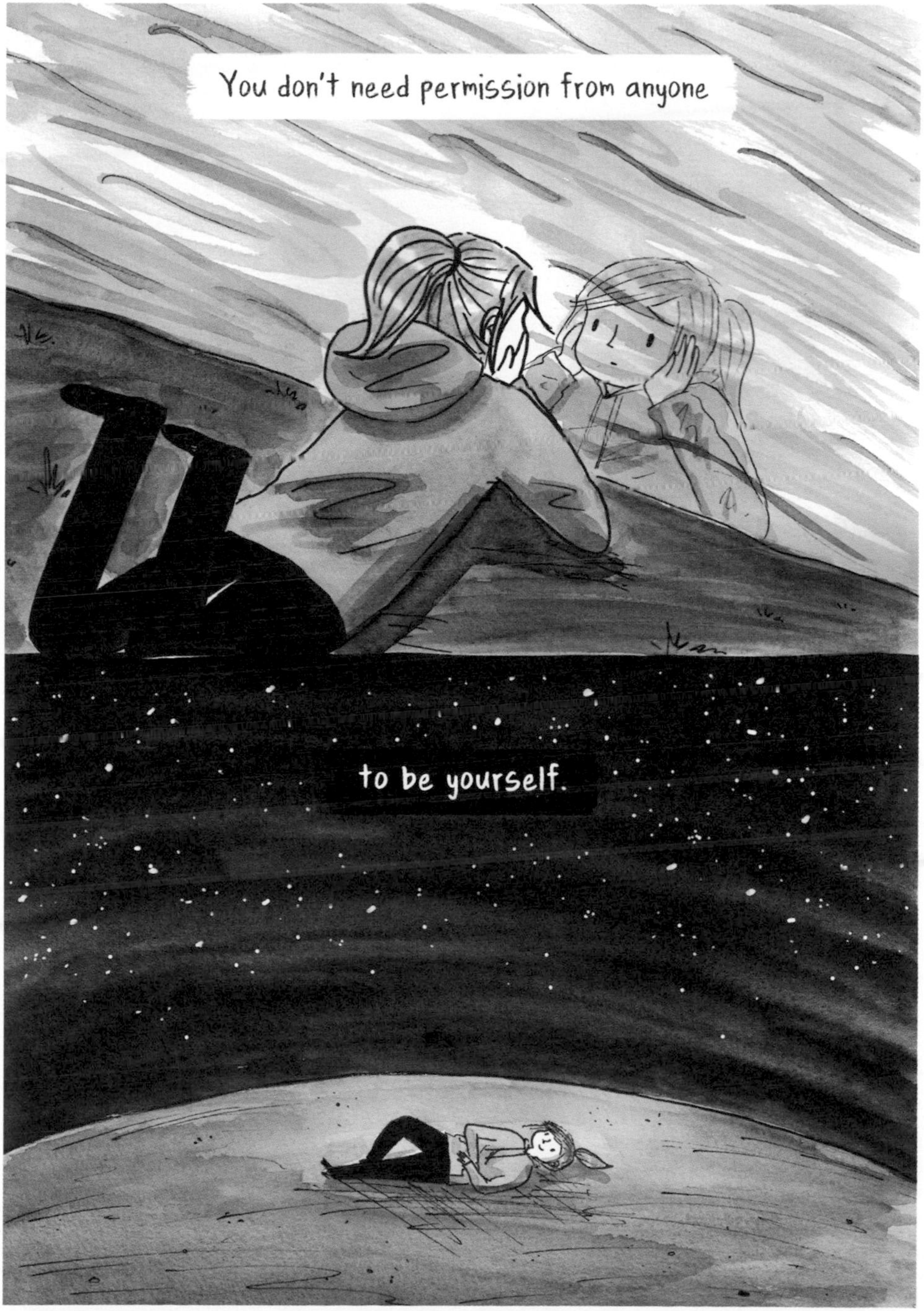
You don't need permission from anyone
to be yourself.

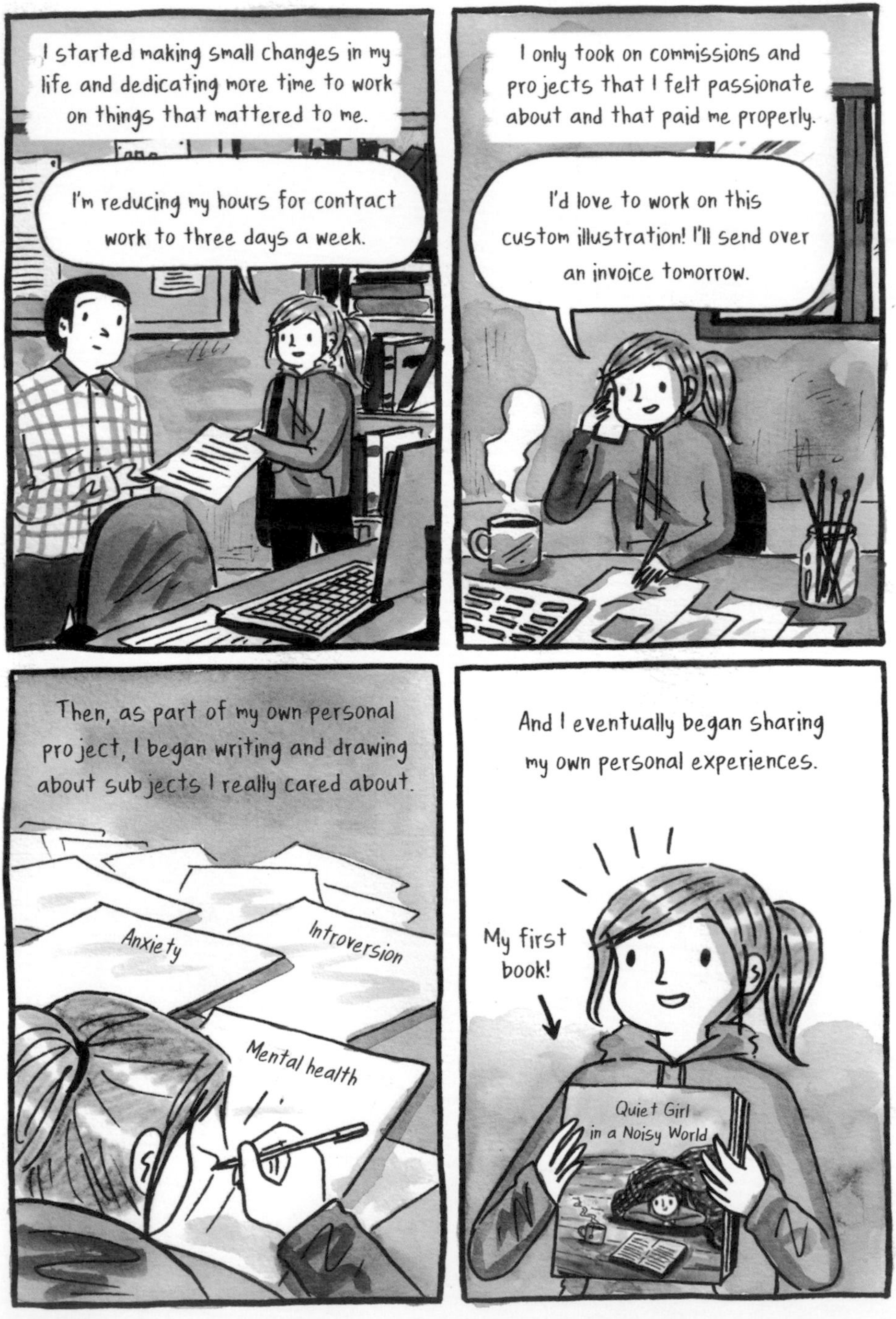
I started making small changes in my life and dedicating more time to work on things that mattered to me.
I'm reducing my hours for contract work to three days a week.
I only took on commissions and projects that I felt passionate about and that paid me properly.
I'd love to work on this custom illustration! I'll send over an invoice tomorrow.
Then, as part of my own personal project, I began writing and drawing about subjects I really cared about.
Anxiety
Introversion
Mental health
And I eventually began sharing my own personal experiences.
My first book!
Quiet Girl in a Noisy World

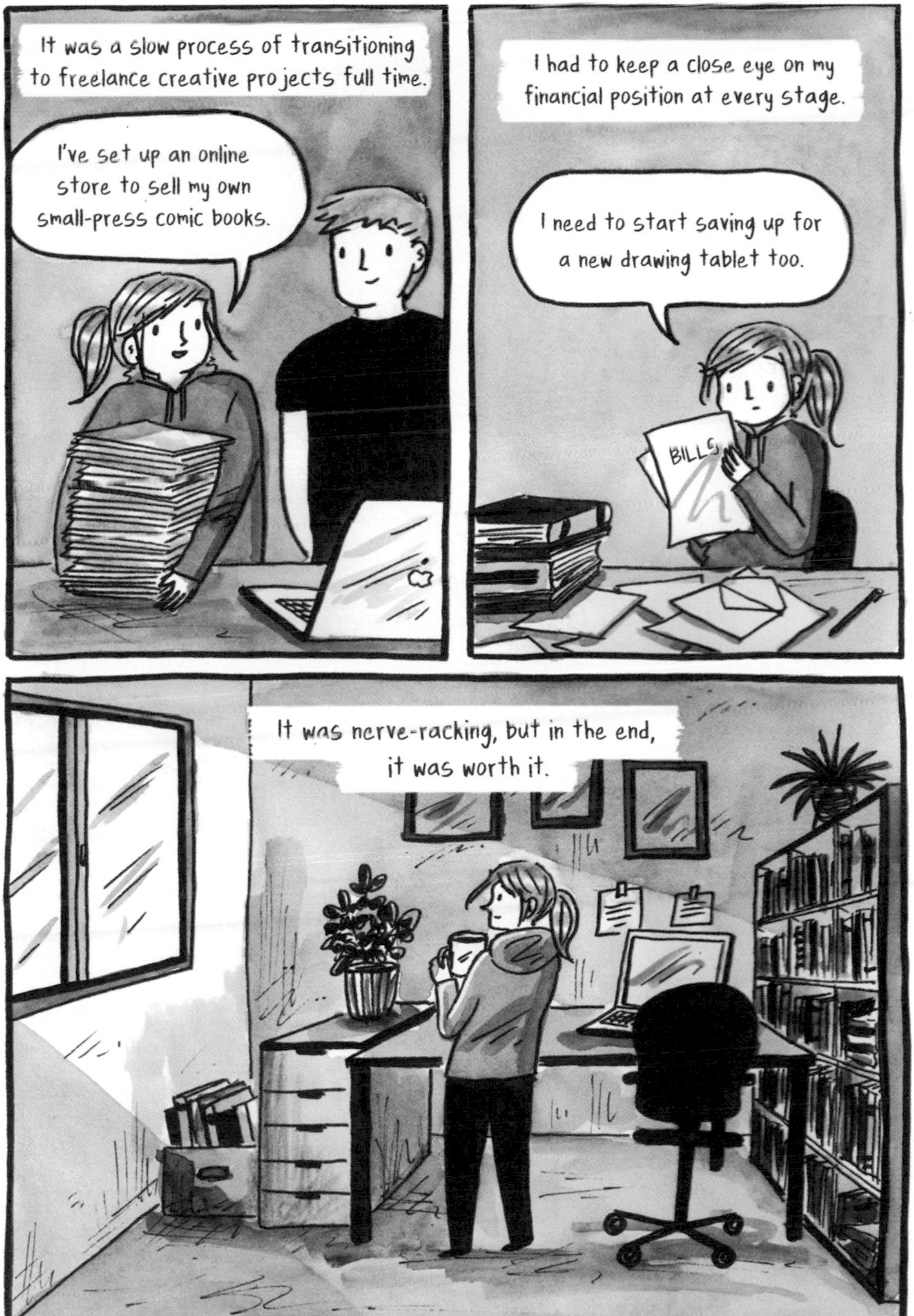
It was a slow process of transitioning to freelance creative projects full time.
I've set up an online store to sell my own small-press comic books.
I had to keep a close eye on my financial position at every stage.
I need to start saving up for a new drawing tablet too.
BILLS
It was nerve-racking, but in the end, it was worth it.

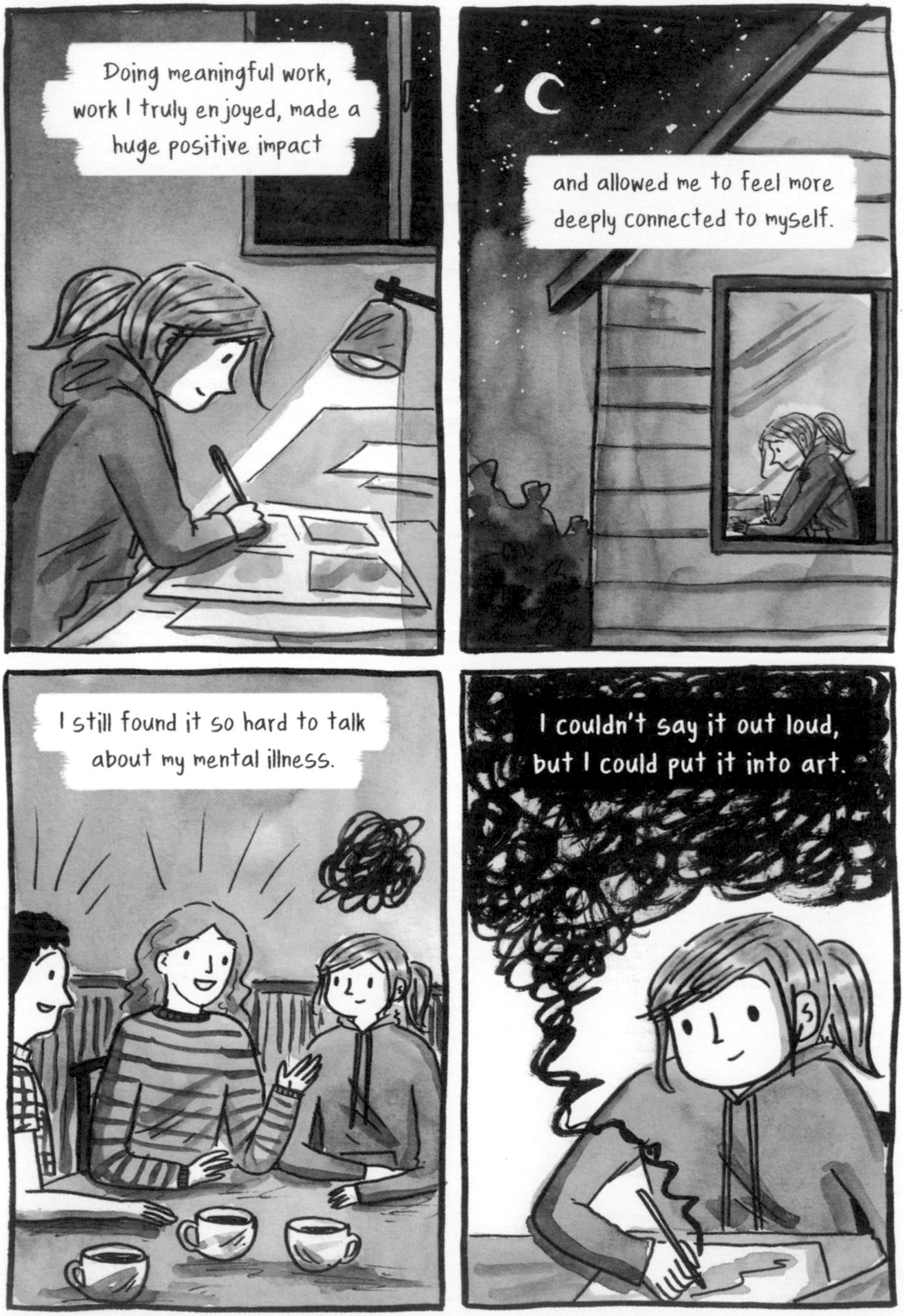
Doing meaningful work, work I truly enjoyed, made a huge positive impact
and allowed me to feel more deeply connected to myself.
I still found it so hard to talk about my mental illness.
I couldn't say it out loud, but I could put it into art.

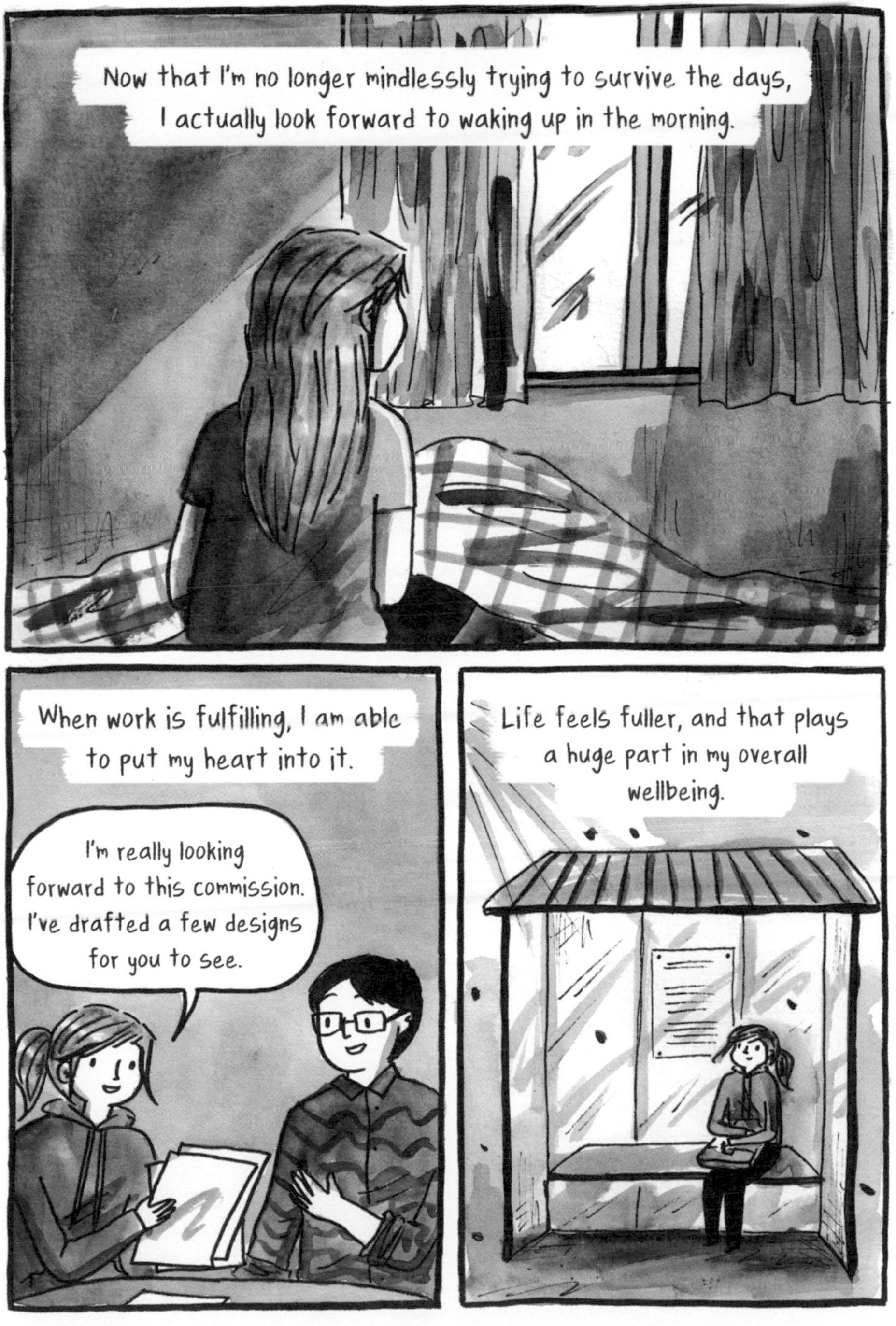
Now that I'm no longer mindlessly trying to survive the days, I actually look forward to waking up in the morning.
When work is fulfilling, I am able to put my heart into it.
I'm really looking forward to this commission. I've drafted a few designs for you to see.
Life feels fuller, and that plays a huge part in my overall wellbeing.

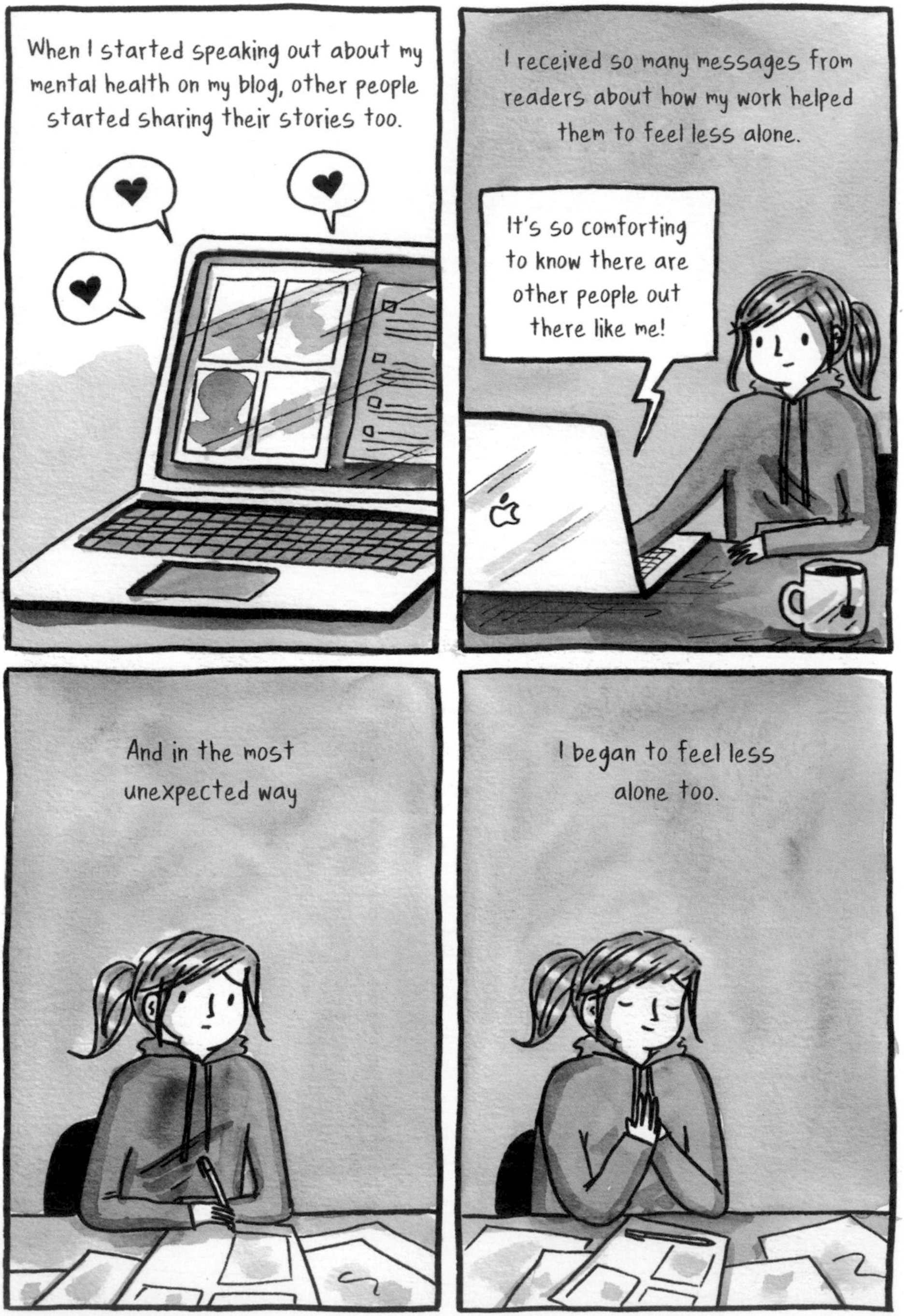
When I started speaking out about my mental health on my blog, other people started sharing their stories too.
I received so many messages from readers about how my work helped them to feel less alone.
It's so comforting to know there are other people out there like me!
And in the most unexpected way
I began to feel less alone too.

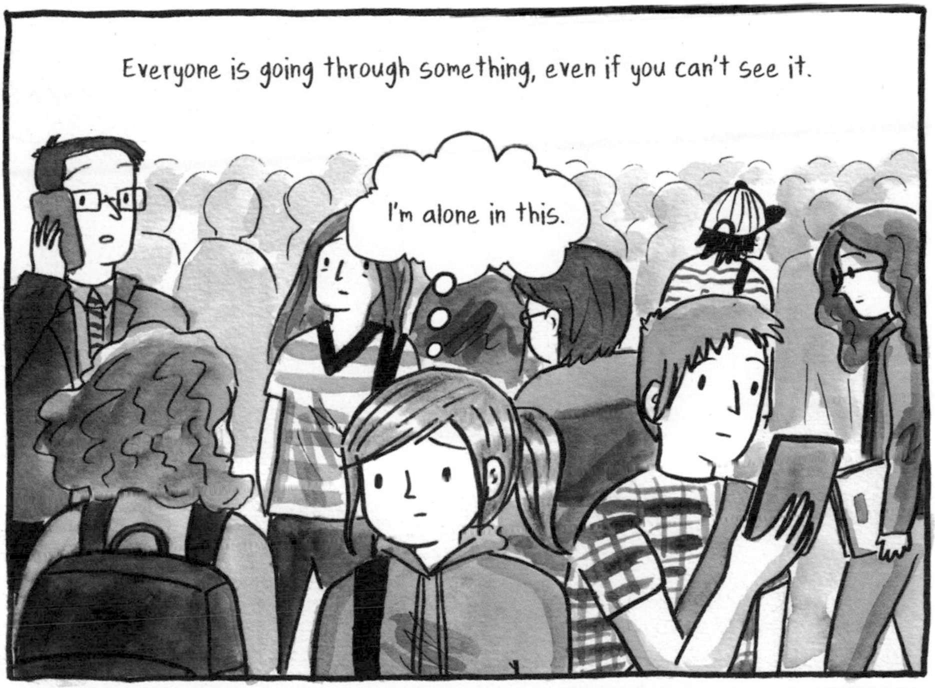
Everyone is going through something, even if you can't see it.
I'm alone in this.

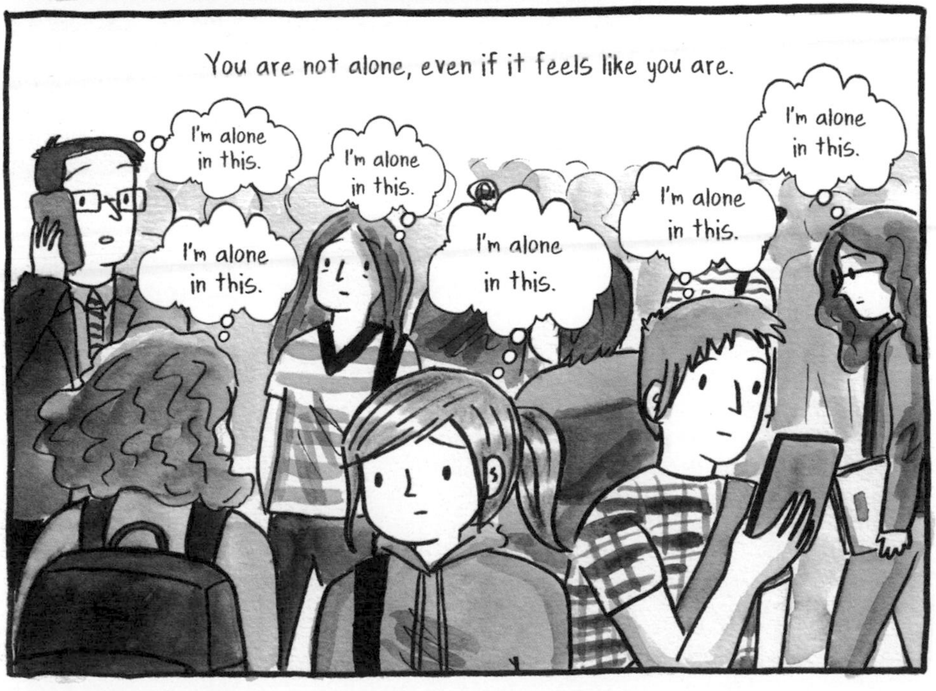
You are not alone, even if it feels like you are.
I'm alone in this.
I'm alone in this.
I'm alone in this.
I'm alone in this.
I'm alone in this.
I'm alone in this.

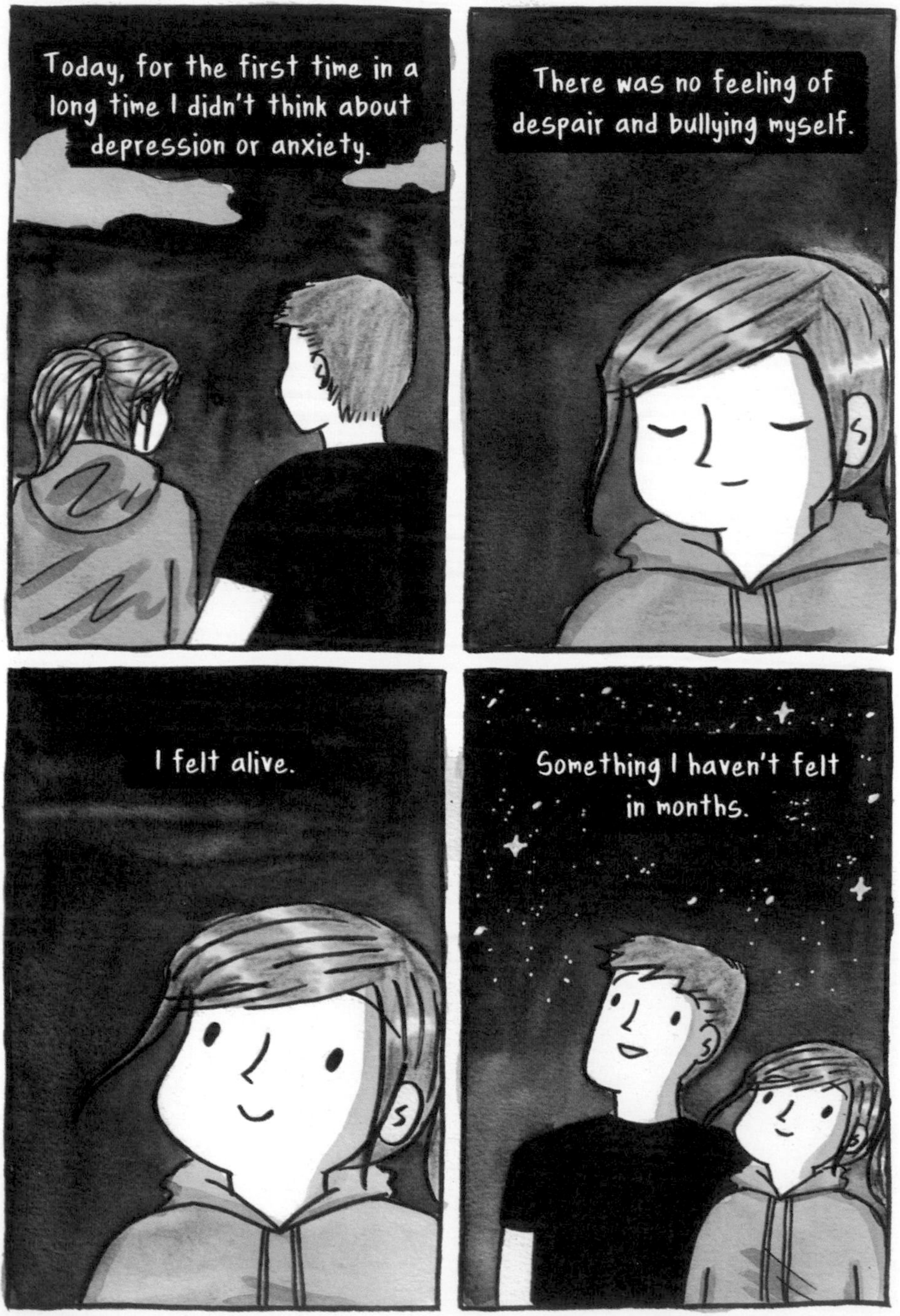
Today, for the first time in a long time I didn't think about depression or anxiety.
There was no feeling of despair and bullying myself.
I felt alive.
Something I haven't felt in months.

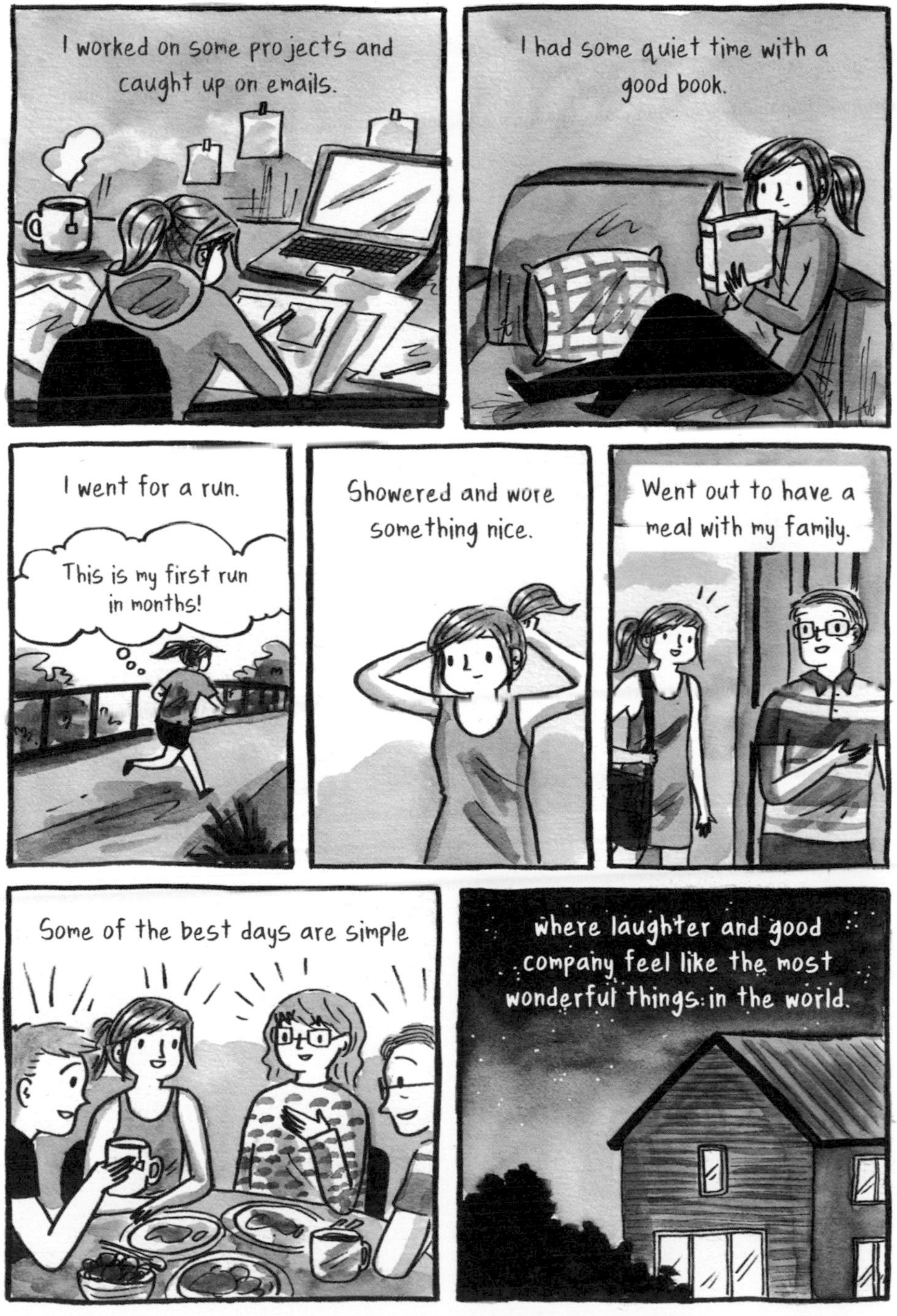
I worked on some projects and caught up on emails.
I had some quiet time with a good book.
I went for a run.
This is my first run in months!
Showered and wore something nice.
Went out to have a meal with my family.
Some of the best days are simple
where laughter and good company feel like the most wonderful things in the world.

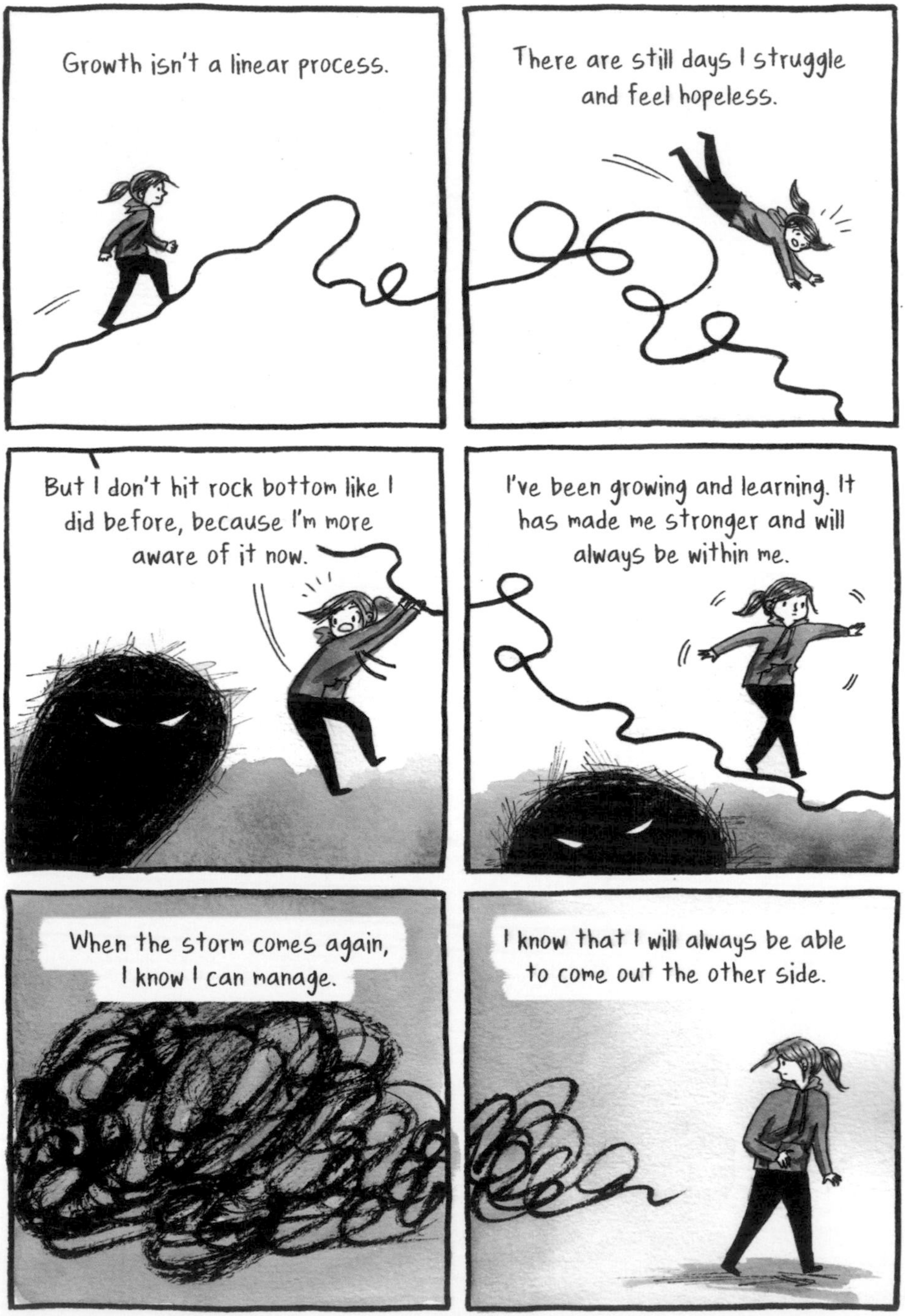
Growth isn't a linear process.
There are still days I struggle and feel hopeless.
But I don't hit rock bottom like I did before, because I'm more aware of it now.
I've been growing and learning. It has made me stronger and will always be within me.
When the storm comes again, I know I can manage.
I know that I will always be able to come out the other side.

Stop being afraid about what could go wrong.

This won't
work out.

It will be a
huge failure.

I will disappoint
everyone.

I'm wasting time.

Because there are also a lot of things that could go right.

This could
work out.

I will learn a lot from
the experience.

If I keep practicing,
I can get better.

I will be inspired to
follow my dreams.

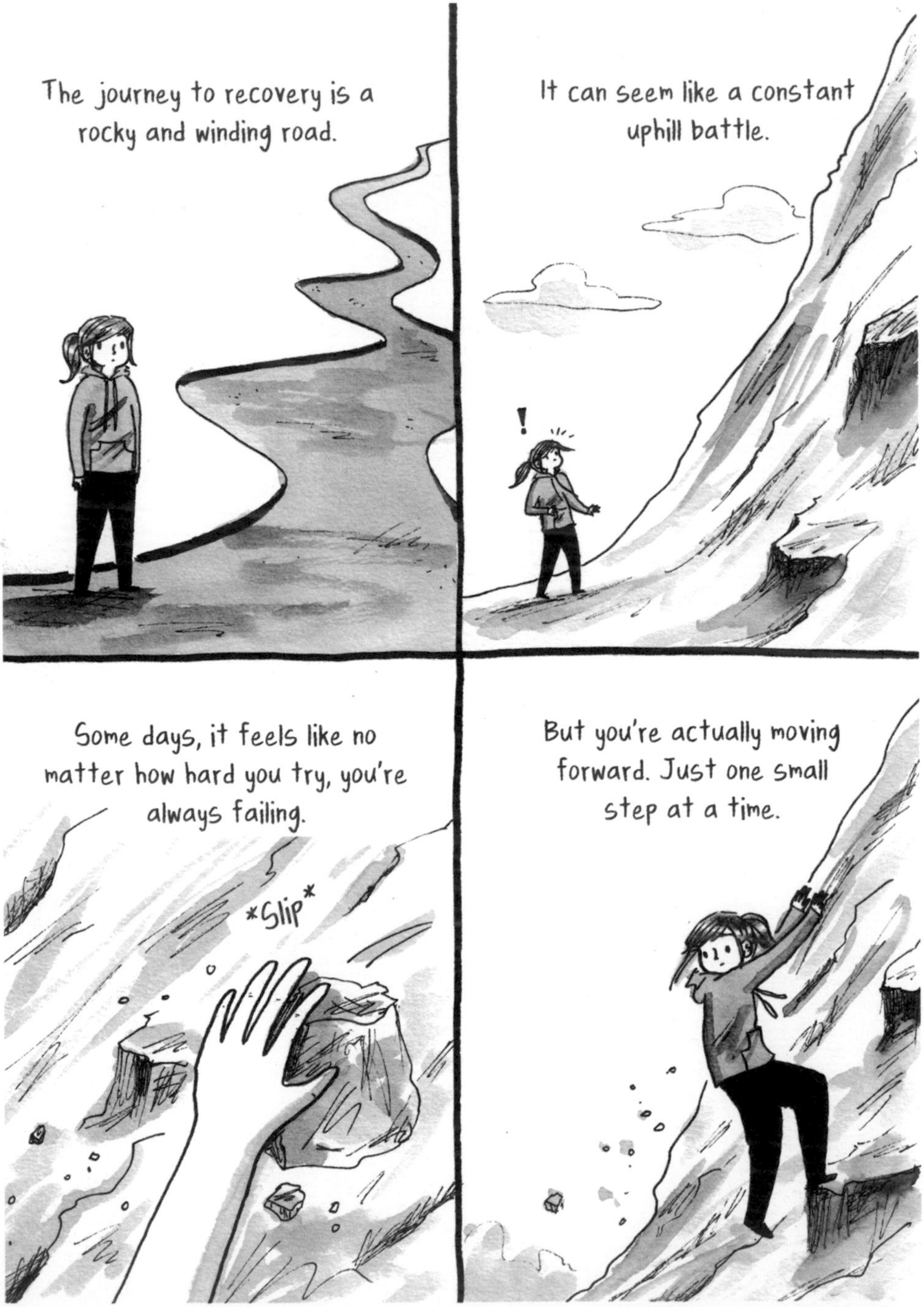
The journey to recovery is a rocky and winding road.
It can seem like a constant uphill battle.
!
Some days, it feels like no matter how hard you try, you're always failing.
Slip
But you're actually moving forward. Just one small step at a time.

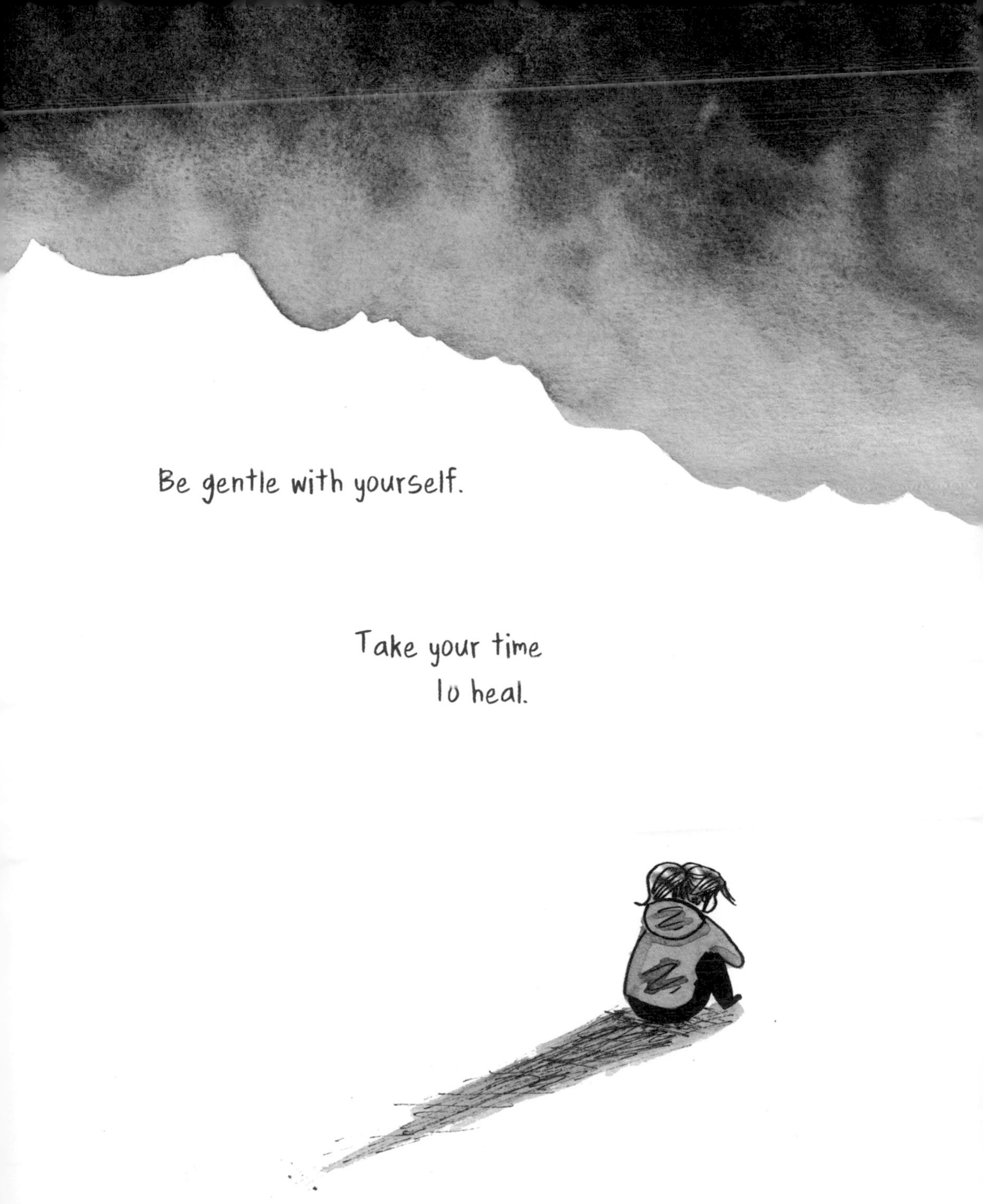
Be gentle with yourself.
Take your time
to heal.

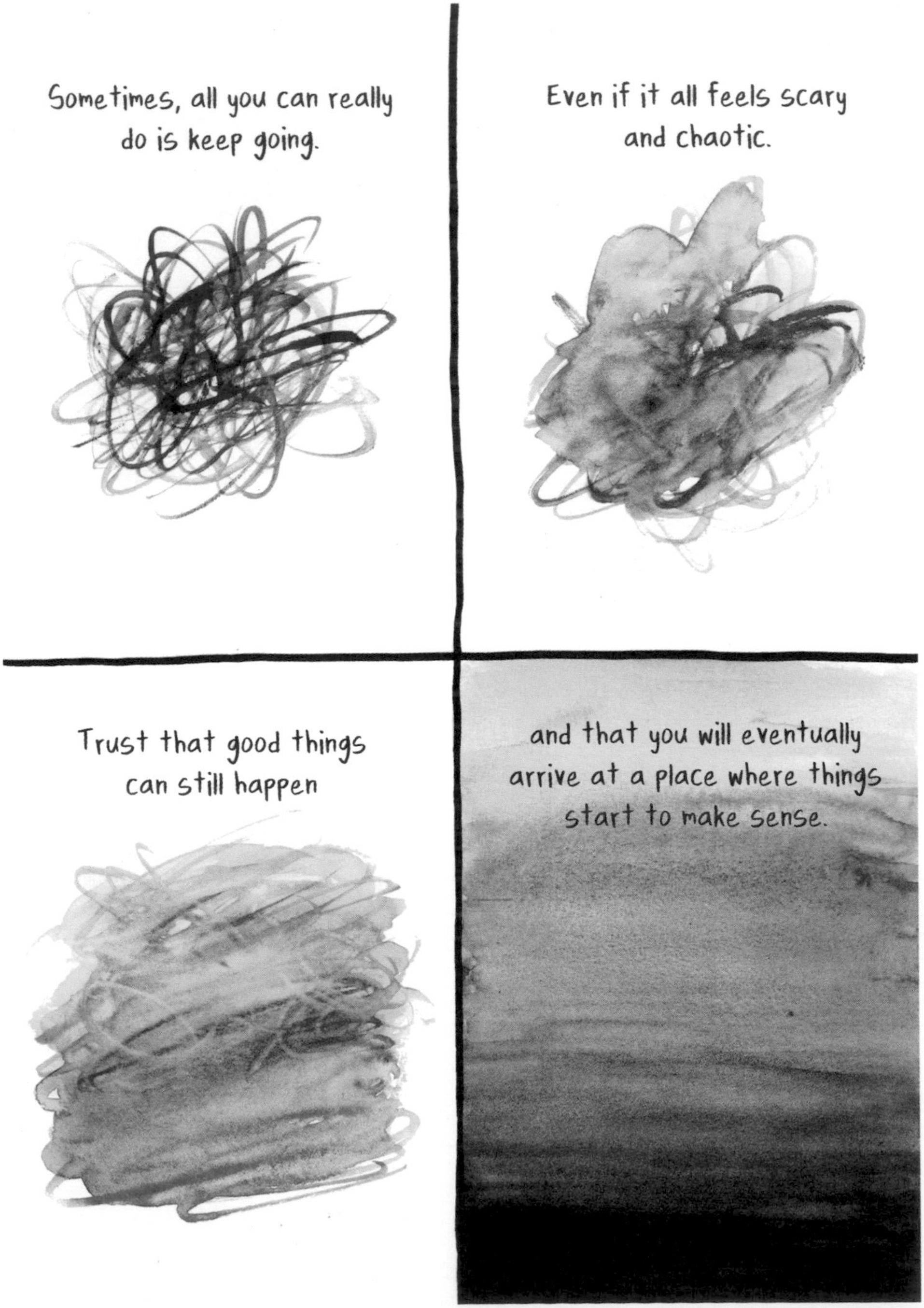
Sometimes, all you can really do is keep going.
Even if it all feels scary and chaotic.
Trust that good things can still happen
and that you will eventually arrive at a place where things start to make sense.

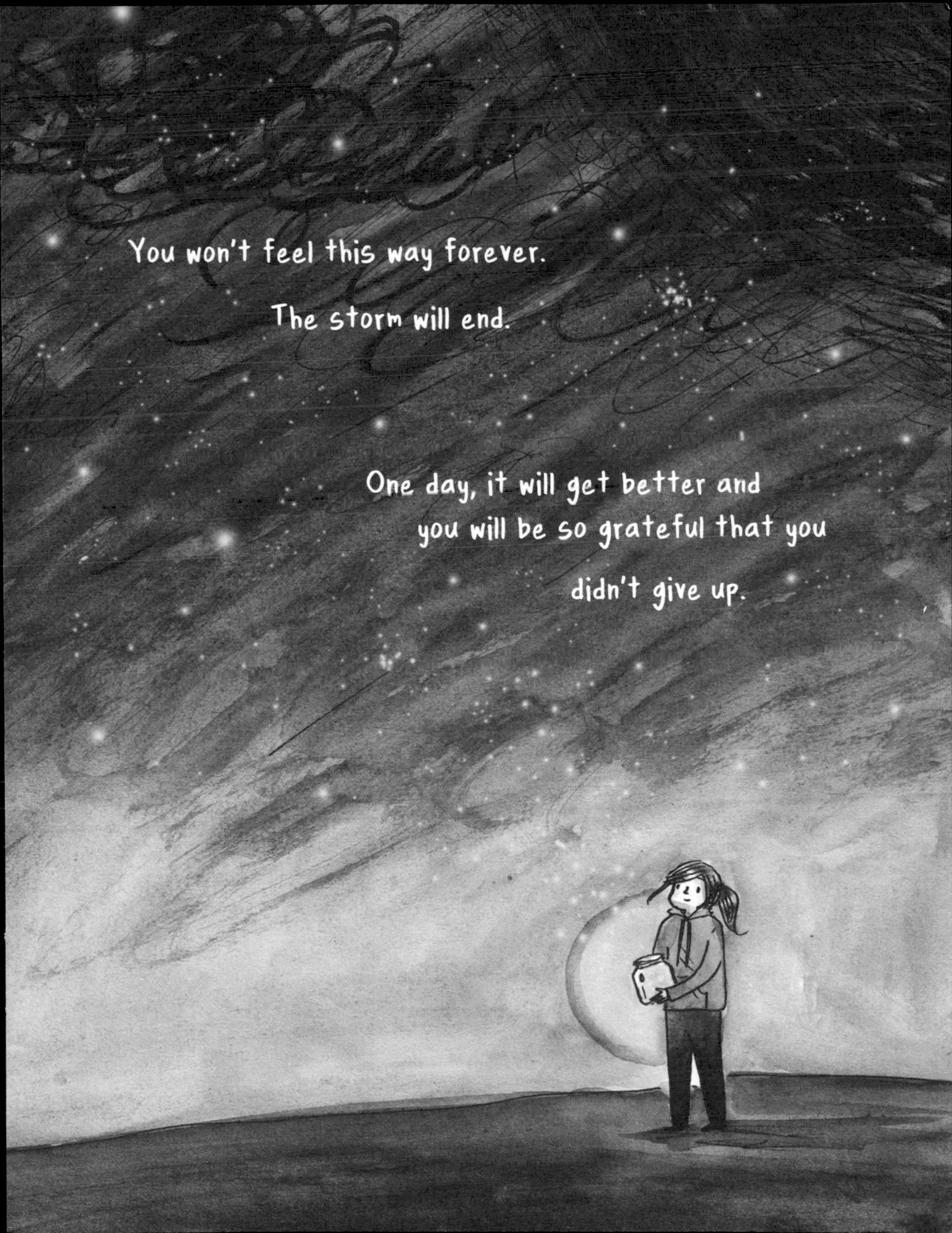
You won't feel this way forever.
The storm will end.
One day, it will get better and you will be so grateful that you didn't give up.

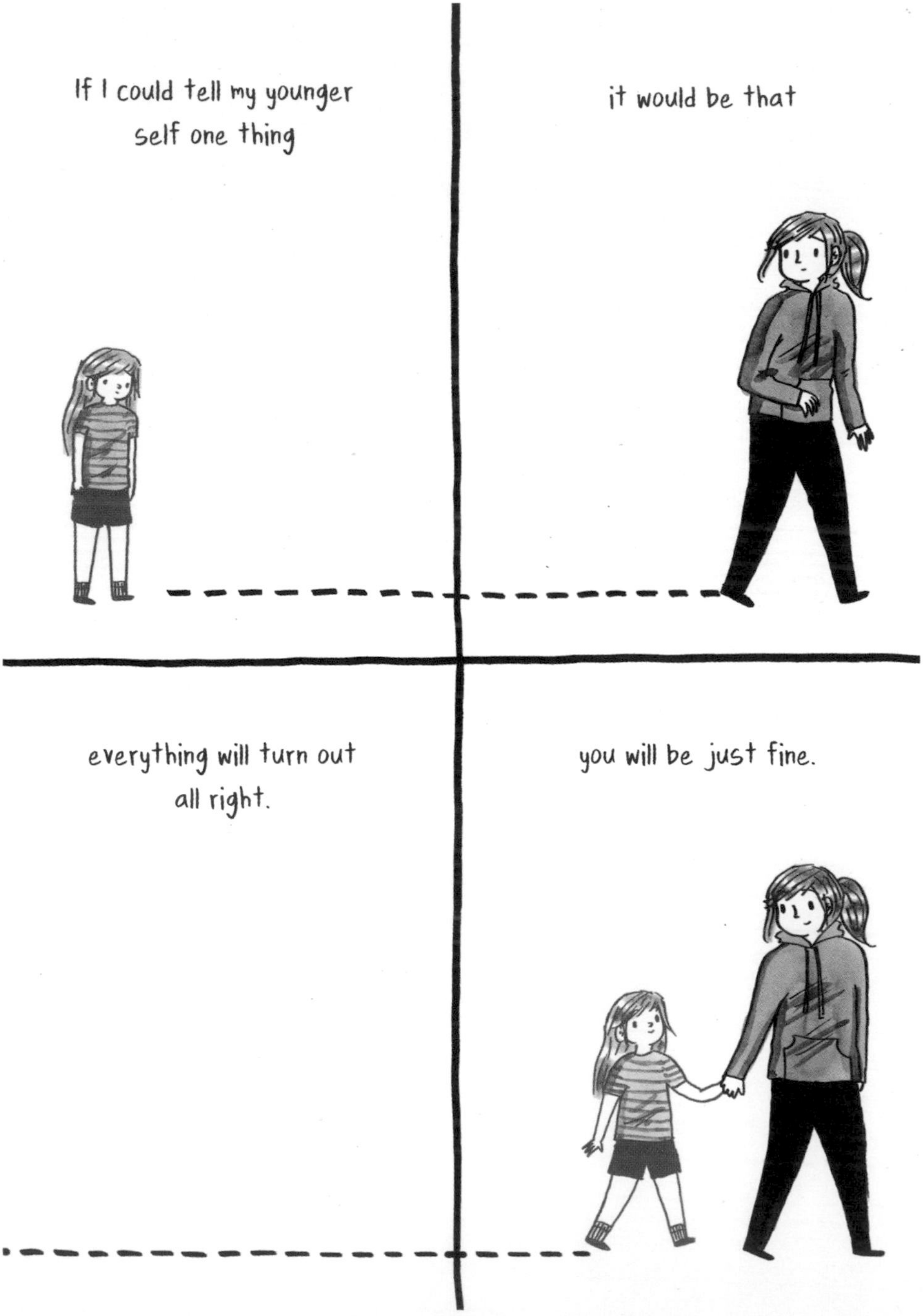
If I could tell my younger self one thing
it would be that
everything will turn out all right.
you will be just fine.

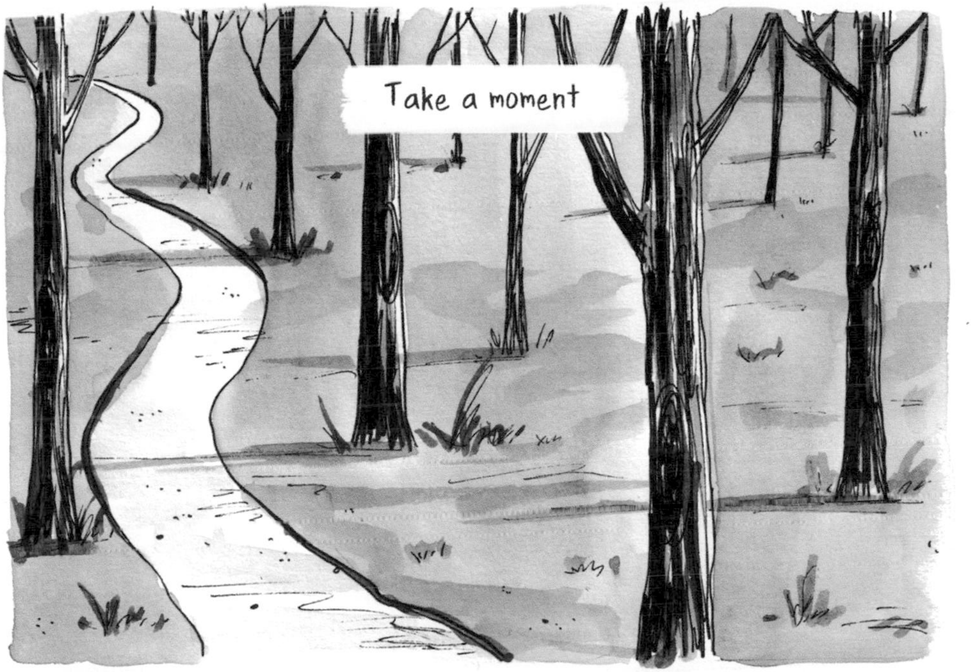
Take a moment

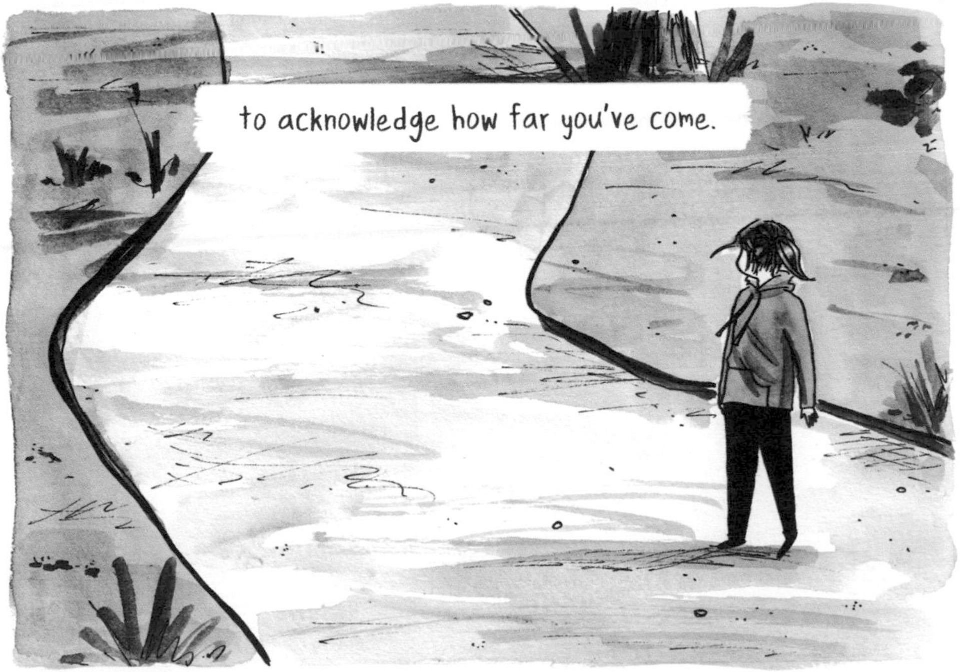
to acknowledge how far you've come.

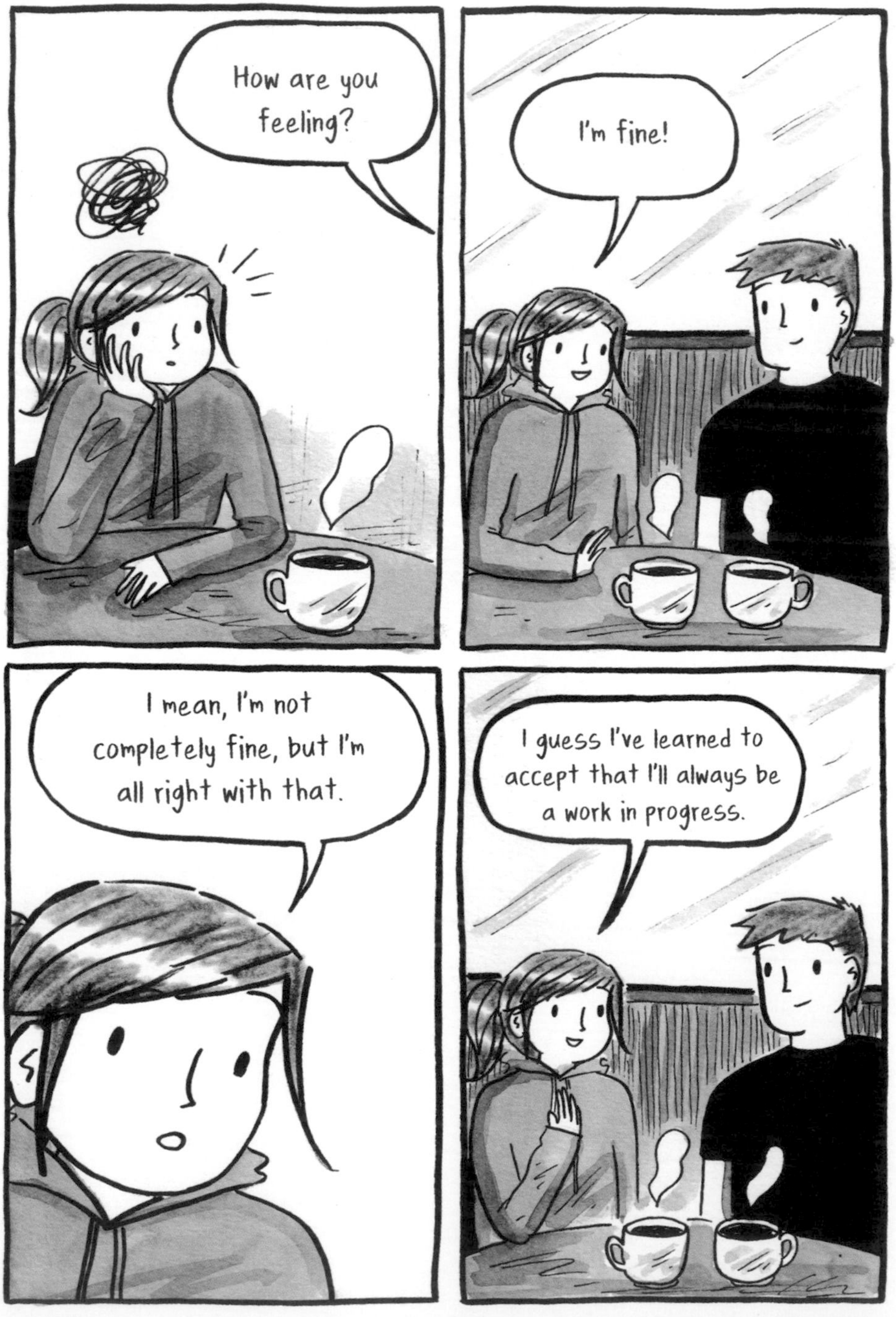
How are you feeling?
I'm fine!
I mean, I'm not completely fine, but I'm all right with that.
I guess I've learned to accept that I'll always be a work in progress.

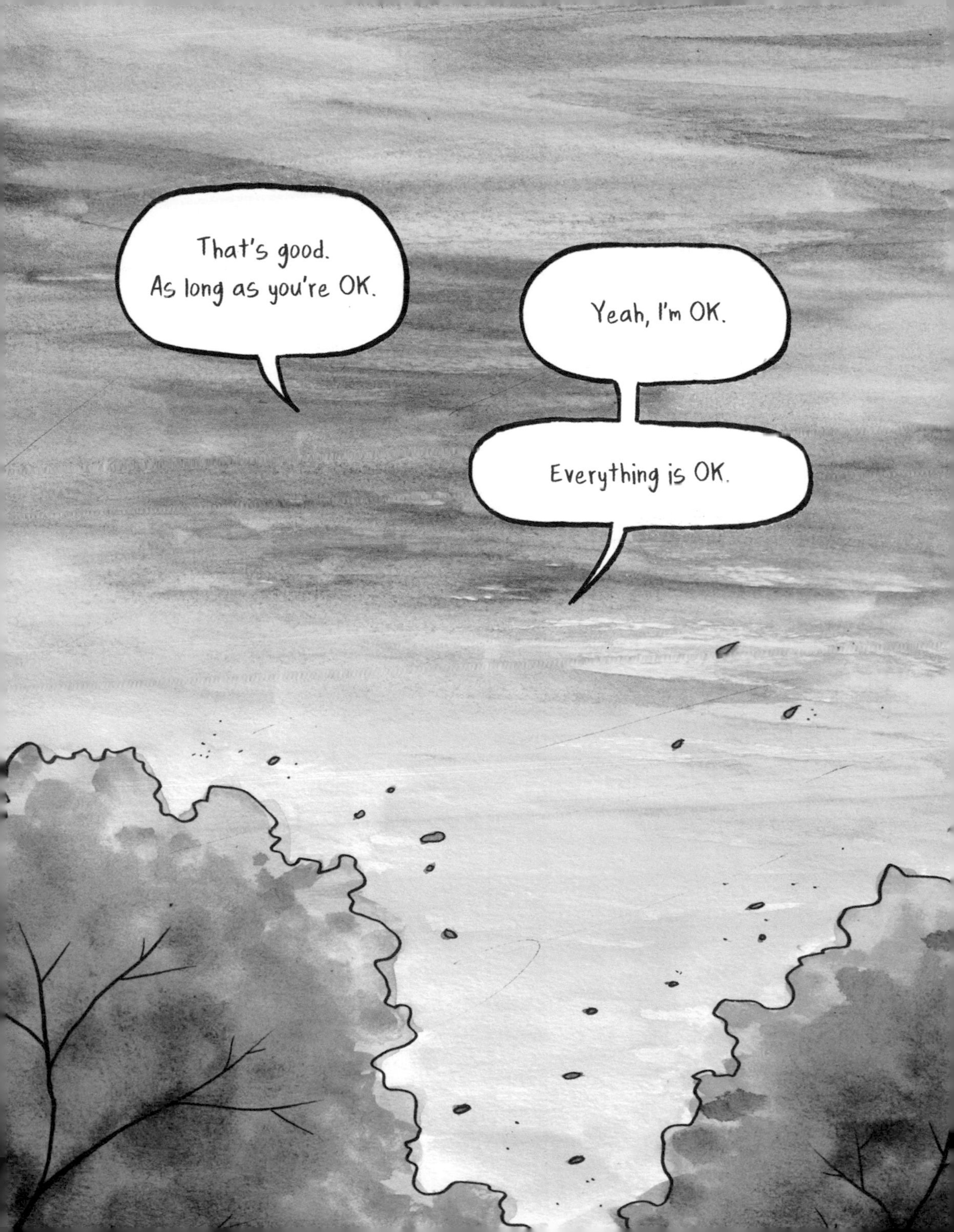
That's good.
As long as you're OK.
Yeah, I'm OK.
Everything is OK.

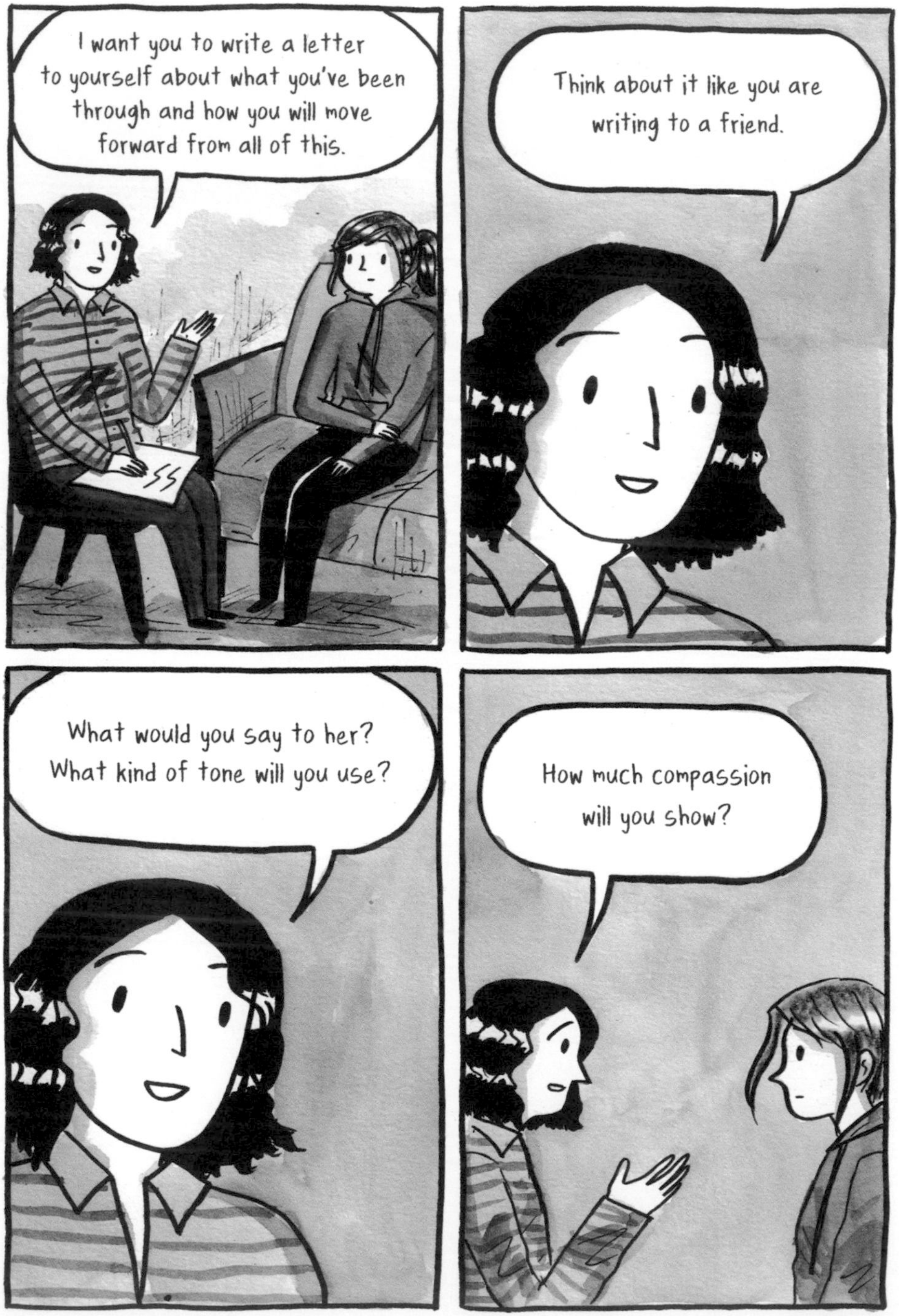
I want you to write a letter to yourself about what you've been through and how you will move forward from all of this.
Think about it like you are writing to a friend.
What would you say to her? What kind of tone will you use?
How much compassion will you show?

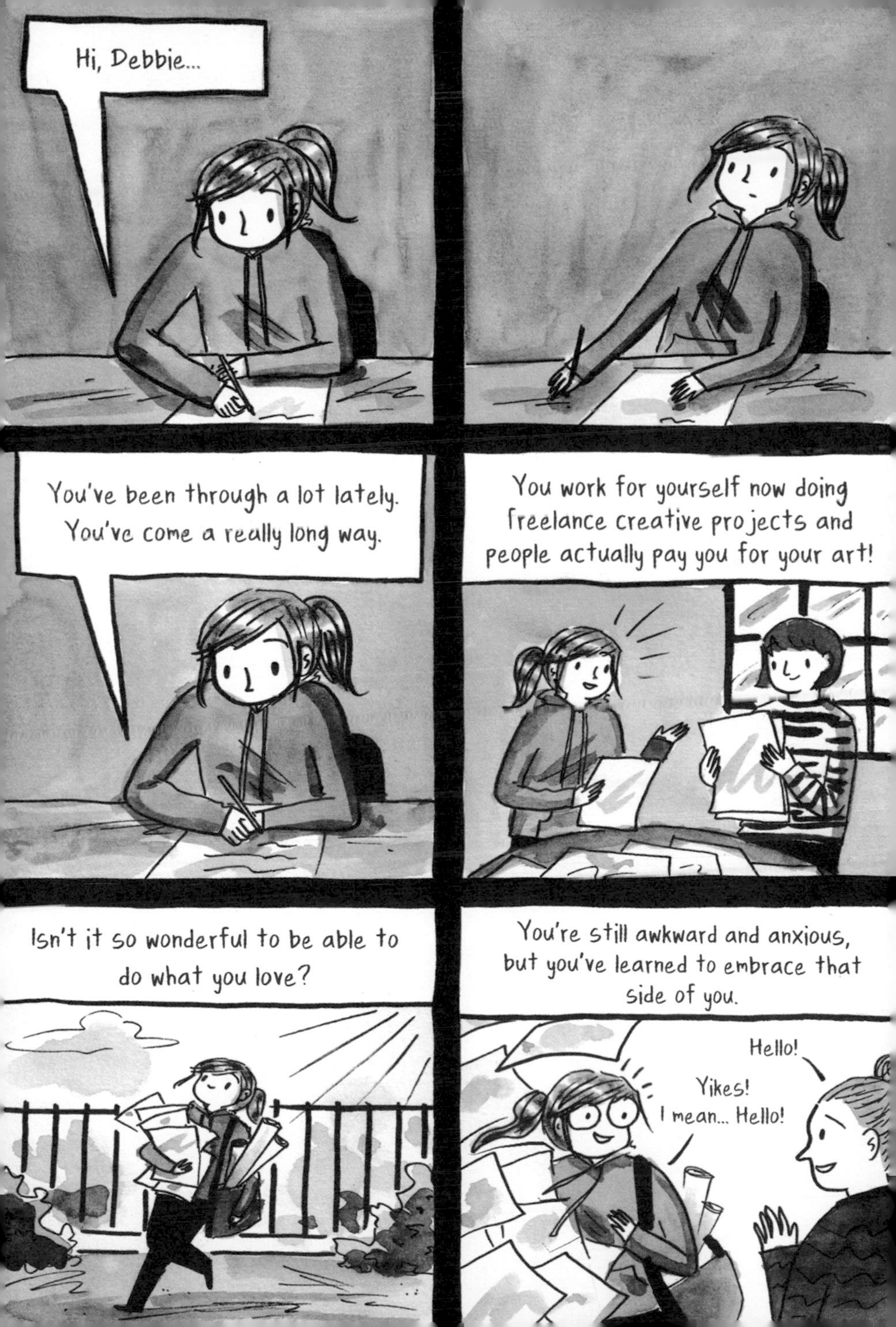
Hi, Debbie...
You've been through a lot lately. You've come a really long way.
You work for yourself now doing freelance creative projects and people actually pay you for your art!
Isn't it so wonderful to be able to do what you love?
You're still awkward and anxious, but you've learned to embrace that side of you.
Hello!
Yikes! I mean... Hello!

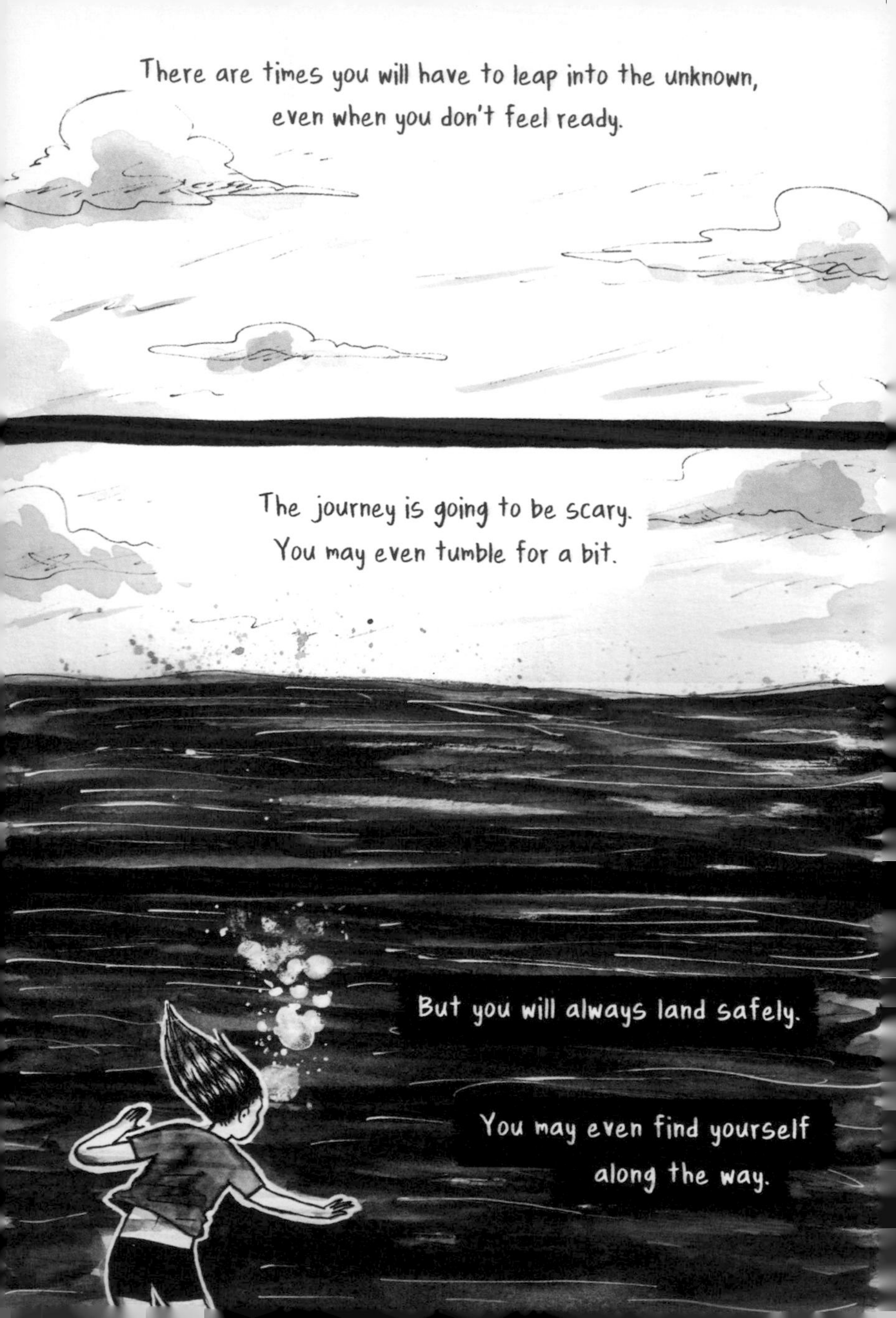
There are times you will have to leap into the unknown,
even when you don't feel ready.
The journey is going to be scary.
You may even tumble for a bit.
But you will always land safely.
You may even find yourself
along the way.

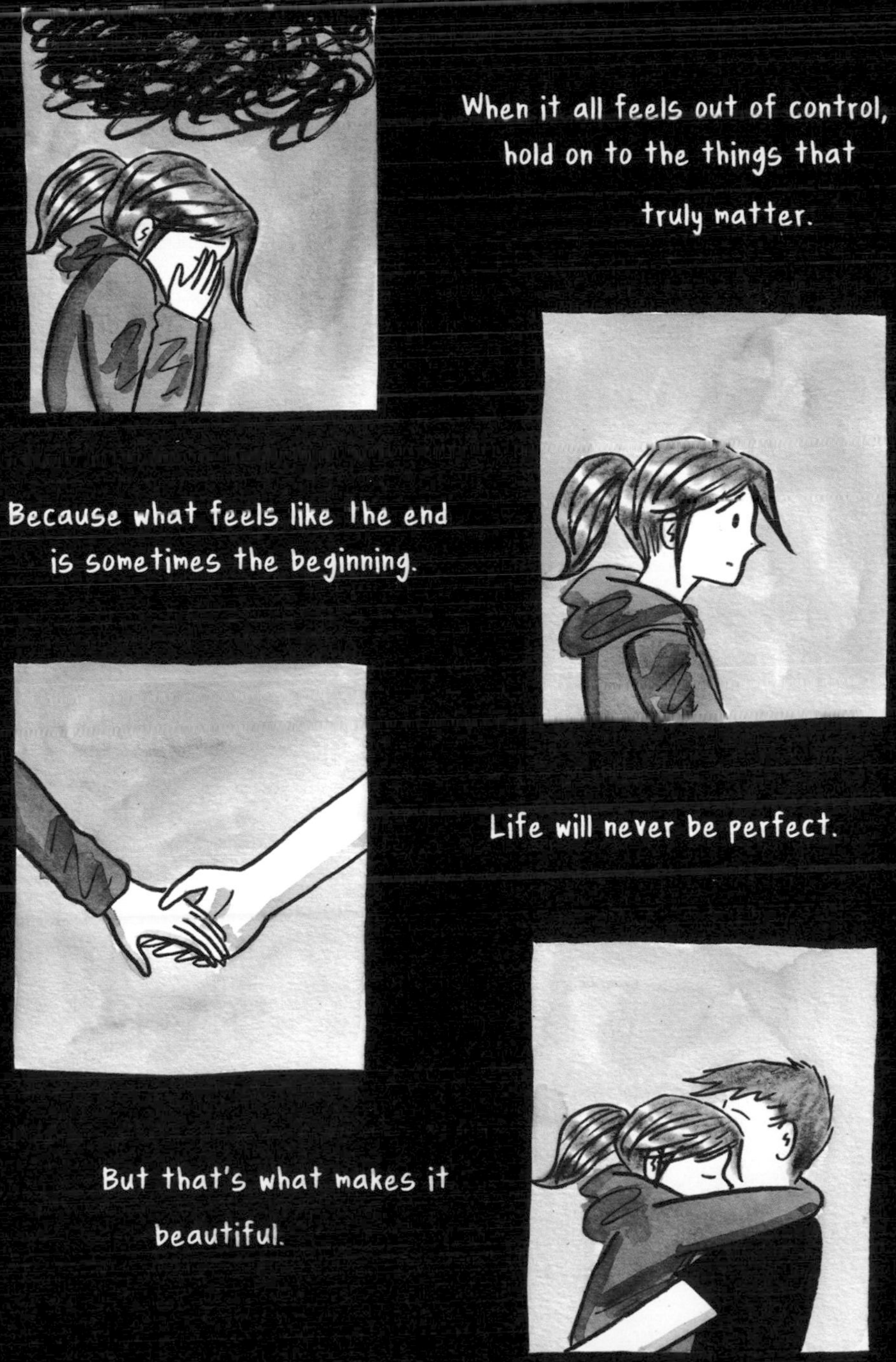
When it all feels out of control,
hold on to the things that
truly matter.
Because what feels like the end
is sometimes the beginning.
Life will never be perfect.
But that's what makes it
beautiful.

Oh, and remember back when you were
having a really tough time

and you thought to yourself

"How will I ever get through this?"

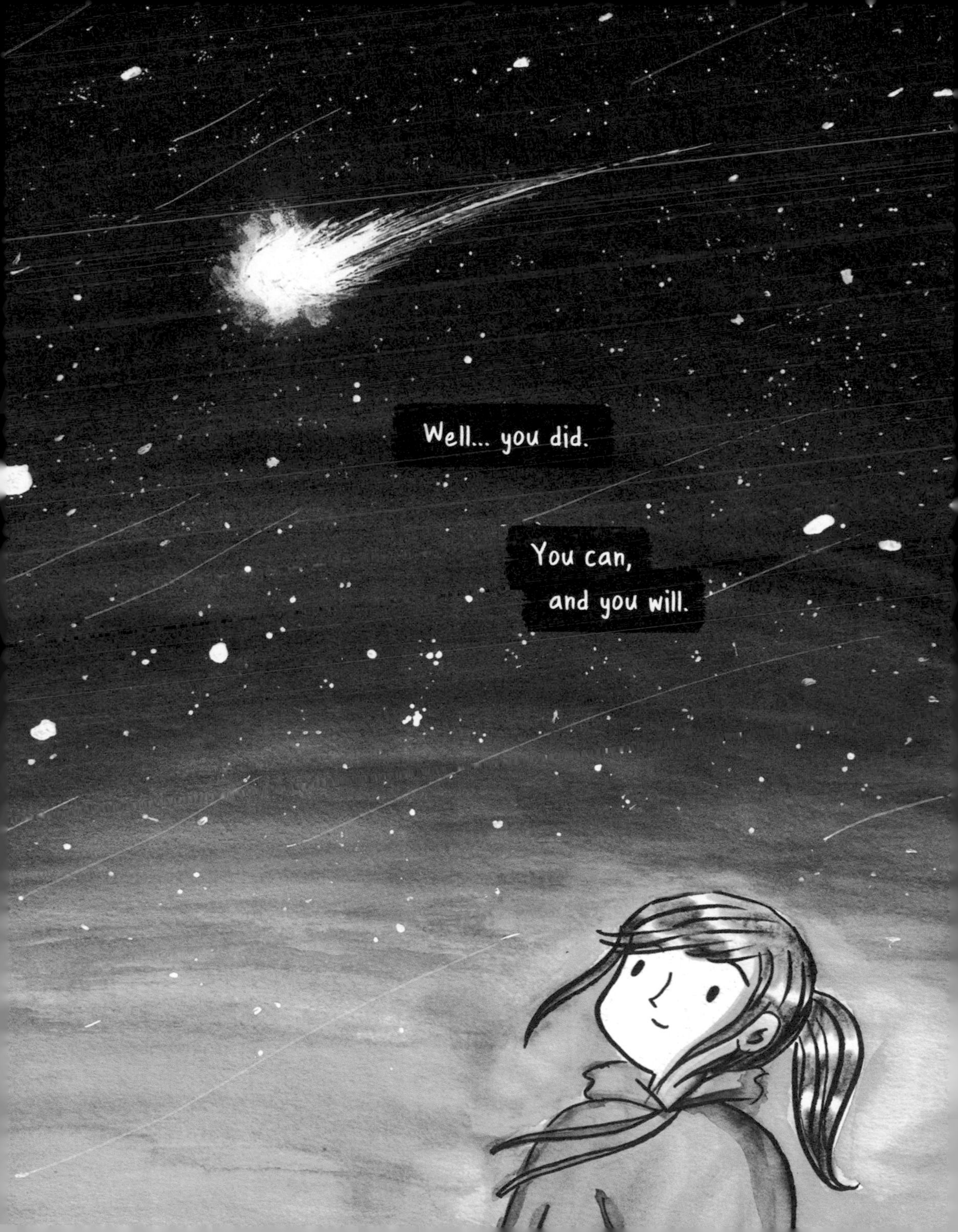
Well... you did.
You can,
and you will.

Acknowledgments

To my husband, Jason, for always being there for me during
the darkest of times.

To Laurie, the most amazing agent, for your attentiveness,
patience, and support.

To my editor Patty and everyone at Andrews McMeel, for giving me
this chance to share my story.

To my sister and brother, for always lending a listening ear
no matter how trivial my problems are.

To the NHS Mental Health Service in the UK, without which I would
not have been able to access the therapy sessions I needed.

To all the readers who follow my work and encouraged me over
the past few years. I am so deeply grateful for all your support.
Thank you for reading my stories.

To my mom and dad, for everything.

Debbie Tung is a cartoonist and illustrator. She draws about everyday life and her love for books and tea. Debbie is also the author of *Book Love* and *Quiet Girl in a Noisy World*, which was listed as a recommended read in *O, The Oprah Magazine*. Her comics have been shared widely by *Huffington Post*, *9GAG*, *Bored Panda*, and *Goodreads*, among others. She lives in Birmingham, England, with her husband and son.

Also by Debbie Tung

Quiet Girl in a Noisy World

Book Love

Happily Ever After & Everything In Between

You can see more of Debbie's work on her website
(www.debbietung.com) and social media (@WheresMyBubble).

Andrews McMeel Publishing
a division of Andrews McMeel Universal
1130 Walnut Street, Kansas City, Missouri 64106

www.andrewsmcmeel.com

23 24 25 26 27 RLP 10 9 8 7 6 5 4 3 2

ISBN: 978-1-5248-6327-2

Library of Congress Control Number: 2022931503

Editor: Patty Rice
Art Director: Tiffany Meairs
Production Editor: Elizabeth A. Garcia
Production Manager: Tamara Haus

ATTENTION: SCHOOLS AND BUSINESSES
Andrews McMeel books are available at quantity discounts with
bulk purchase for educational, business, or sales promotional
use. For information, please e-mail the Andrews McMeel
Publishing Special Sales Department: sales@amuniversal.com.